NATIONWIDE APPLAUSE FOR
YOUR FILM ACTING CAREER

"A classic work on the business of acting."

— *PUBLISHERS WEEKLY*

"The next time anyone asks me how to break into the business, I am just going to recommend that they buy *Your Film Acting Career*."

— *THE CELEBRITY BULLETIN*

"Incredibly informative and marvelously witty — a rare combination."

— *LAWRENCE B. MARCUS, SCREENWRITER*
(THE STUNTMAN, PETULIA, ETC.)

"Full of solid advice for folks who are bull-headed or confident enough to tackle Hollywood."

— *CATHERINE RAMBEAU, DETROIT FREE PRESS*

"A nuts-and-bolts handbook [that] takes a very pragmatic look at breaking into the business. M.K. and Rosemary Lewis bring their years of experience to bear on the subject, anticipating most every difficulty the novice will encounter . . . A thorough overview of the business side of acting."

— *MARK LOCHER, SAG NEWSLETTER*

"If only M.K. Lewis' marvelously informative handbook had been around a few years ago when I first came to Hollywood from San Diego, maybe it wouldn't have taken me 20 years to hit my stride!"

— *MARION ROSS*

"*Your Film Acting Career* is brutally honest and necessary advice that no novice can afford to miss. This is mandatory reading for any actor who is even considering taking a crack at Hollywood."

— *TONY SHEPHERD, DIRECTOR OF TALENT AND CASTING,*
AARON SPELLING PRODUCTIONS, INC.

"An excellent book. I suspect that it will end up being a [standard] textbook."

— *HAROLD GREENE, KABC-TV, AM LOS ANGELES*

"This is a splendid book — bright and breezy with just enough factual detail — a great gift for a star-struck teenager or a regular viewer of TV and movies and a must for the rookie trying to get through his first jobs. It's a lively textbook from a couple who graduated from the school of hard knocks."

— *CHRISTINA VELLA, TEMPO*

YOUR FILM ACTING CAREER

HOW TO BREAK INTO
THE MOVIES & TV &
SURVIVE IN HOLLYWOOD

FOURTH EDITION

M.K. Lewis
& Rosemary R. Lewis

GORHAM HOUSE PUBLISHING
Santa Monica, California

SAMUAL FRENCH TRADE, Distributors
Hollywood, California

Published by Gorham House Publishing,
2118 Wilshire Blvd., Suite 777, Santa Monica, California 90403 U.S.A.

Distributed by Samuel French Trade,
7623 Sunset Blvd., Hollywood, California 90046 U.S.A.

Foreword by Kathleen Nolan
Illustrations by Rosemary R. Lewis
Printed in the United States of America

Publishers' Cataloging in Publication Data
Lewis, M.K.
Your Film Acting Career.
Includes appendix, maps and index.
1. Moving-picture acting — Vocational guidance.
2. Acting for television — Vocational guidance.
I. Lewis, Rosemary R. II. Title.

Library of Congress Catalog Card Number: 97-094182
ISBN 0-929149-02-5

10 9 8 7 6

Fourth Edition

To Marguerite and Jozef
for the talent and background,
and
To Mama Ru and Papa Ru
for their loving support.

CONTENTS

FOREWORD

For me, the choice to become an actress was clear almost at birth. I never longed to be a doctor, firefighter, scientist or politician. I like being an actress. Acting is a joyous adventure.

Over the years I have eagerly read or reviewed countless books on the technique of acting, most being exclusively geared to the stage actor. Some of them have been excellent, for example Uta Hagen's *Respect for Acting*, Stanislavski's *An Actor Prepares*, etc. Sanford Meisner, to me without question the master teacher, has a book [Author's note: Sanford Meisner is now deceased. His book, *Sanford Meisner on Acting*, is available.]

Any serious actor should have more than a passing knowledge of the technique and craft expressed by these formidable artists/teachers. In my opinion, one should also possess a sound background in theatre and film history from the earliest times to the present. The Greek theatre, German playwrights, Scandinavian filmmakers should be studied, and certainly much emphasis should be placed on our cousins in the English-speaking world. However, an actor's research should not ignore American theatre, film and television. We tend to belittle our own cultural contributions, when, in fact, they have been enormous — in all fields.

It is most useful to be familiar with the approach other actors take to their work. The recently published *Actors On Acting* is excellent.

We have also experienced a proliferation of "star turn" books in recent years, written with or without the actor's permission. If one cares to wade through the sex lives, illnesses, traumas, and disappointments over which these actors have triumphed, one might receive some small measure of information about how it all came together for them — but I seriously doubt it. *Being a voyeur does not prepare one for a career.*

I have had the privilege of addressing university students in recent years and have been astonished by their lack of information about the artists' role in the United States — no practical application to add to Strindberg and Brecht. The mere mention of unions, agents, or how to survive outside the ivory towers seems to be considered pedestrian and out of place. In most universities, the film department is separated from the theatre department. Television, cable and satellite television are only touched upon in the communications departments. A curious exercise in "territorial rights" seems to block the student from the interchange which is essential for making decisions that affect life choices in the arts.

We come to New York or Hollywood ill-prepared to survive the shock of the commercial world.

M.K. and Rosemary Lewis' book deals exclusively with the film capital — Hollywood. It was not written by renowned stars or academicians. It was written by two people who have worked the system and, in an intelligent and entertaining fashion, have chronicled that experience. As a professional actress and longtime advocate of the actor's role in American society, I welcome their contribution.

Wherever and however our creative lives begin, we must have a foundation of preparation — total preparation. To "wing it" is more an expression of how we got by than how we prevailed.

Is the "joyous adventure" for you? The chapters that follow are a map with clues. Only you have the answers within you.

If you decide the answer is yes . . . relish the journey.

Welcome!

KATHLEEN NOLAN

KATHLEEN NOLAN has appeared in every form of entertainment — showboats, tent shows, repertory companies, Broadway, film, and television. She came to national prominence as Kate on the long-running TV series The Real McCoys. After 16 years' service on the board of directors of the Screen Actors Guild, she was elected president of SAG in 1975 and served two terms — the first woman president in its [then] 50-year history. She has been a presidential appointee to the Corporation for Public Broadcasting and a panelist for the National Endowment for the Arts.

PREFACE

It's enough to make you stand in the middle of the patio of Mann's Chinese Theatre, shouting . . .

"How do you crack this town?!?"

Each year, hundreds of actors point themselves in the general direction of Hollywood and Vine. Thousands more all over the country are thinking about it. Their shapes, sizes, talents, educations, and egos are as varied as their chances, but almost all have one thing in common: no idea how to start (or establish) a career.

Maybe you're among them.

Even if you've been to college, you're probably as lost as the 16-year-old starlet with stars in her eyes. You can graduate with a Ph.D in Drama (having written a dissertation on the costumes Minnie Maddern Fiske wore in *Our American Cousin*) and still not know what a *Daily Variety* looks like or be able to recognize an agent if he fell on you.

"The universities are pumping out well-trained repertory theatre actors that the world never needed in the first place," says drama critic John C. Mahoney.

This lack of knowledge often leads to paying phony "agents" to take you on; using photos that belong in a high school yearbook; attending so-called "acting classes" that do you no good and sometimes great psychological harm. And on and on.

Ultimately, your pocket — not to mention your mind — gets picked so much that you either jump on a bus or off a building, shouting all the way down . . .

"How do you crack this town?!?"

Even "old pros," newly migrated to L.A., can get totally frustrated. Suddenly what you did for years not only doesn't work any more, it works against you; sometimes it hurts you. And as you walk away from that stern-faced guard at Warner Studios, that *creep* who wouldn't let you onto the lot to drop off a picture, for crying out loud, you might just be tempted to cry out loud . . .

"How do you crack this town?!?"

In an effort to help, years ago we began to teach a course called "The Hollywood Actor's Survival Seminar." Over those years, besides drawing on our own experiences, we've engaged in hundreds of hours of interviews with producers, directors, agents, casting directors, personal mangers, publicists, and the like — even a cinematographer or two — so our students would hear the opinions of the most important people of all — those who do the hiring. And some student would inevitably say, "You know, you ought to write a book."

Well, here it is. We can't promise it'll make you "crack this town" — but it might help to bend it a little.

M.K. LEWIS has been teaching over 25 years at his own studio and in Europe. He also has taught at the California Institute of the Arts, Sherwood Oaks Experimental College, and both theatres which he founded. Now devoting himself to teaching and writing, he has appeared in, directed or written hundreds of theatrical productions (including *The Hero*, which he wrote and directed, at the Walnut Street Theatre in Philadelphia).

His film and TV credits include *Hard Times, Death Hunt, Raise The Titanic,* episodes of *Policewoman, Baretta, Delvecchio, The Blue Knight,* etc.

A former member of the SAG Conservatory Committee and a frequent guest speaker at SAG Seminars in Los Angeles, New York, Washington, etc., he has been interviewed by over 40 radio and TV stations nationwide and in Europe *(German Network television, The CBS Morning News, AM Los Angeles, The Michael Jackson Show,* as well as *People* magazine, *The Los Angeles Times,* etc.).

ROSEMARY R. LEWIS is a writer-cartoonist who has worked in public relations, TV (WDSU-TV News) and newspapers (as action line columnist and feature writer for the daily *New Orleans States-Item).*

She illustrated the book *Never Heave Your Bosom in a Front-Hook Bra* by award-winning humorist Liz Scott (in the guise of zany New Orleans housewife Modine Gunch), continuing a long-distance partnership that began with the cookbook *Getting Into New Orleans' Seafood.*

With acting credits of her own *(The Blue Knight, General Hospital,* etc.), she and M.K. Lewis founded the Hollywood Actors Survival Seminar, upon which their book is based.

ACKNOWLEDGEMENTS

Hollywood is a selfish city?

This book, both the original and revised editions, could not have been written without the generosity of hundreds of members of the Hollywood community. Many graciously took the time to speak at one of our seminars (a few more than once); to grant us interviews at their offices or over the phone; to appear as guest speakers at other seminars or classes we attended. And they all had one thing in common . . .

. . . They all donated their time.

Grateful thanks to: Ellie Abrahamson, Laurel Adams, Donna Allen, Eddie Applegate, Maxine Arnold, Simon Ayer, Kevin Baar, Sean Bainbridge, Vikki Bandlow, Arthur Bartow, Deborah Barylski, Fran Bascom, Angela Bath, Miriam Baum, Mel Becker, Paul Bengston, Jim Bennett, Bob Bergen, Barbara Best, Noel Black, Merritt Blake, Mel Blank, Samantha Botana, Susan Bragg, Buddy Bregman, Kevin Michael Brown, Michael Campus, Pamela Campus, Reuben Cannon, Diana Carpenter, Bonnie Carstensen, Louise Chamis, Warren Christansen, Don Ciminelli, Jerry Cohn, Susan Conners, Patrice Cormier, Cynthia Ann Crawford, Diana Daves, Becki Davis, Sally Dennison, Debbie Devine, Karen DiCenzo, Angie Dickinson, Bernie Distler, Michael Dixon, Pat Doty, Georg Duuglas, Sylvie Drake, Bill Eaton, Bill Edwards, John Edwards, Van Epperson, Pamm Fair, Jane Feinberg, Kim Fellner, Mike Fenton, Margaret Ferier, John Fisher, Roxanne Fitzgerald, Larry Fonseca, Jerry Franks, Bud Friedman, Tracy Fuller, Joseph Garber, Melinda Gartzman, J. Carter Gibson, Edmund Gilbert, Susan Glicksman, Susan Goldstein, Lora Granett, Jim Green, Bob Harbin, Simon Harvey, Marci Helzig, Nancy Hereford, Norman Herrman, Bob Hester, Patrick Higgins, Sharon Himes, Bobby Hoffman, Beth Holmes, Judith Holstra, Tawn Holstra, Richard Irving, Myrna Isenberg, George Ives, Tracey Jacobs, Carrie Jacobson, Cathryn Jaymes, Marsha Jeffer, Janet Joe, Lance Johnson, Steve Joseph, Kathy Juden, William Kayden, Johanna Kelly, Gary Klopus, Eileen Knight, Viva Knight, Kat Krone, Harvey Laidman, Elna Lawrence, Terry Lichtman, Marci Liroff, Bob Lloyd, Morgan Lofting, Bruce Logan, Pegge Logefeil, Beverly Long, Judy Lowry, John C. Mahoney, Philip Mandelker, A. Morgan Maree,

Sandy Martin, Leslie Martinson, Andrew McCullough, Renee McGill, Mickie McGowan, John Mekrut, Frank Messineo, Arlin Miller, Pamela-Beth Morris, Rose Morris, Dennis Moss, Mike Muscat, Don Nagle, Gary Nelson, Patti O'Brien, Fran O'Bryan, Cliff O'Connell, Al Onorato, Tom Ormany, Harry Orzello, Gigi Parker, Penny Perry, Don Pitts, David Ralphe, John Randolph, Steve Ray, Barbara Remsen, Michael Rhodes, Ruth Robinson, Andrea Romano, Jack Rose, Buddy Rosenberg, Doris Ross, Tama Rothschild, Brady Rubin, Ira Rubin, Joel Rudnick, Karen Rushfield, Doris Sabbagh, John Sanchez, Mona Lee Schilling, Sylvia Schneble, Barbara Schultz, Mort Schwartz, Terri Semper, Ralph Senensky, Jerry Shea, Barry Shear, Walter Shenson, Bill Shephard, Tony Shepherd, Marilyn Sherman, Sandra Siegal, Deborah Sills, Kathy Smith, Mary Spencer, Lea Stalmaster, Ron Stephenson, Danny Stewart, Viola Kates Stimpson, Mac St. Johns, Susan Sukman, Arne Sultan, Dale Tarter, Judy Taylor, Liz Temkin, Roz Tillman, Melissa Tormé-March, Bob Towers, Howard Trustman, Tony Turano, Doug Turner, Renee Valenti, Michael Van Duzer, Colee Viedelle, E. Duke Vincent, Roy Wallack, Herb Weil, Louise Wein, David Westberg, Howard Wexler, Dick Wieand, Bob Wollin, Susan Wright, and Brad Yates.

Thanks too to Laurene Kernan, Joan Meyer, Lucy Pegues, Anne Edwards Talltree and especially Mark Locher of SAG, Michael C. Donaldson and David Perren.

We'd also like to thank Brandt Aymar who years ago put us on the starting line, Peter H. Karlen for giving us the "get ready," Dan Poynter for giving us the "get set," and Gwen Feldman, Jim Fox and Leon Embry of Samuel French Trade for giving us the "go."

For additional help with the fourth edition, we'd like to thank Joe Bays, David Beeler, Sam Christensen, Keith Gonzales, Lawrence A. Mandley, Thomas Mills, David Perren, Brad Yates. Also, William Jones of the Actors' Fund and Linda Davine, Pierre R. Debs and Tawanda Lewis of the Screen Actors Guild. And, especially, Gary LaVon and Christine Sheppard for the hard work done so cheerfully.

Also thanks to Andrea Balen and Petra Gallasch for the many blessings they've brought to so many actors and for opening up a part of the world to us.

And finally, thanks to Evan Andes for the work, the laughs and the charm and, of course, to Britt and Steve Wachsman, Bruce Findley and Terry Madden for being there, and Joe for the inspiration of July 1, 1978.

And above all, to all our students, American and European, who over the years have taught us more than we could ever teach them.

AUTHORS' NOTE
FOR THE NEW EDITION

What's new?

As we said in the last edition, the forest continues to be the same, but the trees keep changing — and now they're *wired*.

It's high-tech time, baby. The so-called "new media" is translating into "new work." Actors are finding career information via computer — we've added a new appendix of websites — and getting themselves submitted for roles at the touch of a mouse. Fax machines are giving them a leg up on their auditions. Voice mail and beepers are keeping them in closer touch with their agents. And all this is happening faster than a zip drive can zip.

On a calmer subject, we continue to grapple with the problem of past contributors. Many have changed titles; some have left the industry; a few, sadly, have died. However, the advice given is just as important today as it was originally, and the person's position in the industry at the time he said what he said is what makes the quote relevant. So we continue to leave the quotes and titles as they originally appeared.

We've also opted to continue to use the universal "he." Once again, and for the record, the role of women continues to expand in this industry, from casting director to studio exec. (And also for the record, one of us is a very universal she.)

So what's new?

Like we said last time — pull up a shady palm tree and read on. Only now, don't forget to plug the palm tree in.

I
PREPARING TO GO AND GOING

A SPECIAL NOTE TO NEW YORKERS

What I've learned is that there are several
different definitions of the word "actor." In
New York theatre it's what will make the
literature work; in Hollywood, it's what sells.

Beth Holmes, Commercial Casting Director

"Culture shock" is about to take on a new meaning.

Strike: bumping into people, "studio" apartments, insanely ridiculous rents, subways, hangouts for actors, galoshes, cattle calls, "youse guys," theatre/theatre/theatre, walking, Nathan's hot dogs, the Tavern on the Green, Goldenberg's Peanut Chews, Macy's Thanksgiving Parade, and pretzel vendors.

Superimpose: bumping into cars, "single" apartments, *sanely* ridiculous rents, buses that come *every* other vernal equinox, skateboards, movies/movies/movies, driving 30 miles to "do lunch," Pink's hot dogs, Spago, sushi, the Rose parade and sheepskin seatcover vendors.

Most important, as to your career, you'll get on the plane and, somewhere over Tucumcari or between the third and fourth peanut, *somebody will change the rules.*

No longer will you be able to indulge in the "starving artist" look so often worn as a badge of distinction in New York; you'll have to clean up your act. You'll have to lose that "edge" so typical of New York actors — it won't play in L.A. You won't be able to make the rounds as openly. You'll be permitted only one agent to rep you for each endeavor (TV, commercials, etc.). You'll be encouraged when your Big Apple credits and training are very well received, and exasperated when you constantly hear, "But do you have any *film* on yourself?" You may be respected by your New York peers, but, unless you're a name, it's back to work proving yourself all over again to the boys in the Universal Tower. Your cold reading technique probably will have to change from theatre-expansive to office-intimate. Those stints as an extra you're so used to doing will now have to be done almost on the sly — if at all. The New York sneer at those "non-acting" film actors will have to be replaced by training in, and respect for, acting *for the camera*. And you'll find even more emphasis on your looks.

Everything in this book is as valid for you as any other actor coming from Seattle, Chicago, or West Nowhere. The difference is in the training and experience you may have, not in what you'll need to do.

It's not only the Dodgers who have gotten into a whole new ballgame.

AND A SPECIAL NOTE TO OUR "FOREIGN" COLLEAGUES

A number of years ago, two women, Andrea Balen and Petra Gallasch, formed a superb workshop for Europeans called The Hollywood Acting Workshop (HAW). HAW takes place in L.A. about every six weeks and consists of a number of American instructors teaching actors from Germany, Austria, Switzerland and other European countries about working in front of a camera, functioning in Hollywood, etc.

Now why do we bring this up? Well, through working with HAW, and corresponding over the years with our readers around the world, we have learned how easy it is for a non-American actor to get "caught up" in the idea of not just studying here, but actually working here. So, we have two very serious words of caution: GREEN CARD.

It's one thing to come here and study; quite another to come here to *work*. The problem of obtaining a green card or a visa to work in this country is a *huge* one, not to be blthely ignored whether you're from Calcutta, Canada, or Cologne.

Also, if you have an accent, you'll need to either get rid of it or learn an American accent. If you don't, you'll be limited to playing only those roles that feature your ethnicity.

Please, save yourself a lot of grief. Only come to the USA to pursue a career in acting the same way you would pursue a career in anything else: solve the green card/visa problem first.

1 MAKING THE DECISION

> *Before I take on a client, I look for three things: talent, guts, and imagination.*
>
> Barbara Best, Publicist

Welcome to the job-getting business . . .

. . . That's the *real* business there's no business like.

And if you're in the midst of packing, certain Hollywood had better batten down its hatches because you're the best damn actor this side of Laurence Olivier, we'd like to shake your hand, pat you on the back — and tell you to stop right there.

There's a fundamental flaw in your thinking. You're confusing being a *good* actor with being a *working* actor.

Working actors know they're good, but they also have come to grips with one very essential fact: If you're thinking of becoming a professional actor, above all understand that you're really thinking of becoming *a door-to-door salesman — of yourself.*

An actor's true vocation is selling and job-getting: his avocation is acting. Most would-be actors either fail to understand this or they've never been told it. They spend all their time honing their craft and little or no time on the business of acting. They sit by unrelentingly silent phones, idealistically waiting for someone to "pick up on" their talent. Occasionally this happens, but more often than not they begin to feel like Edgar Allan Poe's famous "Purloined Letter" — there they are, sitting out for all to see, and nobody knows they're there.

Eventually they quit, believing they were failures as actors. They weren't. They were just poor job-getters.

So if you're thinking about becoming a professional actor, put aside your talent for the moment and examine your basic personality. Can you sell? And — equally important — can you live with the idea of being a salesman? Do you have the emotional make-up of a go-getter?

If you can't answer yes to that, we'd honestly recommend you remain a non-pro. You'll probably be a happier man or woman if you don't act for money.

Now don't misunderstand: we're not saying that being an actor is one long toothache. There are many rewards to the profession, not the least of which is being a member of a very exciting, highly creative community.

But that community, to say the least, is overcrowded. There are about 90,000 members of the Screen Actors Guild (SAG), 85 percent of whom earn less than $15,000 a year. That doesn't include the other acting and related unions, and it doesn't include you (probably) and the thousands of others who are trying to get into them.

And even being the greatest talent and the greatest job-getter won't guarantee success. Consider the following rather daunting little story:

Years ago, we attended a seminar for beginning actors. The guest speaker looked over the sea of eager faces, sighed, and said, "Of all the people in this room, I would say that 75 percent will have quit by next year; 20 percent more will have given up by the following year; and in five years, two — maybe three — of all of you will still be pursuing a career in acting."

Regardless of whether or not he was right, the point is that this is a business for survivors.

"Patience and perseverance are 45 percent; timing and luck are 45 percent; and talent is ten percent, as talent should be a given," says personal manager Melissa Tormé-March. "There are so many people in L.A. who are unbelievably talented, but if they don't have the patience, perseverance, timing and luck, their talent is irrelevant."

Put another way, it's like being in a lifeboat with 90,000 other people — a boat that can accommodate only two or three hundred (that's about how many roles are available in any given week in Hollywood). You're going to have to figure out a way to stay in the boat, to make enough money to keep yourself afloat all the while thinking up ways of pulling yourself out of the crowd so that Hollywood will sit up and take notice of you.

That means this is no business for the meek or anyone whose pride can't stand more than the average quota of bruising. After all, in terms of type, there will always be at least 25 other people who can play the same roles as you. You have the right to think of yourself as special — you are. Now convince everybody else.

You're going to have to be smarter, quicker, and a better hustler than the other guy. (That doesn't mean you'll need to sleep with anybody; let's get that out of the way right now. You're out to make *friends* — not lovers.)

Director/cinematographer Bruce Logan put it this way: "I went to a seminar where all the guest speakers were studio executives, and the buzzword there was '*relationships*.' I mean the word 'relationships' must have come up 150 times in eight hours. That's the way this industry works." And part of making those "relationships" work involves not only being a good actor, but a good talker as well. In show business, the people who talk the best, work the most.

In short, either develop good business sense and a strong helping of "street smarts," or in five years or so plan to be a member of that frustrated crowd continually streaming to the exit doors. Entertainment attorney Michael C. Donaldson states it beautifully: "A lot of people are drawn to acting *just to be known as actors.* They haven't become adults — they just want to play for the rest of their lives. Successful actors are *adults* who do this as a career . . . I really believe successful actors would be successful in almost any other field they might choose."

So, before you finish packing, ask yourself:

CAN YOU HANDLE STRESS?

"You tell me you're an actor and I say no you're not. What you really do for a living is audition," says commercial casting director Beverly Long. "If somebody asks you what you do for a living, you should say, 'I audition.' You only act occasionally. And you will be going on auditions for the rest of your life."

Unfortunately, nobody pays you to audition, so the financial stress of being an actor is obvious. We don't mean starving. That's a lot of artsy-craftsy ragweed that could even by harmful to your career (see "Attitudes," Chapter 9). But you'll have to give up things — the hog just ain't that high.

Besides not being fun, financial stress can hurt. Consider this possibility: ten years after going to Los Angeles, you return home. Your best buddy, who became an accountant, is living in a beautiful four-bedroom house — and you've still got a non-air conditioned flat in Van Nuys. Want to make a sure buck? Go into banking.

Far more than financial stress, however, is the *emotional* stress of being an actor . . .

First, there's the emotional stress of constantly seeking work. "Actors," says commercial casting director Beverly Long, "have to be able in a day to read for a soap opera in the morning; then go downtown to read for a show at the Ahmanson or go read for an 'Equity Waiver' play; then, in the afternoon, go on a reading for a nighttime TV drama; then go on a commercial audition, and be able to adjust themselves to each. And each is going to be entirely different."

We know, you should be so lucky, but her point is well taken. You've got to be up, ready, and doing your best — all the time. Every audition is a first day on the job.

Next, there's the strain of being a businessperson/artist. And a schizoid state it is. In the morning you're making the rounds, pleasant as an anchorman, hiding how much you'd like to have that nasty receptionist's guts for garters. At night, you're in a play doing a role where we've got to see that very anger. When a producer says "Next!" you can't sob into his ashtray or jump on his desk and yell, "YOU CREEP! YOU COULDN'T FIND TALENT IN THE DICTIONARY!" You've got to be cool as sushi, smile and say, "Thank you." But when you're acting you've got to let us see your pain — to invite us to peer inside you — and do it *on cue.* Day in and night out, you'll need the soul of a poet and the hide of a rhinoceros.

During interviews with industry people, one question we almost always posed was "If you had to give an actor a single piece of advice, what would it be?" Said one casting director, "Get a good shrink."

Next, there's the stress of constantly making decisions. Everything from little choices, like which photo to use, to big ones such as firing Charlie — your friend and agent — who isn't getting the job done anymore; whether or not to get married; pregnant; and so on. And these don't get easier as you go through your career — they get harder. A beginner doesn't have to think twice about taking "three lines and a spit" on a TV show. A beginner doesn't have to decide whether or not to buy a condo and pray his one-year-old series gets renewed. A working pro does.

If you can't handle making decisions all the time, become a professional bureaucrat, not a professional actor.

Then there's the stress of often being treated like a beggar. A bum. A social pariah. (That's been true for centuries. In the Dark Ages, when they wanted to burn heretics, they used actors for kindling.) Secretaries will hang up on you. Your own relatives, when things are slow, will constantly be on your back to quit. Even fellow actors will pull a Cyrano on you: they'll look down long noses if they're working (currently) and you're not. And don't look for any warmth from the stars. We've seen some treat bit players as if the entry fee to the human race is having more than ten lines to say in a movie.

And, sooner or later, someone very close to you, someone you really care about, will say, "Why don't you stop fooling around and get yourself a *real job?*"

If you don't have the personality to shrug off all this and much, much more, this profession will drive you crazy, into deep depression, or just plain out. If you can't handle stress, avoid two professions: professional tightrope-walker, and professional actor.

ARE YOU MORE IDEALISTIC THAN PRACTICAL?

There's nothing "idealistic" about doing a deodorant commercial, but it beats heck out of waiting tables. Idealism also has nothing to do with writing a good "covering letter," choosing an agent, selecting a play casting directors will come to see, reading and understanding a contract, or battling it out with a producer for an extra 50 bucks a day. As theatrical casting director Paul Bengston put it: "We call it show business. We don't call it show-art."

That doesn't mean be cynical. You don't have to join the sharks already in the water. Just develop a healthy practical streak; for example, don't always expect to be performing Shakespeare. To paraphrase the old saying, you're going to have to kiss a lot of frog roles before the prince part comes along.

CAN YOU STAND HAVING YOUR LIFE CONSTANTLY UPROOTED?

One day you'll be broke; the next, possibly, a millionaire. You're sitting jobless in your apartment, brooding and ignoring your spouse; a week later you're on location in Oswego aching with loneliness. Your agent never calls, so you decide to quit; inevitably, the phone rings with an offer for a week's work in New York. On the set, you're given a two-page monologue to learn in five minutes, and you do, and everybody tells you DeNiro is in deep trouble; the film comes out and the monologue has been cut to one line . . .

Actor, drop one phrase from your vocabulary: "slow and steady."

ARE YOU THINKING ABOUT "BIG BUCKS"? HOW ABOUT GLAMOR?

Just wait until you experience the "glamor" of looking for an agent. Just wait until you experience the thrill of standing in a cold, driving rain for 12 hours waiting to say your one line (alone, because the "stars" won't talk to you). Just wait until all those big bucks pour in from parking cars to pay the rent. If you're thinking about cocktails and limos you're forgetting: nobody is born a star. Every person in this industry has had to endure being treated like a piece of meat, and a glamor fantasy won't be enough to sustain you through the rough years.

As to "big bucks": a few years ago, a major star appeared on a talk show and frankly stated she couldn't afford not to work. Groans of disbelief could be heard in the audience. But she was probably telling the truth.

Yes, get lucky and you can make a lot of money as an actor and appear on *Lifestyles of the Gross and Greedy*. Maybe that's the reason so many believe that the instant a person appears on TV or in a movie, he is "wallowing in the dough."

Well, a working actor makes in the neighborhood of $500 to $1,000 a day. Sound like a lot of money? You may work one day in an entire year.

And, if you *do* become a "star," you may be paying:

- Ten percent to your agent;
- About 15 percent (and possibly up to 50 percent) to your personal manager;
- Five percent to your business manager;
- Several thousand dollars per month to your publicist;
- And, if you're lucky, after deductions, say 20 to 35 percent to the good ole IRS.

That's 50 percent-plus out of an income that isn't guaranteed. You may get hot one year and not work for the next three . . . but your house payment will still be due.

Does the star's statement sound plausible now?

Director Andrew McCullough boiled it all down when he said, "There is nothing more frustrating than to be 'in the middle.' To say, 'I want to be an actor, but I also want such and such.' I think there has to be an absolute moral and ethical commitment. God has given you certain talents. Now how you use those talents is the most important question of your life. Be careful not to buy that fantasy of stardom, money, and all the material things that commercials pump into your heads all the time: 'To be really first rate I've got to have a BMW, a house in Brentwood, or be beautiful and have great clothes.' . . . To be an actor means you take a spiritual vow when you say: 'This is the only kind of life I can live.'"

ARE THE PEOPLE YOU'RE EMOTIONALLY INVOLVED WITH ALSO ABLE TO HANDLE THIS PROFESSION?

We're not talking about Mom and Dad; unfortunately, they may never understand. But others who live with and see you every day are going to have to have the understanding of Solomon. Remember, they're on the ride too. They too are going to have to fasten their safety belts for all those bumpy nights. They're going to have to tough it out and be positive psychological influences. If not, sooner or later you're going to have a very serious problem on your hands.

"If I didn't have a super wife, I don't know where I'd be right now because she carried me," says one actor about his first years in the industry. "Talk about guilt complexes. There I was in a one-bedroom apartment in North Hollywood with no air conditioning and a nine-month-old baby, while my wife is in Beverly Hills working. And I *know* she'd *much* rather be with the baby." As theatrical agent David Westberg says, "Acting is not a job, it's a way of life."

ARE YOU GOOD AT GETTING WORK IN THE TOWN IN WHICH YOU LIVE? DO YOU KNOW THE PRODUCTION HOUSES, AGENTS, ETC., IN YOUR TOWN?

Can't answer yes? Better get going. Finding and dealing with people who can hire you to act should be a lot easier in Dallas than New York or L.A. If you can't get an appointment with someone who sees ten actors a week, how are you going to get to talk to someone deluged with 100 actors a day?

ARE YOU A MAN?

Things continue to improve for women throughout the industry, including the number of female roles available. Still, the ratio of male to female parts is about 2-1.

ARE YOU YOUNG? ESPECIALLY, ARE YOU A YOUNG WOMAN?

If you're 18, nobody will expect you to have a résumé as long as your arm. But if you're over 30 and still don't have professional credits, better think it over — especially if you're female. "Older" women (by Hollywood standards, any woman over 30) have a rough road to hoe. Here's what personal manager Melissa Tormé-March had to say: "In certain age categories it can be very hard. We had a lady come out from New York who had done a tremendous amount of live theatre and commercials. She's very pretty and very sophisticated and up-scale. She's in her early 40's. Well, I couldn't sell her if my life depended on it. She is competing with [already established stars]. It's tough. It's very tough." Quote from an over-30 actress: "Since there are so few roles, I can't look at acting as a profession anymore. I have to think of it as a hobby."

ARE YOU NON-ETHNIC-LOOKING?

In commercials, from which actors derive one-third of their income, there's an expression: "white bread." That's a blandly good-looking person who typifies the cliché Midwestern American. (That's not a racial term, by the way — a black person such as Bryant Gumbel can be "white bread.") Most advertisers are looking for "white bread" (see Chapter 21) because they want Billy Bud Swiller to remember the beer, not the actor. Consequently, if you're visually distinctive (read "ethnic," "older," "character actor"), your chances of getting a decent piece of the commercial pie are lessened.

Today the job picture is somewhat brighter for ethnic actors of all types — especially in commercials — with opportunities for black actors and actresses showing the most improvement overall. But we're still talking about a maximum of 20 percent of all roles.

DO YOU HAVE A CAPACITY FOR CONFIDENCE? DO YOU LOOK CONFIDENT EVEN WHEN YOU'RE QUAKING IN YOUR BOOTS?

The actor who doesn't work is scared and shows it. The actor who works is scared but doesn't show it.

DO YOU HAVE AN EASYGOING, BREEZY PERSONALITY, OR ARE YOU CONSTANTLY UPTIGHT, SCARED, UNHAPPY, NON-SELF-RELIANT?

Most often you'll be selling your personality, not your talent. Okay, it's not fair. But it's Show Biz. "People are always talking about the 'talent' of an actor," says entertainment attorney Michael C. Donaldson. "To me, the 'talent' to be a successful actor involves what I call 'the three A's' of success — they apply to doctors, lawyers and everyone else — they are: affability, availability, and ability — *in that order.*"

ARE YOU THOUGHT OF AS "LUCKY"? DO YOU REFUSE TO QUIT, EVEN WHEN YOUR OPPONENT HAS HOTELS ON BOARDWALK AND ALL THE RAILROADS?

"I know you're talented, but are you lucky?" said theatrical agent Jim Gibson. Yes, there is such a thing as pure dumb luck. But, more often, there is *smart* luck — luck created by work, guts and (forgive the cliché), a refusal to quit. Director Andrew McCullough tells this little story: "Jack

Lemmon and I started out at Harvard and went to New York where we lived together and tried to get into the theatre. Looking back on it, he worked harder than anyone I've ever known. He would drag me into flea-bitten — I mean *horrible* looking — places that I was embarrassed to be in. And he wore a horrible threadbare raccoon coat . . . And he would go in and con and cajole these secretaries of booking agents, and they hated him. You know, 'Get out! Get out! There's nothing for you today!' And he would say something funny or give them a little present . . . And he had a list of everyone casting in town. He'd write a dozen letters a day. He'd make scores of phone calls every day. And he didn't get parts and he didn't get discouraged. I mean, that was what he did: try. And he did it over and over and over and over again."

Theatrical agent Mary Spencer sums it up: "Don't go around saying 'I never have any luck,' because luck is when *preparation* and *opportunity* meet."

And, finally, as to your talent . . .

WHEN YOU DO COMMUNITY THEATRE, DO YOU FEEL YOU'RE NOT ONLY BETTER THAN YOUR FELLOW ACTORS, BUT YOU KNOW MORE?

You'll be competing with people who have film and Broadway credits. Learn your craft — and the best way is to do play after play. You can go to L.A. to study acting, but, even so, the more training you get before you arrive the better. Theatrical agent Joel Rudnick cautions, "In a lot of ways, if you're 19 or 20, it makes more sense not to go to Hollywood — to go and do regional theatre and do roles that you'd never get to play in L.A.: O'Neill, Miller . . . and develop your craft."

WHEN YOU TRY OUT FOR LOCAL THEATRE, ARE YOU ALMOST ALWAYS CAST? WHEN YOU'RE REVIEWED, DO THE CRITICS ALMOST ALWAYS RAVE?

It's one thing for *you* to think you're good . . .

That's basically it. If you can answer these questions to your satisfaction, and you want to go ahead, we'd say, what the heck, give it a shot. That's better than sitting over a cup of tea at age 65 *wishing* you had.

Maximillian Schell, speaking at a seminar, was asked if he had any regrets. His answer: "I've never regretted anything I've done. It's always the things that I haven't done that I regret the most." Sound like we're encouraging you to be an actor? We hope not. Drama critic John C. Mahoney said it eloquently when we asked, "What advice would you give to actors?": "Get out of the business. It's the only honest loving thing you can say to an actor because ten percent of your profession will ever work or make a living. If you're interested in the stage, one to three percent of the population gives the slightest damn what it is you do. It's an alien activity . . .

"The effort you put in is largely wasted, except in whatever it gives you. Half the effort would pay off in used car sales, marketing, public relations . . . If you start thinking, 'Wow, is it worth it?' you've already answered your own question. Of course it's not worth it! . . . If you stick with it, it's because you feel you have something to give.

"It is proper that everyone think you are crazy. There's no reason why you should demand that anyone ever understand your commitment or your dedication. And your mother and everyone else is right — you wouldn't have to work that hard, and you could be rich, if you were in any other business . . .

"I'm very fond of actors, but they are *real* stupid to do what they do. There is no good reason to do it unless you approach it like a monk . . . You may always be happy doing it, but you should only have a good job besides . . . The cruelest thing in the world is to encourage an actor. If you can, *in any way*, discourage an actor, you should."

We'll add that we know you could take everything in this book, throw it out — in fact, do everything all wrong — and still wind up signing autographs on Oscar night. In this industry there's no such thing as no such thing. "The one thing I've found, the longer I'm in the business," says actor John Edwards, "is that there's no general way it happens. Everybody comes through different doors. Which means you have to keep at it in this business, because eventually something weird will happen your way." (For example, actor Lawrence A. Mandley tells this story: "A production company had hired an actor to do a voice-over spot and midway through the session they realized they weren't happy with their choice. A friend suggested they call me. I was asleep and they got my answering machine, on which I playfully was using several different voices ranging from high pitched and nasal to my actual bass-baritone. When I awoke I had a message from the producer offering me the job. I got residual checks from it for over a year. My answering machine had been my audition.")

This book will give you the business knowledge you need, and a few tricks of the trade to help that "something weird" come your way perhaps a bit faster. But we can't make you into a person who turns this knowledge to his advantage. That's your job. In other words, *we'll* supply the knowledge; *you* supply the talent, guts and imagination.

2 PREPARING TO GO

Be sure you can afford to be an actor.

Vikki Bandlow, Theatrical Agent

Make your plans at least a year in advance. Many things will require that amount of planning, and it's just better for your brain.

GET A CAR

A fuel-efficient one. You can't do justice to your career in L.A. without "wheels" — the distances are too great. If you don't drive, consider going to New York instead.

SAVE MONEY

One look at the complete budget in Appendix 1 and a glance at your personal expenses and you'll see why we say give up the luxuries and save, save, save. Besides, doing without will be terrific training.

GET INTO THE "RIGHT" UNION(S)

Thousands of aspiring actors go to New York or Los Angeles knowing nothing about the unions. They learn fast.

New York agents tell them, "Sorry, can't help you if you're not Equity." Hollywood casting directors put out casting notices saying, "SAG *only.*"

"Well, I'll be dipped!" they say as they realize Equity isn't owning a home, SAG is not a physical condition, and non-union people will starve. So they try to join. And what do they hear? "You can't join until you've got a job," and, "I can't hire you unless you're union." Eventually, this gets old — so old that they quit.

Pity. Getting in isn't impossible — with a little information and ingenuity. If you can, join the unions before you leave home. But if you can't, don't despair. You may find it *easier* to join the unions in L.A. than in your native Cleveland.

Our point? Before you buy that plane ticket, read our chapter on the unions (Chapter 7); it could alter your plans for a year — or more.

NOTE: For a complete budget and prices, fees, addresses, phone numbers and websites of items mentioned throughout the book, see Appendix.

GET FIT

If losing pounds will make you a beautiful leading lady or a handsome leading man, start exercising. Otherwise, you'll constantly hear you're "hard to place" (cast) because your face says one thing, your body another. If you're a character type your weight may be less important and you can pig out longer at the dinner table. Still, remember commercial casting director Pamela Campus' observation: "Fat thighs do not sell peanut butter."

Anything else about your appearance you don't like? Fix it or learn to live with it. Don't go out on interviews feeling bad about yourself — they're tough enough without that added baggage.

You commercial types especially — get your pearly whites pearly white. To paraphrase Ms. Campus, broken teeth do not sell toothpaste.

And, finally, you don't need a wardrobe that would make Gucci go into jealous convulsions, but get yourself at least one good suit/dress and one good casual outfit.

GET RID OF ACCENTS

No, it's not a crime to have an accent — it's just limiting.

If there aren't any dialect coaches where you live (or even if there are), record announcers who don't have an accent, and work to sound like them. "A cheap way to do it is to get yourself a tape recorder and read something — a play, a scene, a newspaper article — into it every day for ten minutes," suggests theatrical agent Pat Doty. If you can't manage this by yourself run, don't walk, to the nearest dialect coach the minute you arrive in L.A.

GET A JOB SKILL

"The longer my old college chums are in the business, the more realistic they become," says one actress.

Don't expect Hollywood to fall into a swoon over your pending arrival. In fact, it's a fairly safe bet that, from the time you get your SAG card, it will be at least a year before you get your first paying acting job.

You can type, wait table, sell wedgies, etc., without the job getting in the way of your career, but these kinds of jobs are only a temporary solution. If you're smart, you'll find something enjoyable (anything from résumé shot photographer to interior decorator) that won't interfere with acting and pays more than a prune danish — an alternate specialty/skill, almost as much fun as acting, that will carry you during those (inevitable) dry spells. True, hit it big and savings and investments can tide you over. But the average working actor needs a supplementary income. Waiting tables when you're 20 is kicky — but when you're 40 it's a kick in the pants.

If you're without an independent income, and unless you're far enough along in your career to chance your savings on the "switchover to L.A." period, at first plan to get (and keep) a *full-time day job*. It's fantasy to leave your days "free for auditions." What auditions?? Unless you get hot fast in commercials (possible, but so is winning the lottery) you'll need your nights free for classes, theatre and showcasing.

Note: we said *and keep* your job. The first time you get an audition, or, holy cow!, an acting job, tell your current employer your Aunt Bertie just died and you've got to go and do some serious mourning. The next time, terminate Uncle Fritz (what the heck, you don't like him anyway). Only when you've gotten enough work to bump off the entire clan should you give serious consideration to part-time work.

Also, pass on getting a job within the industry. You'll make contacts all right, but as what? A go'fer? A bookkeeper? Okay, now try to get them to think of you as an actor. Says television stage manager James Hamilton, "I wouldn't recommend actors getting into production. It's very hard to prove yourself as an actor in that setting."

ESTABLISH CREDIT

Anyone who believes all Californians are "laid back" hasn't met a banker. Before you leave try to obtain one or two major credit cards — they, a driver's license, perhaps a passport, will be needed to open an account.

You might even have your current bank transfer some of your money to a Los Angeles bank of your choice a few weeks before you leave.

BECOME COMPUTER FRIENDLY

The days when an actor could get away with thinking a fax machine is Joe Friday's telephone and a website is a place where ducks hang out, have crashed. As in every profession, information is power and using a computer is another way to get that information. You don't need to know how to program the next rover to Venus, but at least learn to surf the Internet — as you'll see, many of the places and services we'll be talking about have their own websites. Might learn how to use a fax machine too.

TRAVEL LIGHT

Wait until you know where you're going to live. Why add hassles?

WHAT ABOUT PICTURES (RÉSUMÉ SHOTS)?

A photographer in Walla-Walla can't know what Hollywood is looking for. Wait.

SHOULD YOU CHANGE YOUR NAME?

Not if you're thinking of becoming "Rock Granite" or "Jasmine Julep." Those days, thank Arnold Schwarzenegger, are over.

"Iznik Prlrdj" is acceptable in today's Hollywood, if you want to drive people crazy trying to pronounce it. However, if you've got an ethnic name and a non-ethnic face, a nondescript monicker could eliminate your "ethnicity" and increase opportunities.

Before doing anything check with the national offices of SAG, AFTRA and Equity. If another union member has first dibs on your name, you'll have to change it — even *if it's your real name*.

Whatever you do, do it now — before you have résumés and photos printed up and certainly before you get a few roles under your belt. Changing then will be a big headache for you and your agent.

All done? You're ready to go. Take a deep breath (it'll probably be the last pure air you'll get for a long time), kiss Mama good-bye, and point yourself in a generally westerly direction . . .

3 ARRIVAL IN L.A.

My biggest hurdle in starting out was taking care of my personal basics — a place to call home, a reliable car, some money in my pocket and, most important, some peace of mind. Without those I was only getting in my own way.

Kevin Michael Brown, Actor

Seasoned travelers admit that moving to a new city can be mind-boggling. Not some actors: they hit town Monday night, and by Tuesday morning they're running around on rubbery legs trying to pursue a career, making mistakes that may take years to repair.

Don't do that. Settle in. The only gun you're under is the one you hold on yourself. You're starting a career that's supposed to last for decades. Spare about six months to get the lay of the land.

Don't get in your way either.

ARRIVAL

- *By air:* There are several airports in L.A., but you'll probably arrive at Los Angeles International Airport (LAX), located on the west side of town.

  Before getting your luggage, you might stop at the transportation information booth outside of your terminal to check options. What's available to get you where you want to go inexpensively tends to vary by the year.

  Certainly the cheapest way to finish your journey is by city bus, but be ready to suffer. Distances in L.A. are a whole other planet. Take the airport shuttle "C" to 98th Street and Vicksburg Avenue, then transfer.

  There are also a variety of shuttle services: hotel buses, commercial vans which carry you (and others) directly home, and flat-rate taxis for splendid isolation. Rates vary by destination. Advice from your local paramedic: check costs before jumping in the back seat. Of

---

NOTE: *For addresses, phone numbers, websites, prices, fees of items mentioned throughout the book, see Appendix.*

course, you can rent a car. Liberty, Rent-a-Wreck and Ugly Duckling car rental services are among the less expensive, though not all these can be rented at the airport. You might want to rent from a "major" overnight, then switch to a cheapie.

- By *bus*: Greyhound-Trailways Bus stations are in East L.A., downtown L.A., Hollywood, Glendale and North Hollywood.

- By *train*: AMTRAK's main stop is Union Station in downtown L.A., but trains stop throughout the L.A. Basin.

TAKE A MINI-VACATION

California is just flat-out beautiful. Before you start hitting the career fast-track, ski a mountain or walk a beach. Clears cobwebs.

Locally, you might want to check out Six Flags Magic Mountain, Knotts Berry Farm, Universal Studios Tour, and the venerable Disneyland. Have a drink at the legendary Polo Lounge in the Beverly Hills Hotel — big deals are still cut over scotch and water. For a look at another kind of sabre-toothed tiger, there's the LaBrea Tar Pits. Some freebie attractions: Mann's Chinese Theatre (Rita Hayworth's feet couldn't possibly have been that small), Rodeo Drive (nobody's budget can possibly be that large), and Venice and Muscle Beaches (to see the L.A. everyone thinks is L.A.).

BASIC L.A.

"What city, please?" That's the first thing you'll hear when you dial Information. And they're not kidding. Seventy miles wide, the "Big Orange" is just like the cut-open fruit: sections lying all around no obvious core.

Cross a street and you'll find yourself in another city — Santa Monica, say, or Beverly Hills. It's very confusing at first, but later you'll find these divisions helpful. The city or area name immediately pinpoints locations in what is otherwise a sprawling metropolis.

Take downtown — the usual "core" of any city. It exists, but, unless you work there, it'll have as much import in your life as Idaho. Since there are high-rise office buildings, stores, theatres, etc. in every area of town, you could comfortably work and live in one area and never have to leave it except to visit friends, do special shopping, or go to a particular show, museum or restaurant.

The city is fluid, restless, always on the go and changing — fast. Blink twice and you'll miss the construction of a new building. (At a restaurant in

any other city, you watch your hat. In L.A., you watch the restaurant.)
Anything with ten years on it is a landmark or a tradition.

The people? As a group they're friendly, positive, laid-back yet, para-
doxically, career-oriented. You're judged not by your family tree but by
how well you cut trees down, how much you're paid to do it, and what
kind of car got you to the forest.

Architecture? A zany patchwork quilt of every style importable and
imaginable — from English Tudor to Spanish Hacienda to Modern Disneyland
— cheek by jowl, connected by a palm tree.

The weather? Gorgeous. Oh, there are a few rainy weeks in winter and
foggy ones in spring, but nobody takes them seriously. Sound boring?
Take heart. The ground *moves*. For swimmers, the ocean is often Antarc-
tica; for lovers and philosophers it's Eden. The city's legendary smog has
been institutionalized — via the South Coast Air Quality Management
District (AQMD), which "manages" what is quaintly called the Pollutant
Standards Index (PSI). The index is usually at its lowest in winter, at its
highest in summer and early fall. (You want it low. During the worst
months you may feel you're coming down with the flu. You're not. The air
has merely become unmanageable.)

Food? Anything you want, from fast food to Vietnamese, with a premium on ambiance, chic, novelty, and especially, nifty names. (Thin is
"in" anyhow.)

Entertainment? If you want to see it, it's here: everything from female
mud wrestling to the Los Angeles Philharmonic. (One day we'd like to see
female mud wrestlers *versus* the L.A. Philharmonic.)

And there's no movie you can name that won't be playing somewhere
within the year. Same goes for just about any item on the face of planet
Earth: if you want to buy it, there's a store waiting eagerly to sell it to you.

Los Angeles was aptly summed up by drama critic John C. Mahoney:
"This town is an enormous smorgasbord. You can walk around and create
your own city — like a sandwich." It can be one gigantic headache or
Christmas present depending on your attitude, how hard you work at
making it home, and how energetically you search for people with interests in common with yours.

There's one interest, however, that all Angelenos have in common.
They've had a love affair with it long before Isis got the yens for Osiris. It's
a status symbol and, according to psychologists, an "extension" of its
occupants. They travel in it, eat in it, use it as a baby sitter, make love in it,
and even worship in it — the car.

So if you want to know about life in L.A., we must start with . . .

TRANSPORTATION

- *Autos*: One blessing of this car-itis is that the city's freeways and streets are usually in decent condition and well-marked. There are often special lanes for turning left and blue street signs giving advance notice of the next major avenue. You can pick up street and freeway maps at a gas station, auto club (Automobile Club of Southern California AAA), or bookstore. A favorite is the Thomas Bros. guides.

  The curse of L.A. car mania is gridlock. If you want to speed along on the open road, try Texas, because those free-wheeling freeway days are a memory in the Big Orange. The problem gets worse with each word you're reading, so give yourself plenty of travel time. (Figure rush hour from 7 to 10 a.m. and 3 to 7 p.m. Rest of the day is semi-rush. Best time to leave to beat the Friday rush: Tuesday.)

  Since it rarely rains, suntan oil builds up on arms and motor oil builds up on roads. Add water and things can get slippery. Be extra careful when it drizzles.

  You probably know you can turn right on a red light, but for more on traffic regulations and car registration information, pick up free copies of the *California Driver Handbook* and the *Vehicle and Vessel Registration Handbook* at the nearest office of the State of California Department of Motor Vehicles (DMV).

  Twenty days after you become a resident or get a job you must register your car and obtain a Certificate of Compliance (smog certification). That may mean bringing the old clunker up to snuff. Anyway, look for any gas station sporting a smog check sign.

  Your car is your lifeblood. Keep it in good working condition and expect dents — on your wallet. Everything about automobiles costs more in L.A. — from mandatory insurance to registration, from gas to maintenance.

- *Buses*: Primary system is the Metropolitan Transportation Authority (yep, Charlie, it's the MTA).

  Transit-wise Angelenos catch the bus *prior* to the one that's supposed to get them to their destinations on time. In addition to traffic delays, scheduled buses sometimes simply never come. (The schedulers used to write for *The Twilight Zone*.)

  Riding buses across this vast city is a time-consuming, exhausting affair. You can't pursue a career effectively leaving the driving to them. Get a car.

- *Cabs*: Hope you're a millionaire.

TEMPORARY HOUSING

If you're thinking in terms of a month or longer, you might look into The Oakwood, which is sort of an apartment-hotel. They've got four locations in L.A. Call their 800 number and they'll send you a brochure. It won't include prices; for those you'll have to call the specific location you've chosen.

If you prefer motels, shop around. You might find one that's not much more expensive.

FINDING/RENTING AN APARTMENT

Types of apartments:

1. *Efficiency*: One small room, bath and kitchen.

2. *Single*: One larger room, bath and kitchen (equivalent to a studio apartment in other parts of the country).

3. *One bedroom*: Two rooms, bath and kitchen.

Rent will depend on size, location and amenities. Be prepared to be hit up for the first and last month's rent, a security deposit, sometimes a cleaning fee. There may be no lease, a six-month lease or a one-year lease. You'll probably pay gas and/or electricity; they'll pay water. If you use air conditioning, you'll heat up your electric bill.

You'll find a greater selection if you stick to unfurnished apartments. These almost always include a stove. But often, of late, no fridge. That's right — no fridge.

If you don't mind driving, you can live anywhere you want. However, since many of the studios and casting offices are in the San Fernando Valley (called simply "the Valley") or the Hollywood area, we recommend the following locations on the basis of proximity:

- *West Hollywood, Hollywood Hills:* Most centrally located; not bad; rents vary, tend toward expensive.

- *Hollywood:* Central location, but a number of seedy areas. Wide range of rents.

- *The Valley:* Includes Studio City, North Hollywood, Universal City, Sherman Oaks, Van Nuys, Burbank, Glendale, and others. These areas get hot and smoggy; in summer you'll need an air conditioner. Rents vary.

- *If you don't mind driving and have some money:* Anything west of West Hollywood (Beverly Hills, Westwood, Culver City, West Los Angeles, Brentwood). As you move west, the apartments and neighborhoods get nicer, cooler and more expensive. Best chances for bargains are Culver City and West Los Angeles.

- *If you don't mind driving and want to live at the beach:* Santa Monica, Manhattan Beach, Venice, Marina Del Rey. Rents generally on the high side. Really pricey: Pacific Palisades and Malibu.

- *If you don't mind driving, period:* Pasadena, Montrose, the West Valley, La Crescenta, Flintridge, etc. Generally, the farther out you go, the lower the rents.

Figure out where you'd like to live, then buy a neighborhood newspaper. Unless you want leftovers, find out when these papers hit the stands and be there to catch them in mid-air.

You could check with a real estate agency in the area, perhaps even an "apartment finders" service. The former probably won't charge, the latter will. The value of either is variable, and you can often do better on your own.

In fact, a good way to search for an apartment is just to drive around. Sometimes all the advertising that's done is a sign on a lawn.

When applying for an apartment, identify yourself by your other job: secretary, office manager — even writer if all else fails — rather than actor. Writers are respectable; they smoke pipes. Actors conduct black masses on the bellies of virgins.

Other tips:

- Get an apartment that includes a parking place.

- You want a washer-dryer on the premises. (The "corner" laundry may be a mile away.)

- To avoid air-conditioning, rent a ground-floor apartment. Heat rises.

- If money is tight, consider apartment-managing, house-sitting, and of course, the time-honored roommate. For all three, scan bulletin boards of colleges and the acting unions, the trade paper classifieds, or even take out your own ad. You can try a roommate-finding service, but add a non-refundable fee to your budget.

- L.A.'s Secret Law: there must be a Dragon Lady (of either sex) in every third building. To avoid him/her, size up the manager/owner

— whoever lives on the premises — carefully. Lots of rules? Kill the deal. You're not renting a cell in Folsom Prison.

GETTING A PHONE

In L.A., Ma Bell has two daughters: Pacific Telephone and General Telephone. Which daughter you marry depends on the area in which you live.

Neither requires a deposit, you'll pay for installation, and both your installation and monthly rate will depend on those little extras, so be careful. You'll probably be surprised at how cheap your monthly rate is; then bam! You get your bill and the "toll calls" would choke a horse. That's because your basic service only extends a certain distance from where you live (they claim it's about ten miles, we swear it's next door), and because L.A. is so big, you're going to place toll calls within the city.

Note your heavy toll-calling areas. Then pour yourself a stiff Perrier and call your phone company and see what kind of savings you can muster with whatever thigamajig toll plan they're offering this week. You'll need them to explain it about six times.

Other services:

- *Call Forwarding*: You're going out. You "program" your phone with the number where you can be reached. When someone calls, their call will be routed to the phone you're near.

- *Call Waiting*: Busy signal prevention. You're adding an additional line onto the same phone number, and can receive two phone calls at the same time.

We used to talk about the area codes you'd be using most. Then Ma Bell went freakazoid with new area codes. (Pretty soon you'll need an area code for your bathroom.) All we can say now is, when leaving messages be sure to include yours, and when it changes in the next 48 hours be sure to correct it on your résumés, letters, etc.

GETTING A JOB

Temporary work is the solution if you need a job quick. Check the no-fee temporary agencies listed in the phone book, trade paper classifieds and union bulletin boards.

But unless your career is already past the early stages or your name is DuPont, ultimately you'll need a full-time job. Don't get one you hate — that's a morale killer. And don't take a job that has you in and out of town or demands a lot of overtime. If there's no time for your career, why are you in Hollywood?

Give your agent your work number and never pass up an audition because you're needed at the word processor. It won't compute and your relationship will suffer.

But don't tell any other industry person you do anything but act full time. We once heard a casting director say actors with regular jobs "aren't professional." May all the elastic in his underwear crumble at the Oscars. Most actors work from time to time, and this attitude reveals a terrible (but unfortunately not uncommon) case of the smugs.

FOOD

Eating out is an expensive little pastime, so get a place with a kitchen *pronto*. When grocery shopping, think big — large often equals cheaper.

Distances make it hard for actors to hang out New York-style, but there are spots such as Duke's On Sunset on the Sunset Strip, DuPar's Coffee Shop and Jerry's Deli (a touch of Manhattan) near CBS Studio Center in Studio City, Lucy's Cafe El Adobe near Paramount, Canter's near CBS-TV and other restaurants near the major studios. Medium-priced shop-talk places include Hampton's in Hollywood and the Broadway Deli in Santa Monica. Drop by and you'll get a mouthful of burger and an earful of "biz."

FURNITURE/FURNISHINGS

A newspaper called *The Recycler* is available at most newsstands and contains ads for just about anything people want to sell or swap. You can get some great buys — especially if you can dicker. Same with garage sales and swap meets. Be ready to pay cash.

Best Buy, Circuit City, The Good Guys, The Office Depot, Office Max, The Home Club, and The Price Club are just a few of the stores that offer name-brand merchandise at low prices.

CLOTHING

Want to dress from head to foot without paying an arm or a leg? Discount clothing stores abound, especially in downtown L.A.'s garment district in the neighborhood of Los Angeles and Ninth Streets.

Others, called "re-sale stores," sell lightly-used clothes, often with de-signer labels. Some of the more interesting in this category are It's A Wrap, in Burbank; Reel Clothes & Props and Studio Wardrobe Services, both in Studio City (the latter on the CBS studio lot, no less); and Reel Clothes & Props II, the Sequel, in Sherman Oaks. All sell wardrobe from movie and television shows — some of them pieces worn by the stars. With care, you can pick up some incredible bargains and have everyone wondering how you, Paul Oldfellow, can afford to dress like Paul Newman.

ESTABLISHING CREDIT

Whether or not you brought plastic with you, establish credit within the city.

Go a bank and open a savings account. Let's say you put in $1,000. Then go to the loan officer and tell him you want to make a $1,000 loan, using your savings account as collateral. (You're guaranteeing the loan will be paid back, because if you default, the bank simply grabs the money in your savings account.)

Then, pay it off in about a year. It won't give you the credit rating of a Rockefeller, but it'll help.

Another possibility is to open a charge account at a gas station or department store. If you get one, put some charges on the card and don't pay it off right away; make only minimum payments. After a few months, you've established at least some credit. (Another tip: not all credit card companies check financial histories. Apply, apply, apply.)

INFO LINE

This free service is available 24 hours a day, seven days a week, and gives information or referrals for housing, community services, emergency food, medical treatment, just about you name it. They have a toll-free number (see Appendix 3).

SIZING UP THE SITUATION

With an apartment, job, and telephone, welcome to L.A.! Now it's time to get that lay of the land, at a leisurely, get-yourself-together pace. Say, three months. You'll know when to get moving; you'll get itchy.

Some places to size up:

- *The unions*: That is, SAG, AFTRA, Equity. Check out their bulletin boards. You'll find all sorts of interesting information, from photographers advertising rates to apartments for sublet, cars for sale, announcements of a free seminar or two.

- *Samuel French's Theatre & Film Bookshops, Larry Edmunds Bookshops and Elliot M. Katt's Bookstore:* Plays, books and other items on acting and film will beg, "Take me home!" And you will. For scripts, posters, movie collectables, visit Movie World and The Collector's Bookstore, among others.

- *The American Film Institute:* It's there for the advancement and preservation of motion pictures in general, and for training filmmakers in particular. It's also the home of the SAG Conservatory Program, which we'll talk about later. The Institute has its own library, with fascinating books and film scripts. Don't be surprised to see actors working on auditions for a student film. Goes on all the time. More on this later, too.

- *Those live TV shows:* Excellent research for an actor. Call the stations and find out how you can get tickets to what's currently in production. When observing, avoid watching the TV sets around you. Watch the actors and what they are doing live.

- *USC, UCLA*: USC's film school is good; its neighborhood ain't. UCLA is a beautiful, sprawling campus adjoining an area called Westwood Village — one of the few walking areas in L.A., with one of the largest collection of first-run movie theatres in town. Speaking of . . .

- *Walking areas*: Two other nice places for a stroll and a flick are the Third Street Promenade in Santa Monica and "City Walk" in Universal City. To jog, bike, skate or walk for exercise you can't beat San Vicente Boulevard from Brentwood all the way to the ocean in Santa Monica.

- *The studios*: Pass by all the major studio lots (see Map). You'll be auditioning at these places and it'll help to know where they are. Without a pass, you won't be allowed onto the grounds (unless you've got the chutzpah to take a manila envelope with you, wave knowingly at the guard, and hope he thinks you're delivering something. Less daring civilians can take a studio tour). If you do get on, don't burst into anyone's office hoping to get discovered. These are busy people — with long memories.

- *Theatres, plays*: See play after play. If you're worried about cost, find out when previews are held; they're usually cheaper. Go to enough theatres, see enough plays, read enough reviews and you'll know where you'd eventually like to strut the boards.

- *Acting classes*: No, don't take a class yet — but look around. And, of course, attend all the freebie seminars you can.

- *The trades*: We'll go into these in more detail later, but take a gander at *Back Stage West/Drama-Logue, The Daily Variety* and *The Hollywood Reporter*. They're available at most newsstands and by subscription.

- *Get to know the city*: Get out and around; learn major streets and subdivisions. Try shortcuts. Now's the time to head for Burbank and wind up in Oxnard, not when you're on your way to an audition. Mix. Mingle. Network. Set a schedule. Sitting home doing nothing is the actor's greatest trap; don't fall into it. You're in an exciting city. Add to the excitement.

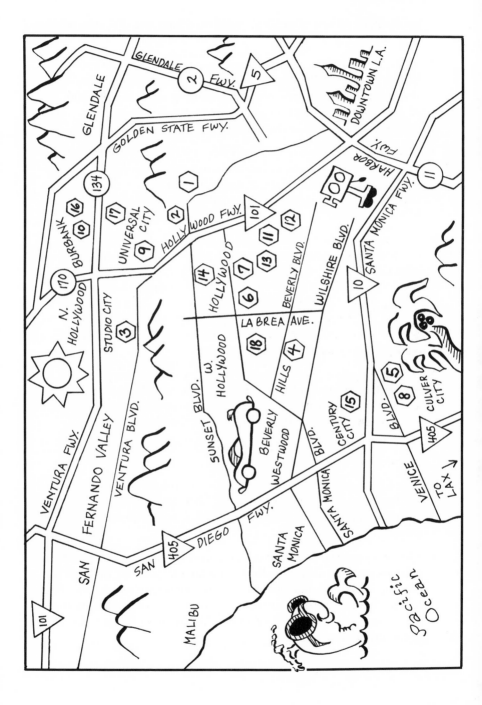

Studio Map Key

(Map not drawn to scale)

1. ABC Television Center, 4151 Prospect Ave., Los Angeles 90027

2. American Film Institute, 2021 N. Western Ave., Los Angeles 90027

3. CBS Studio Center, 4024 Radford Ave., Studio City 91604

4. CBS Television City, 7800 Beverly Bl., Los Angeles 90036

5. The Culver Studios, 9336 W. Washington Bl., Culver City 90232 (also Columbia/TriStar Television)

6. Hollywood Center Studios, 1040 N. Las Palmas Ave., Los Angeles 90038

7. Hollywood National Studios, 1043 N. Seward St., Los Angeles 90038

8. Sony Pictures Entertainment, 10202 W. Washington Bl., Culver City 90232 (Includes Columbia/TriStar Motion Picture Companies)

9. Universal Studios, 100 Universal City Plaza, Universal City 91608

10. NBC Television, 3000 W. Alameda Ave., Burbank 91523

11. Paramount Studios, 5555 Melrose Ave., Los Angeles 90038

12. Raleigh Studios, 650 N. Bronson St., L.A. 90004, & 5300 Melrose Ave., L.A. 90038

13. Ren-Mar Studios, 846 N. Cahuenga Bl., Los Angeles 90038

14. Sunset-Gower Studios, 1438 N. Gower St., Los Angeles 90028

15. 20th Century Fox, 10201 W. Pico Bl., L.A. 90035 (Mailing address: P.O. Box 900, Beverly Hills 90213)

16. Walt Disney Studios, 500 S. Buena Vista St., Burbank 91521

17. Warner Brothers Studios, 4000 Warner Bl., Burbank 91522

18. Warner Hollywood Studios, 1041 N. Formosa Ave., W. Hollywood 90046

II
THE SUPPLIES YOU'LL NEED

SUNGLASSES ✓
TUXEDO
HOME IN BEL AIR
MERCEDES (VINTAGE)
TAN
DESIGNER JEANS
DESIGNER SHOES
DESIGNER PAPER TOWELS
CANNES BUMPER STICKER
BATHROOM TELEPHONE
CAR TELEPHONE
HALL CLOSET TELEPHONE
KIDNEY-SHAPED HOT TUB
CAVIAR ON KIWI FRUIT

4 A LIST OF SUPPLIES

*I used to always summarize by saying,
"Persevere." But "perseverance" isn't in my
summary any more. After all, you have to
know what you're persevering at, and you've
got to have the right materials. So, in
summary: Picture, Résumé, 'Equity Waiver' Theatre,
Cassette, Agent, Producer, and Casting Director.*

Buddy Bregman, Producer-Director

Here's a list of supplies you'll need during your first year. In the Appendix, you'll find a complete budget with dollar amounts for every item mentioned.

We've divided your supplies into three categories:

1. *The Musts*: Obviously, items you can't function without.

2. Other *Items*: You can survive without them, but they can help a lot.

3. *Chicken Soup*: You can spend an entire career without ever having any of these items. But, if you've got the money, like chicken soup, they can't hurt.

Take a look at the budget in Appendix 1, toss in your personal expenses and you'll have a pretty good idea not only of where to start, but of what you're going to have to/want to do and earn at least for the next year.

A point that bears repeating: Figure you'll earn your first money as an actor about one year after the date you get your SAG card (unless you're fantastically lucky). Don't quit your job and declare that you are "now an actor." Keep (or get) that job; acquire the items you'll need; learn some basics about the business; and save your money.

Except for theatre, showcases and classes (each has a chapter of its own later in the book), the next four chapters will go into detail about all the items below.

• THE MUSTS

Telephone
Headshot session
Headshot printing (500 theatrical, 500 commercial)
Résumés (typing, printing 500)

Union(s) initiation
Union dues
Postage
Envelopes (good-looking manila, some regular)
Academy Players Directory listing
Answering device/voice mail/possibly beeper (see below)
Good stationery
Thank-you notes
SAG agency list
Datebook
Theatre, showcases, classes

• OTHER ITEMS

Card file & notebook
Directories
Working Actors Guide
Trade subscriptions
Postcards
Beeper
Typewriter
Labels (blank or pre-addressed)
Videocassette (including air-check, stock, editing)
Passport

• CHICKEN SOUP

Desk
Fax
Computer and/or Fax Machine
VCR
Video camera

5 RÉSUMÉ SHOTS

*Q: When an actor comes into your office and
he doesn't look like his résumé shot, what's
your reaction?*

A: I get furious.

Interview with Judith Holstra, Casting Director

Here's how a contractor we know hires roofers: "Any guy can come into the office and talk a good game about all the wonderful work he's done, but me, *I look at his tools.*"

Your agent (and yourself) uses two tools to sell you: your résumé and your résumé shots. If either is bad, you've tied one hand behind his (your) back.

Photos pour into the offices of casting directors, agents, producers, and directors. Some are good, others, fair. Many are atrocious. There are shots of actors taken with a Polaroid-type camera, half-naked Adonises, figures standing at a distance, waving languidly at the camera . . . And these are the people who will complain, "You just can't beat the system." Well, as theatrical agent David Westberg says, "We're dealing in a visual business. The first thing you need to get in the door is pictures. If your pictures are lousy you ain't gonna get in the door."

Unfortunately, putting together good pictures is like assembling a toy train on Christmas Eve — it's a pain in the neck. It's involved, time-consuming and filled with wonderful little aggravations and things to remember.

Take the time. Plow through it, step by step. Others will. Don't settle for pictures that are mediocre. Eventually, you'll have pictures you're proud to submit — shots that will pay you back in satisfaction and, more important, in income.

RÉSUMÉ SHOTS: THE CARDINAL RULE

The days of the "Joan Crawford glamor picture" are long gone. Today, casting directors, etc., are turned off by photos of painted goddesses and costumed gods. What they want now is to see *you* — not how you'd *like*

NOTE: *For addresses, phone numbers, websites, prices, fees of items
mentioned throughout the book, see Appendix.*

to look, but how you honestly *do* look, scars, moles, warts and all.

We can't emphasize this more strongly. Pictures that don't look like you are worthless. Never forget that.

Now, when starting out, you will need:

- At least one good *COMMERCIAL* headshot;
- At least one good *THEATRICAL* headshot.

(You should be able to get both in one session with a photographer.) Before we explain the differences between these two . . .

HEADSHOTS IN GENERAL
(WHETHER "COMMERCIAL" OR "THEATRICAL")

A headshot, sometimes called an "eight-by-ten" (8x10), is a single black-and-white closeup of the actor's face and hair. (Color pictures are a waste of money.) It's eight inches wide by ten inches long, and there is nothing on the back of the photo.

A headshot, again, shows what you honestly look like in street garb. (No sequined evening gowns or Roman togas, and remember, as theatrical casting director Jerry Franks cautions, "Beefcake or cheesecake photos are very offensive.") Women should apply makeup slightly heavier than usual for the shoot, but the result should be a standard daytime look.

In a headshot, look directly at the viewer. Forget cloud-gazing or profile shots (you can get away with a bit of profile, but still look straight into the camera).

Don't try for the kind of photo a model would use. Avoid tricky lighting or "mists" around the face, and don't ask the photographer to airbrush out scars and wrinkles.

Be careful of background(s). You are not selling tree trunks.

And, if the headshot is good, it'll capture your special quality. Lisa Kudrow bubbles. Val Kilmer smolders. As theatrical agent John Mekrut put it, "The overriding consideration is that the picture has to communicate to whoever is looking at it: this is somebody you want to meet."

At least every three years or whenever anything about you changes, you've got to have new pictures done. As casting director Kathy Smith says, "Whenever you change your hair, say from long to short, think of it as a [minimum] $200 haircut." We'd just like to add not to forget weight gain or loss, and getting older.

Actually, sometimes you should change pictures simply to change pictures. As photographer Tama Rothschild says, "I think casting directors get tired after two years of seeing the same shot. They notice if you have a new shot — it's a new interest in your career."

THE COMMERCIAL HEADSHOT

. . . Goes to anyone involved with the making of commercials (agents, casting directors, production houses, etc.).

On a *commercial* shot, you should look straight out of a musical comedy, showing lots of teeth (they need to know you've got good ones) and gobs of happiness in a "Gosh, it's great to be alive" manner. (No smolder here, please.)

In short, you must look happy, warm, and perky — *very* happy, *very* warm and *very* perky. Happy, warm, perky people sell soap. And happy, warm, perky pictures sell people to the people who want happy, warm, perky people to sell soap.

THE THEATRICAL HEADSHOT

. . . Goes to people involved with films, television, non-broadcast media (such as CD-Roms, industrial films and videos, etc.) and stage productions (agents, casting directors, producers, directors).

Here's where you sell your special quality as an actor, whether warm and happy or not. If you're a burly, villainous sort, project that. Don't lard it on to the point where you look like Jack the Ripper, but enough to suggest how you might be used. Ask yourself:

- *How am I normally cast?* Do I play a lot of calculating women? Weak little men? Villains? Moody young heroes?

- *What have my friends told me about my acting personality?* Do they talk about my warmth? My wit? My sensuality?

- *Is there a known star I am often compared to?* Comparisons to Kurt Russell suggest a casual, rugged look; James Spader suggests a suit and tie. (We're not talking about imitating anybody. The industry already has a Kurt Russell; it doesn't, however, have you.)

- *What roles on television/movies/stage/commercials could I have done without having to stretch* at all?

The answers will tell you your "type" and what qualities your theatrical headshot(s) should show. Understand this: Hollywood isn't a rep company, it's a business of types. The days of playing Granny (if you're 20) are gone. Sorry.

One other note. Have at least two theatrical shots — one for dramas, the other for comedies. Your commercial shot can do double duty for the comedy.

THE THREE-QUARTER SHOT

Used both for commercials and theatricals, this photo shows the actor head-to-waist, head-to-hip, or even head-to-toes. It has become a near-staple in an L.A. actor's portfolio. (Some actors feel three-quarter shots stand out in a stack of headshots and use them almost exclusively.) Also, since commercial composites are no longer used (see below), many commercial agents and casting directors like these shots as they show the actor's body. (If I'm thinking of calling you in on a McDonald's spot, I want to know that you don't look like you need less beef and more veggies.)

However, the three-quarter shot can be problematic. A good one can help to suggest how the actor might be used, but the very nature of the picture makes the subject's face smaller, and the impact of his expression may also be lessened. Worse, some overly "creative" photographers will pose actors in ridiculously mannered and/or contorted positions that can make it nearly impossible to get a clear idea of what the actor looks like — which is like selling sizzle with no steak in sight.

As photographer Herb Weil points out, "If you're trying to establish something — say, if you're a gal with a tremendous chest or a guy who's muscular — if there's a reason for that kind of shot, fine. Otherwise it's dead space. What's interesting about a shirt, jacket or sweater?" And bear in mind photographer Dick Wieand's warning, "If you're a little over-weight a three-quarter shot might hurt you."

In any case, during your headshot session have the photographer take some smiling, commercial-looking three-quarter shots and some theatrical three-quarter shots. Then use the pictures that show you off best. In short, don't lose any sleep if your commercial photo is a headshot, and don't hit the bottle if your theatrical picture is a three-quarter shot.

One other thing. If you submit a three-quarter shot to the Academy *Players Directory* (see Chapter 8) you'll need to tell them you want the entire photo printed or they'll automatically crop it down to a headshot.

THE COMPOSITE

Composites consist of one large photo on the front with three to six — usually four — smaller photos on the back, showing the actor in various situations and outfits. In past years, this was a popular format for commercial work, but they're no longer used except by models and stuntpersons. It's possible they could make a comeback, but for now, they're outski.

Now that you know what you need, don't necessarily run out and get a photographer. First, give some thought to . . .

PRACTICING

It's one thing to know what you want to project; another to project it — especially if you haven't worked in front of a camera.

Buy a friend a beer and convince him/her to do a mock photo session with you, using any camera capable of taking close-ups. Try different poses, outfits, attitudes, etc., and keep shooting until you get tired or your friend begins to seriously grunt . . .

What you get back from the drug store should tell you quite a bit about how to project yourself. No photographer can pull out "hidden charms" or get silk photos out of a sow's ear of a subject.

FINDING A PHOTOGRAPHER

Q. I've got a friend with a camera. Can he take my résumé shots?

A. We've got a friend with a scalpel. Can he take out your appendix?

In other words, get a pro who knows what the industry is looking for. Finding one is easy. They spend a good deal of time and energy trying to find you. Besides, you can:

- Ask actors. They know who's good.

- Check the trades (see "Trades," Chapter 8). Shooters galore advertise in them.

- Scan bulletin boards of unions, acting schools and other places where actors congregate.

- Pop into photographic print shops. They often have photographers' calling cards, customers you can quiz, and employees with a lead or two.

- You might also drop over to Sam Christensen's Studio in Studio City (see Appendix 5 for address). Sam is a highly respected career consultant who works with actors helping them to figure out how best to sell themselves. He's compiled what he calls "The Hollywood Headshot Gallery": a large list of photographers, with examples of their work, and with space for actors to write in their comments on those photographers. It's open to all actors at no charge, and no one will try to sell you anything.

And finally, to get you started, we list a few of the city's many good photographers in Appendix 5.

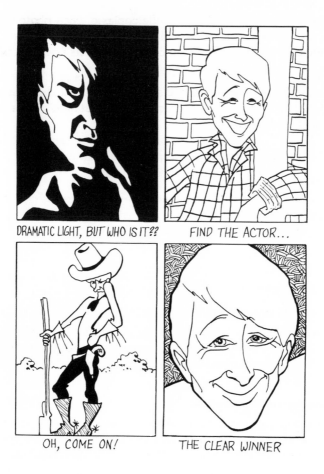

DRAMATIC LIGHT, BUT WHO IS IT??

FIND THE ACTOR...

OH, COME ON!

THE CLEAR WINNER

CONTACTING THE PHOTOGRAPHER

First, some "lingo":

- *Headshot session:* It lasts an hour or two. Figure the photographer will take about 70 (sometimes more) shots of your glorious mug.

- *Exposures, shots:* Other words for "photo" (i.e., 72 exposures equals 72 photos).

- *Negatives:* Few photographers will give their clients the actual negatives, as this is the way they protect the copyright on their work. Rather, you'll get:

- *Proofs, proof sheets*: They're little copies of each photo (about the size you get in a video arcade) on sheets of photographic paper, about 16 to a sheet. You then choose the shots you want blown up into:

- *Print(s)*: These are your 8x10's. One to four of these usually are included in the cost of the session. Beyond that, you'll pay a small fee for each additional print.

Now that you know the jargon, ask him:

How does he work?

Very important. "Posing" you is perfect — for wax museums. You want a photographer who snaps away as you move. He should talk to you, coax you, and, yes, stroke your ego a little.

How much?

What does he include in his price for a headshot session (i.e., how many exposures and prints; how much for extra prints)?

How many costume changes are permitted?

To a photographer, a "costume change" means a change of street garb-type outfits — not cowboy hats and spurs. Four changes are about the most you'll need, but define terms. Taking off a tie is a "costume change" to some.

Is a make-up artist available?

Many photographers offer an additional make-up person at, of course, an additional charge. Tends to be a bit expensive, but making yourself up for the camera can be tricky. Whether to hire one depends on your knowledge.

How long before you get your proofs/prints?

Minimum: a few days. Maximum: two weeks.

Does he keep the negatives?

Expect a "yes," but a few will give them up.

What happens if you don't like your proofs?

Sticky question, but ask — before the first click of the shutter. Most photographers will schedule another session at no additional charge. A few give half or all your money back.

MEETING WITH THE PHOTOGRAPHER

Besides checking to see if you're comfortable with him, you're really there to look at his samples. Don't skim. Scrutinize those shots. Remember, he thinks they show his best work. Notice . . .

Are they clear and bright, or "muddy"? Are the contrasts between light and dark clear and crisp?

The backgrounds: Are subjects in front of brick walls, traffic, spangly paper, etc.? That's distracting and the photographer should know that.

Do the actors jump off the page? Do they excite you? Is there animation in their faces? If it's a commercial shot, does the actor have life and warmth, or is he just smiling? If it's a theatrical shot, does the actor look interesting?

Do the subjects look stiff or posed? Do the same poses keep popping up? (Some industry veterans can guess the photographer from the poses.) Nobody's special on an assembly line.

Has the photographer called attention to himself by using tricky lighting, shadows, etc.? You're the star, dagnabbit!

Again, and above all, *what is going on in the eyes of the actors?* "The first thing I notice in a picture is the eyes. the eyes sell it," advises theatrical agent Sandra Siegal.

(By the way, use this same criteria when choosing your own photos.)

If delighted with what you see, talk to him a bit. Find out if he basically agrees with how you see yourself, and only give him a go if you think you can work with him. (An actress we know went to her session, and the first thing the photographer said to her was, "Gained a little weight, have we?" Guess how her pictures came out.) If he makes you feel defensive, irked, or just in the Universe of the Ungood, pass.

SETTING THE PLACE AND "MAGIC" TIME

Outdoor lighting usually gives more depth to a photo — helps to eliminate that flat "high school yearbook" look. (Some photographers can shoot indoors and make it look like it was shot outside.) If you shoot outdoors, avoid midday. Shadows cast by the sun are too harsh. Actually, you'd be smart to steal an idea from your own industry. Directors have been known to drive producers up the wall waiting for "magic time" — that special twilight cameras love. Makes the hero look heroic and the *femme* truly *fatale*. Well, though some directors think they're God, they don't own that light. See if you can get the photographer to agree to a shoot around this time.

ABOVE, FRONT AND BACK OF A COMMERCIAL COMPOSITE —BUT TODAY IT'S OUT OF STYLE. IN: THE ¾ SHOT AT RIGHT.

PRE-SESSION PLANNING

Decision time. How do you want to look? (You might love that spiked hairdo, but will the industry?) Satisfied with your choices? Fine. Now look that way for as long as you use those shots (probably a year or more). Your hair color, length, and curliness may vary only slightly. Your makeup can't change much either. And moustaches and beards cannot be grown/cut off. Want to change? New photos.

Next, raid the closet. Clothing should suit your type and what you want to project. Medium-to-light-colored clothing is best for your commercial headshot (a quiet plaid under a sweater is a highly saleable commercial look); darker colors are okay for your theatrical headshot. But avoid white or black, loud plaids, prints, shiny fabric — anything that distracts from your face. Skip jewelry too. Pick out a dressy and an informal outfit — provided, again, that either doesn't conflict with your type. Don't be shy. Bring a load of clothes and ask the photographer for his opinion.

Finally, go over in your mind what you're going to do. A good photo session is a combination of the actor's ideas and those of the guy with the camera. Photographer Dale Tarter advises, "It's as important for you to be prepared when you come to see a photographer as it is going on a movie set. *Do your homework.* I love it when an actor knows what he wants."

THE SESSION

Do what you planned. Don't be pushed into poses that are wrong for you. Outside of that . . .

- *Nerves*: If you're a bit shaky, say so. A good photographer will do all he can to calm and reinforce you. (We know one photographer who routinely pretends to shoot a nervous actor for about 15 shots. Then, with the actor over the jitters, he really goes to work. Works like a charm.)

- *Lose glasses and maybe contacts too:* "Specs block the eyes, and contacts reflect light." That used to be our flat statement until actor Brad Yates pointed out: "I found if I didn't wear contacts I couldn't really see the camera, much less focus on it. I think this can hurt the intensity of the eyes." He has a point. Just be careful in choosing your prints that your eyes don't look like you're an alien from the planet "Gleam." As to glasses, you can use them for a specialty shot, but bear in mind theatrical agent Joel Rudnick's comment: "Half the pictures under the category of 'character' in the *Academy Players*

Directory show people wearing glasses. You know, they do various things with them like putting the glasses at the end of their noses . . . and I don't think it works. It just looks hokey."

- *Don't squint:* Occasionally, between shots, squint as hard as you can. Then relax. Feel the difference?

- *Other tricks:* Moist lips photograph better, so, every once in a while, lick your lips. To avoid glassy eyes, look down to the ground. Set your mood. When the photographer is ready, suddenly look up. If he shoots at that instant, you'll have a lively, animated expression.

And, above all, as personal manager Larry Fonseca put it, "Look at the camera — that's where your money is. Look at that camera and say 'Buy me.' Think about something. Feel sexy. Feel mean. Do whatever you want, *but think about something.*"

EXAMINING THE PROOFS

In Universe 27-B, everyone's a millionaire, nobody ever hits a red light, and every shot on all proof sheets is fantastic. In our universe (which continually gets mixed reviews), when your proofs are ready, you'll have to be picky.

Using a lupe or magnifying glass — ideally one with a light — employ the criteria mentioned earlier under "Choosing a Photographer."

Usually the photographer's choices are dead on, but get other opinions. "Actors should never pick their own pictures," says résumé photographer John Sanchez. "They just don't know the industry." Certainly show your choices to your agent and any other industry-wise person you can pin down. Just remember, we said industry-wise. Mom will fall in love with a mantelpiece shot that's a disaster as a résumé shot.)

Don't narrow your choices to one shot. Why? We're sure it's gremlins, but *no picture ever looks the same blown up as it did on the proof sheet.* Have as many shots blown up as common sense and your pocketbook will allow.

GETTING AND CHECKING YOUR (ORIGINAL) PRINTS

You'll think you're going nuts. On one print, a shadow that "wasn't there" on the proof sheet will now be skiing down your nose. On another, those eyes that "jumped off the proof sheet" now look like Dracula at feeding time. Like we said, gremlins . . .

With those *Twilight Zone* prints out of the way, examine the rest, again using the criteria under "First Meeting With the Photographer," and add:

- Are there any spots or scratches?
- Is the focus fuzzy or sharp?
- Is the photo too light or dark?

Sometimes these things can be corrected with a little darkroom wizardry, but if the photographer says "no way," forget the picture. You can't look good blurred.

Okay, with at least two good original prints — one commercial, one theatrical — it's time to say "bye" to the photographer and move on to the printer. Correction: move on to a *good* printer. Remember, the printer you use is as important as the photographer. "I've seen actors go to a good photographer, get great pictures, and then go to a lousy printer," says photographer Buddy Rosenberg. "They take a beautiful job and totally ruin it."

PRE-PRINTER DECISIONS

Since printers tend to specialize, before contacting them know:

1. The finish you want.
2. Whether or not to have a border.
3. The location of your name.
4. The appearance of your name.

The finish:

Among the finishes in wide use are: "glossy," "matte," "gloss-tone," "pearl" and "classic." There is also the "litho." There's no industry standard. Your choice is wide open.

- *Glossy:* Your pictures will look shiny. It's the most-used and usually least expensive.

- *Matte:* (Pronounced "mat.") Your pictures will have a cloth-like look and feel.

- *Gloss-tone:* Sort of a toned-down version of glossy. Open a magazine and look at the photographs — that's what gloss-tone looks like.

- *Pearl:* Rather difficult to describe. Looks cloth-like but shiny. Sort of a jazzed-up matte finish.

- *Classic:* Very close to a gloss-tone or a glossy.

- *Litho*: Actually, this is not a finish — it's a different kind of paper, but the end result is very close to a matte.

Note that matte, gloss-tone, and pearl finishes don't reproduce as well in newspapers as glossy and gloss-tone tends to scratch more easily.

Border(s) or "bleeds":

Borders are the white spaces between the photo and the edge of the paper. You're not selling white space so keep borders narrow, say three-eighths of an inch (except for the border containing your name). If it's in the printer's repertoire, you can also have a black line put between the photo and the border for a slight feeling of added dimension to the picture. (This is often used for three-quarter shots.) "Bleeding" means the photo itself fills up (bleeds off) the paper, leaving no border at all. A variation is the "three-sided bleed" — one border (usually at the bottom) onto which your name is printed.

Name location:

Horrible thought of the day: A producer sits ruefully staring at your picture. He's dying to use you, but he lost your résumé, and your name isn't on your photo.

Name appearance:

If you have no border, your name is on the photo itself. You tell the printer where you want it, and he'll use one of three methods: "knock-out," "overprint" (or "overlay") and "reverse."

- *Knock-out*: That's a small block of white space with your name printed in black letters within the block.

- *Overprint or overlay*: There's no white space around your name. It's directly on the photo, in black letters.

- *Reverse*: Same as above, in white letters.

Don't let your name disappear. If you use an overprint, be sure the spot you choose for your name is fairly light. If it's a reverse, the spot should be relatively dark.

Finally, there's the typeface you want (script, block letters, etc.). If you want your typeface to be special, you could possibly design your own if you've got a good computer and the printer accepts bringing your own typeface to him. Otherwise, you'll have to choose from what your printer has available. In any case, give some thought to what will compliment your image. Don't laugh — typefaces make statements. Corporations spend thousands finding just the right "T." (That doesn't mean your name should look like a marquee in heat. The photo's the star.)

IF YOU PIN US DOWN

Okay, okay, let us up . . . We like:

- A *pearl* finish (we just like the look).
- A *four-way bleed* (calls more attention to the subject).
- A *reverse* or *overprint* (a knock-out tends to draw too much attention on the name).

Remember, that's only an opinion. Like the Valley Girl says, "It's your choice, *totally*."

CHOOSING A PRINTER

Can he do what you want? Okay, now you want to know the:

- *Negative cost*: The printer photographs the photographer's original print, literally taking a picture of a picture, and makes copies from that new negative. (You'll get this negative back.) There's a small fee for doing this.

- *Lot cost*: The number of copies made, i.e., 200, 300, etc. If you have an agent, order about 300. If not, start with 200 — a future agent may like you, but not your pictures.

- *Name imprinting/negative*: In his secret dungeon, the printer spells out your name in the type you've chosen and takes a picture of it. He'll use the negative to make copies. (You'll get this negative back, too.)

- *Extras*: Cropping, bleeds, overprints, lightening or darkening a picture, etc., may or may not cost extra.

A NOTE ABOUT "LINES"

This isn't Photography 101, so we'll simply say that if two printers cost about the same and both can do what you want, go with the one who *uses more lines*. Your copies will just look better. (Ask, "How many lines do you use?".)

AT THE PRINTER — TEST PRINTS

After telling him all the things you want, order a test print — a sample copy. Some printers include test prints, even test wedges (copies of the picture in various lightnesses and darknesses) in your basic cost. If not, pay the small extra amount to have it done. One bad sample copy is a lot better than 300 bad prints.

He'll want a deposit (usually half of the total cost) and will tell you when he'll have your test print (a few days to two weeks). Don't set your watch by any dates a printer gives you. If you're far away, always call first.

CHECKING THE PRINT(S)

Hang in there, you're almost done. Check your test print(s) as carefully as you've checked everything else. Use all the criteria we've mentioned before, and add:

- Is your name spelled right? Is it straight or crooked?
- Is the printing of your name clear or out of focus?
- Are the letters even on all sides?
- Are they "dirty" with white specks or scratches?
- Did the printer do everything you asked for (lightening, additional cropping, etc.)?

Something wrong? Point it out and have another test print done. If you gave the printer a negative (as opposed to a print) and there's a problem, call the photographer. If the negative can't be fixed, choose another picture.

CHECKING THE COPIES

Don't grab 'em and run. After all, this is the last step. From the center of the stack, pull out a copy and examine it, using all the criteria we've mentioned. Unless something very strange occurred, your copies should exactly match the test print.

Satisfied? Go home; take out one of your pictures; pour a drink and toast yourself. You're now way ahead of a lot of aspiring actors. Was it worth it? Here's what casting director Deborah Barylski says: "Every now and then I think 'God, I've got to go through these pictures because I'm going to find a diamond in there.' And I do. It actually happens."

Congrats, now you've got a diamond!

6 RÉSUMÉS

I can tell a phony résumé at a glance.

Mary Spencer, Theatrical Agent

Hand someone a résumé and photo, and you're presenting them a package. Both are your trademarks. Both make a statement about your professionalism. If you're spending hours pouring over your pictures and ten minutes dashing off your résumé, you're wrapping only the top part of your package.

APPEARANCE

Here's the most neglected area of résumés, and it's just as important as what's on it. Some suggestions:

- *Don't use cheap paper:* That'll make you look cheap. Good paper is 20- or 24-weight rag bond. It'll cost more, but it's worth it. (Just ask the printer to show you a sheet.)

- *Type it on a good typewriter/word processor:* Or have it composed and typed by someone who knows the industry. (Acting résumés are different from business résumés.) The small fee you'll pay will be well worth it. (Actually, unless you've been living on the planet "Dodo," you're probably aware of the wondrous things, from typesetting to graphics, that can be done on even an inexpensive computer. Your résumé can now look as good and as professionally interesting as you want it to look, so no excuses, podnuh.) And never submit a résumé with something handwritten on it.

- *Have it nicely copied:* With the advances in photocopying machines, you can photocopy your résumé and it'll look terrific, or have it offset-printed. There's no need to typeset the résumé. Granted, typesetting looks beautiful, but it's expensive and permanent-looking — as if the actor didn't intend to add any more credits. (Still want that look? Check out one of the desktop publishing services in town — a computer and laser printer can do it.)

- *Try a muted color:* It's eye-catching. We like egg white.

- *Cut the résumé to fit the photo:* You submit a résumé and photo by stapling or glueing the résumé to the back of the picture. (No paper clips, spit, bubble gum or tar.) Since the average piece of paper measures 8 1/2" by 11", cut it down to fit your 8" by 10" photo, or ask the printer to do it — *before* he prints the résumé. Don't forget to allow space for this on all sides when typing the résumé. Sound petty? Might keep your pic around longer. To quote a casting director: "Nothing drives me crazier than résumés that are slightly larger than the photograph. Filing them is a real pain in the neck."

  By the way, if you've got a good computer and printer you could print your résumé directly onto the back of your picture (works best with lithos). Plus: looks great. Minus: can look like you never expect to work again.

- *Your name:* Is the first thing anyone should notice. If you think that's obvious, you'd be surprised at the number of résumés we've seen that make you hunt for that lil' item. How large should your name be? Make it the most prominent thing on the résumé, but not so big you look like you've got an ego that dwarfs Mount Everest. (See sample.)

There are four ways to put a name on a résumé:

1. Have the printer do it. Easiest for you, but expensive.

2. Have it done, or do it yourself using a computer and a laser printer. (If you don't own one, many copy stores rent computer time.)

3. Cut your name from the border of your photo, glue it onto the original résumé, and make copies.

4. Go to an art supplies or stationery store and buy rub-on (dry transfer) lettering. It's inexpensive and will give you a professional look that only requires the artistic skill of drawing a straight line with a ruler.

Finally, be sure everything is spelled correctly. If not, you'll look awefully stewpid.

WHAT NOT TO PUT ON A RÉSUMÉ

- *Your age or age range:* Don't limit yourself. If your résumé says you're 20, you're opening yourself to some casting director saying, "Oh, no, this part calls for a 22-year-old." (Bureaucrats can pop up even in this creative industry.) An age range doesn't help either. Limits you to the numbers you put on the résumé.

- *Any dates*: All dates do is date you.

- *Your Social Security number, home address or measurements*: Résumés can fall into anyone's hands. When a producer hires you, he can ask you or your agent for this information. Discretion keeps creepy crawlers from entering your woodwork.

- *Emphasis on your singing and dancing:* This may sound like strange advice, but there are people in Hollywood who believe singers and dancers can't act. Dumb? Sure. But the attitude exists. We aren't saying to drop all those musical comedies from your résumé; nor are we saying you can't put singing or dancing, perhaps, under "Special Skills." Just don't have your experience here a prominent part of your résumé. Make up a separate résumé for nightclub, concert or dance work.

- *Your college and/or community theatre credits:* Stop yelling, "That's all I've got!" and calm down. We're only saying there's no need to go out of your way to indicate those credits are from *community* theatre. For example, put Cambridge Theatre — *not* Cambridge Community Theatre. Then, as you build up your résumé, drop them.

- *Anything cutesy or autobiographical:* For example, "I was born . . ." A résumé is a list of your credits, not your autobiography or a forum to prove you can write comedy.

WHAT TO PUT ON A RÉSUMÉ AND WHERE TO PUT IT

Here's a typical professional-looking résumé. (Of course, your agent may want modifications.) The little black dots or "bullets," by the way, are an easy graphic touch you can add via computer or by hitting the lower-case "o" on your typewriter and then filling it in with black ink.

- *Your name:* Note it's the most prominent thing you see.

- *The agency name, etc.:* Includes the name of the agency; the name of the actual agent who handles you; their address (including zip code); and their phone number (including area code).

No agent? Move your phone number over to this spot.

- *Your phone number:* Use your voice mail/beeper, if you got. Other-wise, put your home phone number, under the word "Contact." (Creepy crawler avoidance again.)

- *Your four vital statistics (often called Stats or Vitals):* Height, weight, hair color and eye color.

- *Your unions:* Use the standard abbreviations.

Credits

- *BCF:* Unlike a typical business résumé, always put your best credits first (BCF) unless they are obviously dated. People read from the top down. Since you don't put dates, there's no need to put a bit part on a soap over a guest starring role in a series, just because you did the former more recently. Don't bury dynamite under a sea of trivia.

- *Your television credits:* Start with the name of the show in capital letters. Then, reading left to right, add the production company followed by any special billing. (Your agent may want you to substitute or add the character name and a one- or two-word description of the character.) No TV credits? Put the next category first.

- *Your motion picture credits, listed under "Features":* Same as above. In this case the actor had no special billing.

(Some would disagree with this order, opting to put features first, followed by television. The arguments on both sides — film has prestige; TV shows you can work fast — are equally valid. What to do? BCF.)

If you've only got a few (or no) feature/TV credits, put industrials, student films, anything that puts your face on film, under the heading: "Film."

- *Your theatre credits, listed under "Stage":* Reading left to right: The name of the play in capital letters, the name of the theatre, and the name of the character. (Add the city if you like — a good idea if they're New York credits. "Sometimes where you did it is more important than what you played," says director Noel Black.)

If you have no TV, motion picture, industrial or student film credits, your stage credits will, of course, be the only credits on the résumé and the list should be longer (about ten of your best credits).

- *Any skills or talents, listed under "Special Skills":* Actors have gotten auditions because the producer needed someone who could ride a horse, speak a foreign language, shoot pool, play a musical instrument, etc. But don't over-do this. We've seen actors list every skill known to Superman, making themselves look awfully desperate. Also, be sure it relates to acting. Forget "expert tax consultant" and

Steven Stunning

Contact: (213) 333-STAR   REVOLVING DOOR AGENCY
                                            Agent: Slam Gently
                                            #1 Superstar Path
                                            Colossus, CA 99999
                                            (213) 321-BOMB

- *HT:*   11'12"   *EYES:* Red   *UNIONS:* SAG
  WT: 22   *HAIR:* Blue   AFTRA
                                                           AEA

- *TELEVISION:*

  NOVA   Celestial Prods.   Guest Star
  I.V.   Flatline Prods.   Guest Body
  AS THE STOMACH TURNS   Rolaids Inc.   Recurring
  I LOVE LOOSELY   Marilyn Chambers Prods.

- *FEATURES:*

  APRIL THE FIFTEENTH
    (PART 1040-A)   MoneyMadd Inc.
  IT CAME FROM OUTER
    DA SINK   Hal Roach Prods.
  A FAREWELL TO ARMS   DeMilo Prods.
  THE CREATURE FROM
    THE BLACK LATRINE   Rotorooter Inc.

- *STAGE:*

  100 CLOWNS   Theatre of Reduced
                         Expectations   Clown #99
  THE BIG SHOW   Performing Theatre for
                         the Performing Arts   Benito
  PERFORMANCE   Performing Theatre for
                         Performing Performers   Performer
  LOOK BACK IN ANGER   Theatre for the Angry   Pissy

- *SPECIAL SKILLS:* Fluent Pig Latin, sleeping, Golden Thumbnail in
  tiddlywinks

"black belt in muffin-making." And most important, *don't bluff* — if you can't really do it, don't list it. "Chopsticks" doesn't make you a pianist.

- *Training*: (Mr. Stunning doesn't need this, as he's got film credits.) Only have stage credits? You might list your training — especially if it deals with the industry (for example, a film technique class); if the class was in New York or a foreign country, which tends to impress; or if the instructor is well known.

- *Education*: That is, your college credits — B.A., M.F.A., etc. Unless these come from outstanding schools of dramatic training (such as Yale, UCLA, USC, Northwestern, Julliard, NYU), they're — well — nice. Please forgive us if we're sounding blasé about four years or more of your life. It's just that a drama degree by itself isn't going to make Spielberg jump into your lap.

SHOULD YOU PAD A RÉSUMÉ?

Talking about the industry in general, television stage manager James Hamilton says, "Don't ever b.s. someone. These people are experts on b.s. They can spot it a mile away." Excellent advice — especially here. Pad a résumé and you're setting yourself up like the Phantom of the Opera: sooner or later, someone will pull off the mask. But, if you're determined, use your noodle. For example . . .

- *New York credits*: Some terrific theatre is mounted outside the Big Apple, but people in L.A. are often disproportionately impressed with New York credits. Fighting fire with fire, you could take a Dallas community theatre credit (say *The Glass Menagerie*) and move it to a New York off-off Broadway theatre. But, remember, *off-off* Broadway. Saying you appeared in *Rent* will only get you evicted — especially if you also don't belong to Equity. And, if you engage in credit immigration to New York, at least be familiar with that city and the off-off Broadway theatres. Smart is *not* listing New York credits and then telling the interviewer how much you enjoyed strolling through Central Park at 4:00 A.M.

- *Motion picture credits*: Hoo boy. You *might* get away with it if you list an obscure potboiler like *The Bloody Hand with the Greasy Hook That Speared Savannah*, Sharp Productions, Atlanta. Even then, you'll meet someone who knows potboilers or Atlanta production and spots it as a phony. We're not kidding. As one agent puts it,

"If you don't have credits, *don't make them up.* You don't know if I was on the set of *Run Jerry Run* 14 years ago when I was in production."

- *Television credits:* No way. *Absolutely* no way.

- *Industrials/CD-Roms/student films:* Here's your best bet for a little padding, if you must. Many cities have industrial film/CD-Rom production houses and/or colleges that do student films. Just be sure you know what you're talking about.

- *Stage credits:* Leave them in Podunk and you can pad to your heart's content — provided you at least read the plays. But frankly, if that's where you are, you're about as ready to do battle in professional acting as a baby is ready to do brain surgery. (You 18-year-olds are off the hook here. At your age, nobody expects you to have a résumé as long as your arm.)

One other thing. Drop all mention of commercials on your résumé — including "Commercials on Request." Current industry thinking is that mentioning commercials on a résumé can only hurt. Film/TV people either don't care or might worry about you being "too big" for the camera (commercial acting is different from "straight" acting). And, when it comes to commercials, no sponsor is going to be ecstatic seeing all that experience you've had — advertising other people's products. (For more, see our section on commercials.)

Okay, now go to work, bearing in mind a quote we really like. It was on a sign hanging in the window of a résumé typing service: "When they ask to see it, it better be good."

7 THE UNIONS

*Okay. I can't get into the Guild without a job,
and I can't get a job without the Guild.
They're not going to screw my head up. I'm
going to beat them at this.*

An Actress

Some actors have been born with silver spoons in their mouths, but no actor was ever born with a union card in his hand. If you think its impossible to get in the unions, we've got some surprises for you. Today, coming up with the initiation fees can be harder than qualifying to join. Stay tuned.

Your main concern as an actor will be to get into AFTRA, SAG, and Equity.

THE AMERICAN FEDERATION OF TELEVISION AND RADIO ARTISTS (AFTRA)

Its jurisdiction is over actors involved in live and taped television shows and commercials, and other TV and radio performers (announcers, disc jockeys and so on; David Letterman and Peter Jennings are members of AFTRA).

THE SCREEN ACTORS GUILD (SAG)

Actors and extras appearing in motion pictures — whether for use in theatres or on TV — and filmed commercials.

SAG and AFTRA are currently separate unions (see below), but they now jointly negotiate with producers regarding commercials. All rules (what you're paid, the shoot, residuals, etc.) are the same regardless of whether the commercial is under AFTRA or SAG jurisdiction.

A WORD ABOUT THE PROPOSED AFTRA/SAG MERGER

For years AFTRA and SAG have been working towards merging into one giant media performers' union. As of the printing of this edition we can only say that a merger is a *possibility*. Merging requires the hammer-

---

NOTE: *For initiation fees, dues, addresses, phone numbers, and other union information, see Appendix.*

ing out of a lot of problems, and, ultimately, 60 percent of *each* union's membership must vote their approval. Since merging means a likely increase in dues a yes vote is no certainty. Anyway, two points: first, if it does happen, much of the information in this chapter may change. Second: if you need a SAG card and a merger becomes imminent, get down to your nearest AFTRA office and join. Then you'll be performing your own personal merger.

ACTORS EQUITY ASSOCIATION (AEA), CALLED "EQUITY"

Actors and stage managers in live theatre.

However, before we talk about membership . . .

A CAUTION ABOUT JOINING ANY UNION

If you need more experience, and/or want to community theatre, avoid joining any union. Once you do, *you may no longer do any non-union (community) theatre*. All three unions have reciprocal agreements on this.

Exceptions are occasionally granted, but more often union members get around this rule by doing community theatre under phony names. Others, living in North Booneyville, just ignore it because they're outside of major centers like New York or Los Angeles. But any union member doing non-union theatre is subject to a stiff fine the first time he's caught and can even be tossed out of the union(s) if he's caught again. That means bye-bye to his career.

In short, join a union and they'll think of you as a pro. If you're not at that level, avoid the unions and get experience — doing community theatre.

A WORD ABOUT INITIATION FEES, DUES AND THE JOINING RULES

The fees quoted in the Appendix are Los Angeles minimums and can vary depending on the union and where you join. Dues for all increase as your income increases. Also, the rules for getting in any or all of these unions can change. Remember, we wrote this in the morning. You're reading it in the afternoon. Check before you do anything.

THE ONE WAY INTO AFTRA

Got the money? You can join. Anyone can at any time. AFTRA has an "open-door" policy. Obtain an application form from your nearest branch, fill it out, and plunk down the initiation fee and dues in cash, certified check or money order. It's that simple.

THE MANY WAYS INTO SAG

At the Hollywood branch (other branches may vary), send a copy of the contract that makes you eligible (see below). They'll check to be sure it qualifies you to join, then schedule an appointment. Bring your initiation fee plus a semi-annual dues payment.

Contrary to myth, there are many "side door" entrances to the Screen Actors Guild, some of which may surprise even experienced old-timers. Again, stay tuned.

The three "fast" ways into SAG

- *"Taft-Hartley"*: You're not a SAG member, but a producer goes bananas over your face and casts you in his union film, TV show or commercial. You just got "Taft-Hartleyed." Now the fun starts. No union can stop anyone from hiring you, but either the producer or the casting director will have to send a one-page "Taft-Hartley Report" to SAG. Included are the producer's reasons for hiring you instead of a Guild member. If the role calls for an Arabic-speaking midget, no problem. But, if his reasons are "because you're good," SAG will say, "Not good enough. There are, Mr. Producer, thousands and thousands of unemployed union members at this moment. Surely one of them is 'good.'" He's then subject to pay "liquidated damages" (basically, a fine) for hiring you, you cur.

  Obviously, getting Taft-Hartleyed depends on how badly the producer wants you. If he doesn't mind the hassle and expense, he'll do it. Most often, this occurs in commercials, low-budget films and network pilots. Occasionally, feature film producers will do it, sometimes even the makers of episodic television shows — especially so-called "reality shows," such as *Unsolved Mysteries*, since the producers don't want familiar faces playing the parts and distracting from the "reality."

- An *"unscripted line"*: In the middle of shooting *Phantom of the Opry*, the director decides he needs somebody in the crowd to shout,

"Kill that demented yodeler!" That's an "unscripted line" — a line that didn't appear in the original script.

Here's what a producer had to say: "I like to tell this to aspiring actors and actresses. If you know a producer or director of a movie, ask him to give you an 'unscripted line.' It can't be in the original script because then SAG will ask why the producer didn't hire a SAG actor to do it. The producer will tell you to be on the set the day he needs someone to yell out a line. He can hire you, on the spot, to do that line, and you automatically have the right to join the Guild." (Be sure to keep the "Day Player" contract you sign on the set — you'll need it to get into SAG.)

If you don't know a producer or director, you might luck into an unscripted line doing extra work. And speaking of that . . .

- *Extra Work:* Since SAG has jurisdiction of union extra work in Southern California and anywhere within 300 miles of New York City, you can get into SAG if you do three days of SAG extra work. (AFTRA extra work will not qualify you to join SAG.) The three days can be any combination of three separate jobs, three days on one job, etc. Simply show SAG the three vouchers you'll get and you're in. Do bear in mind, though, that getting SAG extra work when you're not union is almost as difficult as getting a union speaking part. (In fact they also call this being "Taft-Hartleyed.") Still, many actors have gotten their SAG cards via this route. For more on extra work see Chapter 24.

The many slow ways to join SAG: ("Parenting")

Your "parent" union is the union holding jurisdiction over your first job. (If your first job is an AFTRA sitcom, AFTRA becomes your parent; if it's a SAG film, SAG becomes your parent; if it's a Broadway show, Equity becomes your parent; if it's singing in a union nightclub, AGVA (see below) becomes your parent; if it's doing a concert at Carnegie Hall, AGMA — see below — becomes your parent. Here's the point: You can join one union from another. That is, you can go from your parent union into another union if you meet two criteria:

1. *The time criterion:* You must have been a paid-up member of your parent union for a minimum of one year.

And . . .

2. *The work criterion:* You must be able to prove you worked at least once under that union's jurisdiction (which is what makes it your parent).

Say you join AFTRA on Jan. 1, 1999. Six months later, you get lucky and land a role on that new hit soap, *The Old and the Exhausted.* Since it's taped, it's under AFTRA jurisdiction, and AFTRA becomes your parent union. On Jan. 1, 2000, you will be eligible to join SAG. (You have been a member of AFTRA for a year and have done a job under their jurisdiction.)

And it's not only AFTRA. You can do this from any of the unions mentioned below. (Canadians can parent into SAG through the Alliance of Canadian Cinema, Television and Radio Artists — ACTRA.)

- *Entrance into SAG from AFTRA:* Since you can join AFTRA any time you want, the problem here isn't so much waiting that agonizing year, it's getting that first AFTRA job. Your best shots are commercials, soap operas (they use a lot of new faces) and, possibly, radio work. Also, newcomers often get that first union job in syndicated shows (for the current ones check with SAG, AFTRA or read the trades).

- *Entrance into SAG from Equity:* Unless you got into Equity via the Membership Candidate Program (see below) you've already got a contract from the show that got you into Equity in the first place. Save that contract. You can join SAG once you've been in Equity for a year.

- *Entrance into SAG from the American Guild of Variety Artists* (AGVA): This union has jurisdiction over singers, magicians, clowns, stand-up comics, etc. — anyone who performs in nightclubs, halls, circuses, even someone's home.

  Like AFTRA, AGVA has an open door policy. Just obtain an application, fill it in, plunk down the coin and you're in. Then get the job. How? If you can get anyone to hire you as a singer, dancer, stand-up comic, etc. — repeat, *anyone,* from a nightclub owner to the president of your local Moose or Elks Lodge to your next-door neighbor who hires you, say, to sing at his birthday party — and he's willing to sign an AGVA contract, then call, write or go down to your nearest AGVA Office.

  You and he will sign the contract, and, after you warble "Happy Birthday to You" in C minor, your employer/birthday boy should pay you by check.

Photocopy the check, attach it to your contract, put them both in a vault guarded by Godzilla, wait a year from the date you joined AGVA, and, yes, you're eligible to join SAG.

- *Entrance into SAG from the American Guild of Musical Artists (AGMA):* Not to be confused with the American Federation of Musicians, AGMA has jurisdiction over "classical" singers and dancers, soloists and choral singers (Luciano Pavarotti, for example, is AGMA), and solo instrumentalists who perform live in concert halls, theatres, etc.

Getting into AGMA and getting that first job occur together. Hypothetically, you could form your own group, hold concerts, rent halls, sell tickets, etc., and ask AGMA to represent you. Otherwise, in Southern California, look for work at the Los Angeles Master Chorale, San Diego Opera Company, Opera Pacific Orange County, or Music Center Opera Association.

Once again, save your AGMA contract(s), wait a year from the day you joined AGMA, and you're eligible to join SAG.

THE SEVERAL WAYS INTO EQUITY

The fast way in

A producer hires you as an actor or stage manager to appear in or work on an Equity show. Bring your contract, along with your initiation fee and dues, to your nearest Equity branch, and you're in. Notice we said this was the "fast" way, not the "easy" way.

The slow way in: Parenting

Like SAG, Equity permits joining from other affiliated unions. The time criterion is the same (paid-up member of your parent union for one year). The work criterion: one principal role, one "under five" (AFTRA) or three days of extra contracts. (Note that, unlike SAG, Equity will accept both AFTRA and SAG extra work. Also, if your parent is AFTRA or AGVA you'll also need to provide written proof — a copy of a contract or letter from your parent.)

And the REALLY slow way in: The Equity Membership Candidate Program

If you're a member of SAG or a working member of AFTRA, you're ineligible to join this program. (Exceptions have been granted — you can waive your pro status and do this for 25 weeks and be eligible to join AEA

— but since you can parent your way into Equity, why bother?)

Obtain a list from Equity of theatres participating in this program. Then go job hunting. Once accepted by a participating theatre, send a completed registration form to Equity (there'll be a fee which you can later deduct from your initiation fee, see Appendix 2). You'll work as an actor, understudy, even a production worker, depending on that particular theatre. Complete 50 weeks of this kind of work and you'll be eligible to join Equity.

Your 50 weeks don't have to be consecutive and can be spent at any number of participating theatres over any length of time. Just keep a record and notify Equity when you reach your goal. Also, you can reduce the number of weeks to 40 if you pass a written exam about AEA.

ON BEING CHOOSY

If you stole a peek at the Appendix, you may have noticed that joining these unions isn't exactly cheap. Ultimately, you should get into the three actors' unions (SAG, AFTRA, Equity — and any others that the shoe fits.) But, if you're short on cash and live in L.A., shoot first for your SAG and AFTRA cards. If you live in New York, get your Equity and AFTRA cards. Los Angeles is a film town; New York is a stage town. If you hear that SAG and AFTRA are about to merge and you need your SAG card you might join AFTRA fairly soon — like yesterday.

ANOTHER WORD ABOUT YOUR DUES

Keep your dues up to date. Casting directors notify the unions when they want to cast you. If you're in arrears, that's hassle. So what happens? Bruce Beautiful gets the part.

8 OTHER ITEMS

When I'm casting, I always check "the Book." (i.e., the Academy Players Directory)

Arne Sultan, Producer

You can hammer a nail with a rock. Hammers and the right supplies sure do come in handy, though.

POSTAGE

Send a casting director a photo with postage due and don't be surprised if he refuses more than your mail. If you're uncertain about the postage, wallow in glorious excess.

MANILA ENVELOPES

You'll be using these to mail your résumé and photo(s). Choose sturdy ones. (Cardboard adds protection for the photos. It also adds more glorious excess in postage.)

THE ACADEMY PLAYERS DIRECTORY

"Next to your agent, it's your best agent," says theatrical agent Vikki Bandlow when talking about this powerful opportunity-getter. It's a visual directory of actors now done in three formats. The first and most widely used is the book format, published every four months. The second is the computer disk, called PD-Rom™, their registered trademark, also produced every four months. The third, updated monthly and available to agents, personal managers and casting directors, is an address on the Internet called "*the link*™." One fee pays for all three formats.

To be listed, you must be a member of at least one union or be represented by a franchised agent or bona-fide personal manager (and either will probably demand you be listed).

First, choose your best 8x10 picture and print your name on the back of it as you want it to appear. Next, choose the casting category in which you want to be listed. On the back of your picture, write in the code letters the APD uses for that category: Young Leading Man (YLM), Ingenue (ING),

---

NOTE: For addresses, phone numbers, websites, prices, fees of items mentioned throughout the book, see Appendix.

Leading Man (LM), Leading Woman (LW), Character/Comedian (CCM), Character/Comedienne (CCF), Child Male (CHM) and Child Female (CHF). It'll double the cost, but if you could logically be both, say, an "ING" and an "LW", give thought to listing under both categories.

Also on the back of the photo, put either the letter "F" or the letter "H" ("F" if you've chosen a three-quarter shot and want the entire shot shown, "H" if you're using a headshot or you want them to crop your three-quarter shot down to a headshot. Note: if you're using a three-quarter shot and forget to put an "F", the Directory will *automatically* crop it down to a headshot.

Then bring your shot to the APD offices in the Academy of Arts and Sciences building. There, you'll fill out a rather elaborate submission form that asks for your representation, your contact number (using your pager or home phone is not recommended), whether your photo is new and/or what year it was shot, your unions, professional credits, and, optionally, your physical characteristics, ethnicity and any special skills.

Sign the form, date it, pay your money and you're in, as producer William Kayden puts it, "the bible."

Naturally, the Directory has a deadline for each edition. They send out notices, but don't hold your breath. Check. (Some agencies call clients to remind them about Directory deadlines — think this isn't important?) If you miss a deadline, ask your agent to get your picture and check to the Directory as his deadline is later than yours. And don't forget to put the Directory on your "to be notified" list if you change agents.

Finally, if you're not convinced about the importance of "the Book," just go down to the Academy and look through the volumes themselves. Mixed in with "unknowns," you'll see shots of top stars. Time and again, actors get auditions directly from their Directory listing(s). Theatrical casting director Bob Harbin sums it up: "If you're serious, you should be in there."

Periodically, other services listing actors pop up, some using computers. As it stands, though, the only one you *really* must be in is the APD, and, perhaps, the similar New York *Players Guide*.

ANSWERING DEVICE/VOICE MAIL

You can opt for either — your own machine or voice mail, which is offered by both phone companies for a monthly fee.

If you choose to have a machine (and you don't have a beeper — see below), be sure it has touch-tone message recall: you can listen to your messages from another phone. That way, barring mechanical or electrical failure, the only way you'll miss a message is to forget to check your machine.

One plea: keep your message short and identify yourself by your first name. Actors, in their wonderful creativity, try to make those machines less obnoxious by using everything from cartoon voices to Beethoven's *Fifth* — thus making them even *more* obnoxious. Long, cutesy messages are annoying to people who make 100 calls a day. And it's a serious irk to leave a message for "nameless," wondering if you've reached the right machine. Try, "Hi, this is Mike. I'll be checking for messages shortly, so at the tone please leave your name, number and approximate time of your call."

However, we'd advise giving serious thought to voice mail and having it on a *separate* telephone number which you can list on résumés, your APD listings — anything public — as your "contact number." Considering how easily a phone number can fall into the wrong hands (and, with the Internet, we're talking about *worldwide* wrong hands), this will give you a little more security.

GOOD STATIONERY

Like your photos, the better your stationery looks, the more responses you'll get.

THANK-YOU NOTES

Sending these every time you get an audition, interview, part or shake of the hand, is not only courteous, it's smart. Puts your name in front of the person one more time.

Now, we've seen the glaze over actors' eyes when we talk about thank-you's, so stop yawning and pay attention: An actress attended a seminar at which one of the speakers was a world-famous producer. She sent him a thank-you and, a little while later, received a letter from him. (He's so well known a friend suggested she frame the letter.) It began: "I just read your note and I want to tell you I was very *touched that you took the time to write to me.*" [Italics ours.]

Dr. Watson, that first sentence tells us three elementary things:

A. Yes, he read her note.

B. He (unfortunately, like everyone else in this industry) isn't exactly inundated with thank-you notes.

C. He won't say "Who?" if she ever auditions for him.

SAG AGENCY LIST

You'll need this list of SAG-franchised agents when it's time for the Great Agent Hunt (see Chapter 11). You can pick one up at SAG or, if you've got a computer, you can get the list off of their website (for the website address see Appendix 4).

DATEBOOK

If you're starting out, you'll find it hard to believe anyone can forget an appointment with a casting director. If you've been at it a while, you know it's possible — especially if you're going out a lot. An appointment book will prevent this dire event from crossing your karma. You'll also see later how vital an appointment book can be come April 15.

THEATRE, SHOWCASES AND CLASSES

What you spend on these depends entirely on you, but you will need to be doing *all three.*

CARD FILE

A typical call to a working actor:
Agent: *Have you ever met Slicke Deale, the producer?*
Actor: *Uhm . . .*
Keep a file on every person you meet, the where and why of the encounter, perhaps even your feelings about how it all went.

Also, you don't have to leave information-gathering to the CIA. If, in an article in *Back Stage West/Drama-Logue* (see below), a casting director says he likes actors to stand up for a reading, or if an agent at a seminar rails on about actors calling him in the morning, make — and keep — notes. You'd be surprised at the information you can put together. The more you know about preferences and, yes, quirks, the better. Actor/teacher Mike Muscat says, "I have a five-star system for casting directors: If I've met them, they get one star; if they brought me in, they get two; if they gave me a job, they get three; if they bring me in on a regular basis, they get four; and if they've become a friend, they get five."

DIRECTORIES

You can walk out of Los Angeles' several drama bookstores with armloads of material on everything from acting teachers to which agents accept photos from new actors. We're hesitant to name titles here because these directories tend to come and go with the tides, and they change prices faster than you turn pages.

But here are a few highly-regarded ones that have been around for awhile: *The Hollywood Acting Coaches And Teachers Directory, The Hollywood Reporter Studio Blu-Book Directory* (similar to *The Working Actors Guide*, see below, but more geared to producers), *Breakdown Services C/D Guide* (helps you find casting directors), *Film Directors — A Complete Guide, Pacific Coast Studio Directory* (a quarterly similar to the *Blu-Book*) and *Ross Reports Television* (a monthly, lists Los Angeles and New York productions and personnel).

So go browse. But be sure to pick up . . .

THE WORKING ACTORS GUIDE

If a Pulitzer Prize were ever to be awarded to a directory for actors, this would win hands down. The *WAG* is a brilliantly comprehensive directory that's worth double its price tag. It's such a gold mine we have to give it special mention. Imagine in one book a list of casting directors, personal managers, agents, theatres, acting coaches, publicists, entertainment attorneys, extra casting agencies, production houses, etc., etc. Imagine all that and you've barely scratched the surface. If you can only afford one directory, this is the one.

TRADES SUBSCRIPTION

There are, basically, four trades:

- *Back Stage West/Drama-Logue:* In case you're wondering about the name, *Drama-Logue* was once a separate publication from *Backstage West*. The latter bought out the former but agreed to include *Drama-Logue* in the name — for now at least. (Remember Roebuck?) Anyway, this weekly newspaper is an excellent source of opportunities — who's casting what, etc. — and is especially valuable if you are trying to get into a play. It also runs interviews, news, casting announcements for student and other films, and ads by photographers, acting workshops, voice coaches and the like. For an actor this newpaper is vital. Comes out on Wednesdays. Consider subscribing.

- *Back Stage:* If you live in L.A., you might want to squeeze in an occasional reading of this weekly to keep abreast of the New York scene. If you're thinking of going to New York, or already live there, read it religiously.

- *Daily Variety/The Hollywood Reporter:* These are the daily news-papers for anyone involved in show business on the West Coast. Reading them can be informative, though Show Biz news stories should be treated like eggs — better with a grain of salt. You don't need to subscribe to both; perhaps you don't need to subscribe to either. On Thursdays *Variety* prints a rundown of television shows (staffs, producers, directors, casting directors); on Fridays they print the same information regarding films that are in (or about to go into) production. *The Hollywood Reporter* prints TV production charts on the first and third Tuesdays of the month. You might limit your purchases to those days. However, we've included a subscription.

POSTCARDS

You're in a play; you just changed agents; you want to remind people you still breathe; whatever. A postcard is a photo of yourself, reduced to postcard size, with your message on the back.

We used to be more enthusiastic about postcards. They were cheap and effective. However, they're now so prevalent they've lost some impact. "I get so many of these a day," says casting director Ron Stephenson. "You want my honest opinion? It's a waste of a lot of stamps." And they're no longer inexpensive either (right, what is?). Still, postcards remain the most practical, un-pesky reminders of your existence.

BEEPER ("VOICE MAIL")

You won't absolutely have to have a beeper until after you have an agent and start getting frequent calls for auditions. With the cost of beepers and voice mail declining you might think of getting one sooner rather than later. And when the day comes and (by Zeus!) you're working on the set, be sure your beeper is either a silent one or turn it off. We'd hate to see some poor director spend the rest of his life in jail for murder because your beeper went off in the middle of a take.

TYPEWRITER

If you can't afford a computer, a typewriter is a darn good investment. Your letters will look more professional and you'll feel better about send-ing them. If you add in the fact that the cost is tax deductible, you've got a pretty irresistible argument for buying one.

BLANK LABELS/LABEL SETS

Naturally, you can buy blank labels, but you'll save a lot of typing and some research if you purchase them in pre-addressed sets (to casting directors, agents, commercial casting directors etc.) from Breakdown Services Ltd. (for more information on the Breakdown Services, see Chapter 10). Competing companies offering labels tend to come and go; check *Back Stage West/Drama-Logue* for ads.

VIDEOCASSETTE

Having a videotape of your work is becoming as important as having a good résumé shot. A casting director or agent can see your work without making an appointment to see you or having the distraction of your presence. So copy everything that can be copied, regardless of the size of the part. Here's how:

- *Have it done professionally:* If your initial copy is made on a home VCR, it'll be on 1/2" VHS videotape (standard for all home machines). While VCRs have improved over the years, as a rule they still don't quite produce the quality of picture obtained by using professional (3/4") equipment. (With the advent of HDTV this may change.) The cost of air checking (see below) is relatively cheap, 3/4" tape is slightly easier to edit, and the copies you make from that 3/4" original will look better.

- *"Air-checking" a role:* If it appears on TV, you can "air-check" it (have a copy made). Simply notify any company capable of making 3/4" videotaped copies, telling them the name of the show, the day, time, and its approximate length. They'll do the rest and give you the tape of the entire show, which you'll then have edited (see below) and put onto standard VHS 1/2" copies to loan to industry people. (Expensive 3/4" copies of the original aren't needed.)

- *Copying a movie:* If you don't want to wait the year or so it will take for the picture to become available on videocassette or aired on television, or if you are in something that will never be put onto cassette or TV (industrials, out-of-town commercials, student films, etc.), try to get a copy, at least of your scenes, from the producer or director. Most companies capable of doing air checks are also capable of transferring film onto tape.

  If it's a major motion picture, chances even of borrowing a copy before it's released are virtually non-existent. If it's an industrial or a student film/tape, your chances are better. Industrial filmmakers are much more open to lending you a copy. Student filmmakers, in our opinion, *owe* you a copy: after all, you worked for free. But students are students, so keep after them for your copy like a horse — nag, nag, nag. (For more on industrials/student films, see Chapter 24.)

- *Editing:* Since nobody wants to (or will) wait 20 minutes for you to appear, you'll have your original copy edited down to include only your scenes, the name of the show and your billing (if the billing was special). Once again, only a pro (usually the same person who does the air checks) can do this kind of editing.

  We've included this information just in case you get lucky and win that first job in your first year.

- *Presentation tapes:* Once you've been around long enough to accumulate a number of scenes from different projects, you'll want to re-edit what you have into a ten-minute "presentation tape."

  If you've got a lot to choose from, use the material that shows you off best and, as theatrical casting director Susan Glicksman suggests, "Have your best things first." You won't want to risk somebody turning you off before you ever got "on."

  Don't be too quick to pooh-pooh a bunch of bit parts. Judiciously edited, even they can be surprisingly impressive.

  That's why we say *tape everything*, including, "Check your hat, sir?" in a movie and "Man, that's coffee!" in a commercial. Remember, you don't have to show any particular scene to the industry. If you don't like it, leave it in the can.

  And don't be a critic *before* you tape. If you hate the way you played the king, decide not to make a copy, and, when it's aired, come off positively regal, you'll want to shout, "Off with *my* head!"

- *A word about videotaping prepared scenes:* We know there are companies that will videotape you and another actor doing a scene. We also know you can buy or rent a vid-cam and videotape a scene in a theatre, even at home. Forget it. Any way you do it is too expensive because it's a waste of time. The industry is only interested in seeing tapes of professional work, done under professional conditions (lighting, sets, etc.) — though student films are included here. The quality of the tapes done by companies offering this often leaves a lot to be desired. And a tape on a vid-cam done at home sure won't be better. Besides, if someone wants to see you doing a prepared scene, he can attend a showcase, play, or simply call you in and have you do the scene live.

PASSPORT

Aha! You knew it! Hollywood *is* a foreign country! Well, maybe, but that's not why it's a good idea to have a passport.

First, we're sure you've run into the law requiring proof of citizenship to prospective employers. It's no different in Show Biz. Flashing a passport when you're cast saves a lot of time trying to remember what you need ("Let's see . . . is it my driver's license *and* birth certificate, or . . . ").

Second, what happens if you're cast in a project that's shot in Paris, they need you tomorrow, and you don't have a passport? Maybe the producer can pull some strings and get you one in a hurry, but to lose a role and a trip to the City of Lights because you don't have a passport will cut deeply into your *bon appétit*.

You can renew a passport by mail, but if it's your first time you'll need to apply in person. If so, you can apply for a passport at some Post Office branches. That's especially helpful during the summer. Avoids waiting in looong lines at federal buildings. Allow about three weeks for the entire process.

DESK

You can work on the kitchen table. It's just good for your attitude to have a specific work area, a place that's designated "Career work done here."

FAX MACHINE

There's no question you can pursue a career without owning one of these near-magical devices but, boy, can a fax machine come in handy — especially to get your sides fast when you're up for an audition (see Chapter 17).

COMPUTER

Imagine making changes in your résumé whenever they occur, quickly and without charge. Imagine writing one covering letter, and, with a few keystrokes, "personalizing" it to each of the 100 people you're mailing to. Imagine . . .

. . . Yep, they're wonderful, time-saving gadgets. And you can now outfit yourself with a good computer and printer relatively inexpensively. (With a modem, most computers can serve as fax machines as well.)

And then, of course, there's the Internet which contains the one thing an actor absolutely needs —*information*. Today there are myriad websites you can access — SAG's, *The Hollywood Reporter*'s, etc. (for a list see Appendix 4) — that will alert you to happenings throughout the industry.

Still, if a computer will take a megabyte out of your budget, forget it for now. (Remember, these are under "Chicken Soup.")

VCR

Another "Chicken Soup" item. But it can be of immense help when you're trying to find a scene for a showcase or office scene (see Chapter 18). Also, if you're out a lot, you'll be able to time-shift programs and watch them later. It's important to keep up on the various shows on TV. (We know an actress who was called in to read for a satire of a well-known cop show. She'd never seen it. Think she got the part?)

Actually, having a VCR is becoming more of a necessity every day for actors. (Even the IRS recognizes this — see Appendix 6.) Note: If you're trying to convince Mom and Dad to buy you one, we wrote this so you can put your thumb over the first sentence when you show this to them. That's one you owe us.

VIDEO CAMERA

A *real* luxury item. But, if you get a script in advance and can videotape yourself doing the reading, what you learn from playback could be the difference between getting it or not.

CELLULAR PHONE

This one barely made the list because, for an actor starting out, it's more of an ego trip than a necessity. However, it's true that a cell phone can come in handy if you're stuck in traffic on your way to an audition. Beats pounding on the steering wheel.

That's it. Now you're ready to get started on your career — except for one other supply item: your attitudes.

9 ATTITUDES:
NEED — THE CAREER KILLER

Have 'screw you' money.

Barry Shear, Producer/Director

Here's the single most important sentence in this book — our *best* advice:

Don't need the work. If you need the work, you won't get the work.

It's surprising. Time and again, when you boil down all the stories about how actors get jobs, it's due to an absence of desperation; a lack of need; a sense that the job just wasn't all that important at the time.

We know. You understand the concept, *but* . . . how can you honestly pretend you don't need something when you do?

By honestly no*t* needing it. And (using a slightly cleaned-up version of Mr. Shear's advice), that starts by . . .

HAVING "SCREW YOU" MONEY

The industry wants people who can handle pressure. An actor who needs the job to pay his rent has pressures on him that have nothing to do with the "shoot." (Theatrical agent Maxine Arnold calls this kind of an actor a "desperate-ado.") He blows takes and readings — not because he's bad, but because that job is too important to him.

You can't make intelligent decisions when you're hungry. To advance, for example, sooner or later you're going to have to turn down a two- or three-line "day player" part. Keep doing these and you may wake up one morning to discover that's how the industry views you — as a "day player." (Careers, it's said, are made by how many times an actor says no.) But how can you turn down a part if that's all that stands between you and eviction?

Work, beg, or "glumb" it from your parents — but *don't need the money.*

HAVE OTHER INTERESTS

After an informal survey of working actors, we learned that when they got work it was often because the job or audition "got in the way" of something else, usually having nothing to do with acting. When they auditioned, their minds were partly on that "something else," and they were more relaxed and didn't try as hard. The producer or director saw actors who weren't desperate and hired them, little knowing it was concern over a plot point in a screenplay they were writing or a nagging problem with a sick begonia that kept the actors from being nervous.

We aren't saying don't pursue a career. Sure, make those calls, visit studios, send out photos and résumés, etc. But remember too that life isn't just film running through a camera, and there's a difference between dedication and obsession. "Frankly, the reason I don't handle a lot of actors is because they're too self-involved," says entertainment attorney Michael C. Donaldson. "There's a great line in the movie *To Be Or Not To Be* where one character says to the other, 'Enough about me. Let's talk about you. How did *you* like my last scene?' There's a lot of truth to that. But not so much with successful actors. Successful actors, like successful people everywhere, are involved in the world around them." Or as personal manager Roz Tillman says, "I can't stress enough getting together the basics. I mean the basics of your life. Getting it all together. Don't be a flaky artist."

Have an avocation. Do something that brings in an extra few bucks on the side. Learn a freelance trade that makes you your boss for life. Have a hobby. Smell the begonias.

HAVE COURAGE

"Dare to be hated."   Bette Davis, in a TV interview

We've been to gatherings of actors where the atmosphere was that of a group of desperate, whipped puppies, yapping about their "masters" (producers, etc.).

Well, join the kennel or learn to keep your self-respect.

This industry too has its share of petty, bullying bureaucrats who enjoy "doing a number" on actors. You owe it to yourself not to let them push you around. Someone rude to you? Don't sit there and take it because you're "only an actor" and need the work.

Now, we're not talking about walking around with a chip on your shoulder — then *you're* the bully. Just don't allow yourself to be somebody's doormat. If you do you'll get frustrated, hurt and angry — exactly the kind of actor who doesn't work.

KNOW YOUR PRODUCT

"Defining your image is essential. Nowadays most actors are good actors. The real question is, 'Which of the good actors are you?'"

Sam Christensen, Career Consultant

"Most actors don't seem to know their product," says publicist Mac St. Johns. In fact, some actors don't even know that they *are* a product. "You have to define your personality," says theatrical casting director Paul Bengston. "Not 'I want to be a pirate or a cowboy,' but what you are. What are you selling?"

Let's put our cards on the table — you're a part of a product designed to make money. Producers aren't interested in fulfilling your creative needs. Their title is "producer," not "mommy." Nobody cares if it hurts your feelings to be playing the wallflower when you'd rather be the orchid. You'll be cast for what you are and how you look, not for what you'd like to be or how you'd like to look.

Analyze where you fit in and sell yourself that way. Remember no actor is right for every part. If you look like "Auntie Em," don't try to sell yourself as the next "Dorothy" and then complain about what a rotten business this is when nobody buys.

It's not easy, but try not to take rejections personally. If you were selling a Mercedes, but your customer was in the market for a Cadillac, we doubt you'd take that as a personal affront.

When you don't get that part or agent, it simply means that they weren't in the market for a Mercedes that week.

KNOW YOU KNOW IT

"Know your craft."   Ralph Senensky, Director

There's no way around it. Some dues will have to be paid.

You're going to have to study hard and work at your craft. You're going to have to go through the pain of doing badly before you do well. Make your mistakes before becoming a pro, because, sooner or later, you'll be asked to show what you can do. If you need knowledge and experience, a little voice inside you will scream, "Dear God, I'm not ready for this."

Know you're ready — know it in your gut.

SET DAILY CONCRETE AND ATTAINABLE GOALS

"Try to do at least one thing a day to help your career."
Merritt Blake, Theatrical Agent

Taking off for weekends and holidays, if you do what Mr. Blake suggests, you will have done 250 things to help your career at the end of your first year. That's about 248 1/2 more things than many of your fellow actors will have done. Why?

Well, ask an actor what he really wants, and he'll most likely say, "To be a working actor." Ask him how he intends to achieve that, and his eyes glaze over.

Most actors spend a lot of time spinning their wheels because they don't really know where they're going. Their goals — if they have any — are usually very foggy.

It's a lot smarter to say, "Okay. At the end of my first year, I want to have obtained all the supplies I need; gotten an agent; and gone on one interview."

Personal manager Roz Tillman says, "I encourage my actors to be goal-oriented; to isolate specifically what they want." Then, if you're really smart, you'll break that list down into monthly, weekly and daily goals.

Don't try to set "goals for life." They're not concrete. There are too many unknowns out there that can completely change your life. Make your goals *concrete, attainable,* and *daily.*

We once talked to a recovering alcoholic. This is what he said: "If I thought I could never take another drink for the rest of my life, I'd be back on the booze in a minute. I couldn't deal with that. The only way I can stay sober is to do what Alcoholics Anonymous teaches —*I take it one day at a time."*

GET OFF YOUR OWN BACK

"Don't worry about it. Alfred Hitchcock always used to say, 'It's only a movie.'"
Angie Dickinson to an actor
who had just blown a take.

It can be therapeutic to take a class. Why? By watching others, you'll learn you're not the only one who ever screwed up.

Actors are amazing. If they're not yelling at their agents, they're screaming at themselves. *Everybody* seems to be working better and more.

Try not to get down on yourself. If you do a bad audition/interview/ performance, go home, kick a door and forget it. Nothing is life or death.

Everybody screws up. As theatrical casting director Bob Harbin says, "Be serious about your work, but don't take this business too seriously. There's just too much craziness that goes on."

Babe Ruth struck out far more than he ever hit the ball — but what's he remembered for? Sooner or later, you'll get "good wood" on the ball.

NON-WORKING ACTORS

"Earlier, I heard you say not to hang around with non-working actors. I'd like to hug you for saying that."

Fran O'Bryan, Commercial Agent

Welcome to Negative City. Population: thousands. Points of interest: none. (After all, it can't be done.)

"If you want to be an unemployed actor for the rest of your life I can tell you exactly how to do it: Spend all of your time with unemployed actors talking about how unhappy you are being an unemployed actor," says entertainment attorney Michael C. Donaldson.

The greatest spur in the butt is to be around people who can do and are doing. They'll inspire you to do more. After all, they're living proof that things *can* be done.

What do you learn from people who are failing? How to fail. They're magnificent at finding all the ways things can't be done. Worse, stated or not, they don't want you to succeed. They'll commiserate you into doing nothing.

Birds of a feather . . . need together.

ALWAYS ACT SUCCESSFUL

Q: "What mistake do you continually see actors making?"
A: "Being too hungry."

Ruth Robinson, The Hollywood Reporter

We don't mean act cocky — that's just a mask for the insecure. And we don't mean you'll have to drive a Mercedes or wear Gucci loafers.

Acting successful means giving those in the position to hire you a feeling that they can be confident in you because you know your value.

Present yourself as a successful working pro, even when times are tough. Act like you've "made it" long before you have.

As actor Edmund Gilbert put it: "Be there before you get there."

AVOID NEGATIVE BEHAVIOR

"No matter what, try to be positive."   Jack Rose, Jack Rose Agency

A salesman's creed: "To be enthusiastic, act enthusiastic."

If you think that sounds corny, go to a commercial audition. There, you'll find a roomful of actors who know they have to be bright and "up" if they want to get cast. And, because everyone is acting so happy and perky, you'll find it very hard to be negative or "down." Enthusiasm is catching.

Conversely, so is negativity. Be on your guard against it, in yourself or the company you keep.

Consider this quote from an actor friend of ours: "I never read the trades. The trades make me feel that everybody in this town is working but me."

He has a point. If you find yourself getting upset at all that work out there that you're not getting, then don't read the trades. Not until you can read them again for the positive information you can actually do something about. Too often, actors will read something about a film that has been cast, decide that they weren't up for the part, and immediately pick up the phone to chew out their agent. That's one long series of negative behavior.

Here are some other things to be on the lookout for:

- Don't go to see a movie, TV show, play, or even read reviews of a project you were "up for" and didn't get. (Face it — you're being perverse.)

- Don't listen to stories about how a fellow actor didn't get a part or agent. What a downer! (Our favorite way of handling this was in the following overheard conversation: First Actor: "I'm really miserable. I was up for a part and I didn't get it because . . . " Second Actor (interrupting): "At least you were up for it, baby.")

- Don't listen to anyone who says you'll never make it. (Unless they've shown a remarkable aptitude for walking on water.)

- Don't read bad reviews of a show you are in. (Talk about perversity!)

- Don't fall into "bad mouth" sessions about anyone or any group. (Ever felt better after one of these?)

- Be sure your acting teachers are trying to help you, and not just trying to keep the bucks coming in from a lot of perpetual students, or playing games with your head.

- Don't dwell on the mistakes you made. Dwell on what you learned from them.

- Not a beginner? Stay away from people, groups, or situations that cast you in that light.

- At an audition, don't assume you're wrong for the part. Are you there? Brother, you're right for it.

- Don't get secretly mad at your agent because he has other clients. That's what keeps him in business.

- When criticized, be sure of the other person's motives.

- Don't enjoy someone else's misfortunes.

- Don't listen to doomsayers.

- Don't work for compliments — work for money. That means working to improve your pocketbook, your opportunities or your skills — not merely to get stroked. For example, don't keep working at the same theatre or acting class just because everybody there thinks you're soooo good.

Finally, in an interview on Inside The Actors' Studio, Meg Ryan had this answer to a question about being a woman in an industry that is still so dominated by men (it was directed to women, but anyone could make it a "rule to live by"): "Well, I'd say first be optimistic. Sometimes I see a lot of women get very angry and it stops the creative process . . . I think it's dangerous to let yourself stay in that anger."

And, above all . . . *don't need the work.*

III
THEATRICAL AGENTS

10 THEATRICAL AGENTS — WHAT THEY ARE AND DO

Nobody pays an agent to keep people out of work.

Jim Gibson, Theatrical Agent

Do you need an agent? Only if you want to be considered a pro, get paid more than union scale, and have a shot at better billing. And only if you want to work.

When casting, the studios, casting directors, producers and directors of Los Angeles hate crowds. (It's hard to be laid back in a mob.) Consequently, they've set up elaborate systems to keep actors uninformed. Except for an occasional hot tip from a friend or the trades, without an agent you'll miss out on most jobs simply because *you won't know they're there.*

More important, with an agent you cross a very important psychological barrier. You become a pro; someone (else) in the industry believes in your talent. As voice-over casting director Bob Lloyd put it, "You have to be competitive. Then you have to be able to prove it. And then you need to have someone who believes that and will merchandise you."

And, frankly, one producer said out loud what most industry people feel: "I get leery of actors without agents."

There are about six different kinds of agents, each handling performers in different areas of the business. No matter his special field, he's still a salesman whose product is talent:

- *Theatrical agent*: Television and motion pictures.

- *Commercial agent*: On-camera work in commercials.

- *Legitimate agent*: Theatre.

- *Voice-over agent*: Radio and off-camera work involving only the actor's voice for commercials, cartoons, announcing, and radio drama.

- *Modeling agent*: Modeling and, often, print work (magazine ads, billboards, other print media), although this can be handled separately.

- *Variety agent*: Nightclub work, personal appearances, etc.

As an actor, your main concern will be to obtain a *theatrical* agent and a *commercial* agent — that's where the jobs are.

In Los Angeles, you may sign with *only one agent per category.* (There's no limit in New York.) You may sign with different agents/ agencies in different fields, but you may not have several commercial agents, several theatrical agents, etc.

WHAT A THEATRICAL AGENT DOES

The typical theatrical agent has about 50 actors in his "stable." (That's the term. Well, it *is* a horse race.) Each morning, between slurps of coffee, he looks over one of his primary tools for finding his clients work: the "breakdowns" (from the Breakdown Services, Ltd).

Since acquiring and reading entire scripts is time-consuming, this service has become an institution. It provides agents and personal managers with a summary of all roles taken from scripts about to go into production, including the sizes of all parts and a brief description of every character. The Breakdown Service is not available to actors. And there's no guarantee that any role listed hasn't already been cast. (The Breakdown Service is also available to agents and personal managers on computer and is also used in commercials — see Chapter 22.)

From these descriptions the agent decides which, if any, of his clients are "right" for the various parts. With a typewritten submission sheet, photos and résumés of the actors he's submitting under his arm, the agent then visits the casting director, submits via computer, or has his submissions delivered.

The casting director checks the submissions and says yea or nay based on his reading of the script and what the producer and/or director has told him about the part. Most often, the answer is nay: the part's been cast, the casting director thinks the actor is wrong for it ("Some of the things casting directors say about actors is reason enough to have an agent so you won't have to hear it," says theatrical agent Joel Rudnick), or the casting director doesn't know, like, or trust the agent. (Some agents can't even get in to see some casting directors.)

Faced with a turndown, the agent may try to change the casting director's mind; he may submit another client for the part (theatrical agent Colee Viedelle calls this "the Fuller Brush approach to agenting"); or he'll fold his tent and slip away. Rarely will an agent go over a casting director's head to the producer or director — it's not good politics.

If the agent gets a yea, a time is set for the actor to audition. If the actor gets the part, some serious dickering takes place between agent and casting director, primarily over salary and billing. The actor won't take part in these negotiations; the agent will call an actor only to get a thumbs-up or thumbs-down — but, no matter what the offer, he must call.

For doing all this, an agent receives ten percent of the actor's *gross* earnings when the actor gets paid — and *not a moment before*. He is *never* paid in advance.

The rest of the agent's day is one long series of: phone calls from clients, reading contracts, interviewing potential clients, strategy meetings with fellow workers, etc. And, when the sun sets in the west, he gets to go home, right? Wrong. He's off to see one of his clients in a play.

These dervishes really whirl.

ABOUT LEGITIMATE AGENTS . . .

. . . The agents who handle stage work. The problem is the lack of paying work within the city. "The opportunities to make a living in L.A. theatre are almost nil," said personal manager Larry Fonseca. We know of no agent in L.A. who works stage exclusively. The ones who handle theatre all do it "on the side." Get the picture?

If you want to concentrate on paying theatre, head east. If you ask an L.A. agent to rep you for theatre, be willing to go out of town if you're cast — that's where most of the work will be. But remember, while you're strutting the boards in Birmingham, the rest of your career will be largely on hold. You take the money and make your choice. In any case, the information in this section basically holds true for theatrical and legitimate agents.

A WORD OF ADVICE

Without the right qualifications — good photos, a decent résumé, and a SAG card — unless you're under 21 and look it, *you're wasting your time.* As one agent bluntly put it, "What makes an actor think he qualifies for film work when he's done no films and has few or no theatre credits?"

Postpone the Great Agent Hunt until you've gotten some experience. In the meantime, if you have a good smiling photo, you might try for a commercial agent. Since many commercials don't involve lines, commercial agents are more receptive to a beginner who lacks credits but has a look or personality they think will sell.

Too often, actors in a beginning acting class talk about getting an agent. A one-year-old horse doesn't need a *jockey.* He needs a *trainer.*

11 SEEKING A THEATRICAL AGENT

The relationship between the actor and the agent can be summed up in two words: hot pursuit. It's the actor's job to attack and attack again until he gets the attention of someone in the industry who can do him some good.

Michael Campus, Producer/Director

Put on a hard hat, 'cause some large chunks of stone wall are about to bounce off your head. Agents have far more experience turning you down than you have convincing them to sign you. When you're starting out, merely getting one to see you will be a time for buttered popcorn all around.

When you hear the time-honored "Sorry, we're not taking on any new clients at this time," however, bear in mind that agents are always/never taking on new clients, and there's no room/plenty of room for you.

"Every agent will tell you, 'I don't need any new people,' and every agent will tell you privately, 'I'll take someone on if I feel I can make some money off of him.'" says voice-over casting director Bob Lloyd. And he's right: let Mel Gibson walk into an agent's office, and room will be found for him.

If you can act, have experience and a SAG card, there *is* an agent for you. It just might take many miserable months to find him.

A WORD OF WARNING

To avoid getting ripped off, never sign with any agent who isn't union-franchised. A franchised agent has agreed to abide by all union regulations, and you'll be protected from most unethical practices. Once you're union, in fact, you aren't allowed to sign with a non-franchised agent even if you've gone too long without a sun hat and want to.

If you are interested in a particular theatrical (movies/TV) agency, check the SAG list of franchised agents. You can pick the list up at SAG for free if you're a SAG member; for an extremely nominal fee if you're not. (If you've got a computer, you can go to the SAG agency website for the list

---

NOTE: For addresses, phone numbers, websites, prices, fees of items mentioned throughout the book, see Appendix.

which is updated monthly. For the website address see Appendix 4.) If you find that the agency isn't on the list, call SAG (ask for "Agencies"); perhaps the agency received its franchise in between updates. If the agency you want is legitimate (stage), call Equity.

Most agents hire additional personnel, called *sub-agents*. SAG and Equity list them as such, and they need not be franchised as long as the agency for which they work is franchised.

A word of warning: You may run across so-called "agents" or "agency-finder services," with impressive-sounding names like "Galactic Representatives International." They prey on the unwary actor. They guarantee jobs; demand money for ads in their "magazines," which, they promise, will be seen by everyone in the industry from Louis B. Mayer (So what if he's dead?) to the washerwoman at William Morris (Who knows? She may be casting something next week); set you up with photos for a mere $1,000 or so; offer acting classes that teach you to stand in a corner scratching and moaning. The very worst of the lot can even be fronts for prostitution. How can you avoid the sharks in the water?

If an "agent" ever asks you for money, run, don't walk, out of his office. An agent on the up-and-up makes his money from one source only: *ten percent of what you make, after you make it.* Your best protection is that franchise. If the agent isn't franchised, don't sign. Period.

THE SIMPLEST WAY . . .

. . . To get an interview with any agent is to have a producer, director, casting director or even a represented fellow actor put in a good word for you. If you know someone in the industry, *ask.* Bear in mind, however, that a referral won't guarantee the agent will sign you (or even see you). As theatrical agent Joel Rudnick cautions, "We're always looking at people. But signing and looking are two different things."

THE BEST WAY: PERFORMING YOUR WAY TO AN AGENT

Why the "best" way? Because, even including referrals, there is no stronger introduction to an agent than having him see and like your work. And you can do that by doing (in best to weakest order) . . .

- *A movie or TV show:* Are we kidding? No, actors do luck into these even without agents. Just be sure you've got lines — extra work doesn't count. You may be surprised to find your movie/TV show does you little good before it opens/airs; when it does, however, work hard and fast. Send out letters or postcards, wait a few weeks, then call back.

To avoid making an agent sit through 50 minutes waiting for your three-minute TV part, include in your letter the day and time of the show and approximately when you appear. (You can get this information from the producer's office. Television books well in advance.) Call *every* agent a day or so before the show airs to remind him. After it airs, call back and ask for an appointment. We know — *aargh*. But don't waste the opportunity — it may be five years before you get another like it. Don't make the romantic (or lazy) mistake of sitting back, waiting for agents to contact you. Go after them.

- *Prepared scene/cold reading showcases:* Non-existent a few years ago, today they are one of the best ways to be seen by an agent (or a casting director). See Chapter 18, "Showcases and Office Scenes."

- *99 Seat ("Equity Waiver") theatre:* You may do this kind of theatre whether you are union or not. The theater will seat less than 100, and, if it's a good production and well publicized, your chances of being seen by industry people are fairly decent.

  Understand, it's possible no industry person will come even if the show gets good reaction. But it's certain that no industry person is going to go to your apartment to watch you do your dramatic interpretation of a couch potato.

  You "old pros," new only to Hollywood, may balk at this. You may feel you've proven yourselves on stages all over the country, and advice to do more stage work — in small theatres, no less — is insulting and a waste of time. After all, you came to Hollywood for film work!

  Do it anyway. Nobody wants to buy a ham in a poke — unless they see you act, how do they know if you're an experienced, interesting actor or one who's merely left audiences comatose from coast to coast?

- *Equity productions:* In Los Angeles, if you're in an Equity show, there will be industry professionals in at least some of your audiences. Unfortunately, there's little paying theatre in the city, so you've probably got a better chance of getting into a movie or TV show.

- *Community theatre:* Not only off-limits to union members, it's also often difficult to get industry people to come to community theatre.

Agents aren't all that interested in seeing a cast composed mostly of insurance executives doing theatre as a hobby; their chances of picking up a client are slim. Still, you might get lucky: someone may come to the show because he's a friend of a cast member. Be sure the theatre keeps a guest book (buy one for them if they don't), and check it every night.

When you do any kind of theatre, as opening night approaches, send out letters or postcards (maybe even e-mail) to every casting director and agent in town. A sample:

Dear _____ :

This is to invite you and a guest of your choice to the upcoming production of PLAY at THEATRE & ADDRESS . We open on DATE and close on DATE . Performances times are _____ .

I play CHARACTER , and appear ONLY IN ACT I ,
THROUGHOUT THE PLAY, ETC.

(Please call (THE THEATRE/ME) and make a reservation to insure that we hold two good seats for you.)

Please come. I believe you'll have a thoroughly enjoyable evening.

Sincerely,

If you go over your allotment of complimentary tickets, are doing a major show, or the theatre doesn't give "comps," shell out for them yourself.

THE DIRECT WAY . . .

This method isn't a lot of fun, involves a lot of work, and gets old fast. It's only got one thing going for it: it does work. Take the list of franchised agents, scratch off the top dogs such as William Morris, ICM, Creative Artists, etc., and mail your picture, résumé, and a cover letter to the first ten remaining agencies on the list. A sample:

Dear _____ :

Your agency has been recommended to me a number of times in my search for representation in Los Angeles. A look through the *Academy Players Directory* seems to indicate you have no one quite like me, so I enclose photos and résumé for your consideration.

I'll call in a week or so, and hope we can get together for a chat.

Also, do you have a favorite "Equity Waiver" theatre?

Very truly yours,

The above sample appeared in the first edition of the book, as a *guideline*. We hoped no one would be silly enough to copy it. Boing! An agent we know received an exact duplicate, copied *word for word*.

Please, come up with your own letter, keep it brief, and use just about any approach that's comfortable, without getting silly, negative, braggadocios, or out-gushing Ol' Faithful.

As personal manager Melissa Tormé-March observes, "Clever letters attract people." For example, one of the most effective cover letters we've ever seen was sent to commercial agents by a light-skinned black actor:

> Hi! I am seeking commercial representation and would like you to consider me as a client. I am new to Los Angeles, just in from Washington D.C., and am enthusiastic about commercial acting. I have heard wonderful things about your agency, and, although I look more like wheat toast, I think I am the 'white bread' you are looking for.

Need we say he got a lot of replies?

"I think you have to figure out why I'd be interested in you," says director Andrew McCullough. "It really has to be on the basis of 'I have something to contribute.' I mean, so many letters come in, pitched on 'I would like to act.' *Well, so what?* I think that's why so many letters fail."

And one other thing: remember, your letter reveals something about your common sense. "Anyone who can't spell 'Dear Mary Spencer' is out," dryly notes theatrical agent Mary Spencer.

So, send out ten résumés, résumé shots and Pulitzer Prize-winning cover letters in one week. Then, the following week, pick out the *next* ten agents on the list, repeat the process, and, *in addition*, start calling the *original* ten agents you wrote. For the next six months or so, you'll be calling and mailing to *ten agents a week*. Expect 99 percent rejection. And a few "Can you call us back?" responses. And back . . . and back . . . and back . . .

Sound awful? It is. That's why there are more unrepresented actors than represented ones. Many actors try this approach for a week or so, quit, then wail, "Ya can't get an agent."

A variation is the old dropping-in method. Usually, it doesn't work, but you never know. You may not get to see an agent, but you can leave your photo, résumé and a personal impression — if only on the receptionist. And all that walking is a great way to lose weight.

Whether dropping by or phoning, you're going to be talking to a lot of secretaries. This brings us to . . .

SECRETARIES AND THE BRICK WALL SYNDROME

Today's secretary/casting coordinator/receptionist is tomorrow's agent/ casting director/producer. Taking them for granted is like eating ice cream on a diet. You'll be aghast at where it shows up later.

Assistants control access to agents, casting directors, and producers. Whether they throw broken glass or roses in your path is up to you.

When commercial casting director Beth Holmes was a casting coordinator (see what we mean?), she said: "I think actors know to be friendly to me because I have the first waste paper basket."

Because they constantly deal with actors — in person and on the phone — they've developed pretty good defenses. You'll sense that tone of indifference the minute you start talking. Without getting obnoxious, find a way to catch their attention. Learn and use their names. Ask questions. Try to involve them in conversation. Most of the time they'll be too busy to talk and, if they are, leave or hang up.

Every once in awhile, though, you'll catch a secretary during a lull. Then it's time to try to make a friend. What you are striving for is a businesslike amiability — a scaredy-cat, "I'll-just-die-if-you-reject-me" air isn't going to sell you any better than a hotshot approach. As casting coordinator Tawn Holstra put it: "The thing about telephones is that the fears of the people on the other end comes through. I mean, I'm not going to bite you. You can ask me things and you don't have to be afraid of me. There's nothing I can do to you on the phone. *Nothing.*"

And, when you talk to anyone, bear in mind these two tips from theatrical agent Vikki Bandlow: "When the actor calls, he usually calls in slow motion. Get it out." And: "Everything's so heavy in this business. If someone can get me to laugh on the phone, I'll have him in. I love to laugh!"

OTHER METHODS OF GETTING AN AGENT

Classes/seminars

Seminars with agents as speakers can be helpful. Ask questions. Make the speaker notice you. Afterwards, go up and introduce yourself, and see if you can wheedle an appointment. We've seen it work.

If you're well-trained, you might take a class that has "industry nights" when agents, etc., are invited to come and watch/teach/comment. (Don't confuse these with classes that *promise* jobs or recommendations — avoid those!) Warning: if you're not ready, industry nights can backfire, emphasizing your limitations instead of your strengths.

You could also ask your instructor (especially if he's a casting director), or even a fellow student, for a recommendation. Be aware that the teacher usually is flooded with such requests and has only so many favors he can ask of his connections. (On the whole, however, take classes to learn, to stretch, to take chances in private, away from judgmental industry eyes — not to impress in hopes that someone will do something for you.)

Serendipity

Actually, when seeking an agent you're limited only by your own imagination. Actors have sent flowers (rather obvious) and have taken out billboards on Sunset Boulevard (*very* silly). A fresh approach such as one suggested by publicist Barbara Best can be charming: "To a single agent of your choice, send one genuinely funny greeting card every day for 30 days. When you're done he should certainly be interested at least in meeting you!"

The real key to getting an agent is how hard you try.

INTERVIEW WITH A THEATRICAL AGENT

Lo and behold — an interview! Now, the agent isn't yet ready to sign on the old dotted, but you have at least piqued his interest. There's something about you, your pictures, résumé and/or a performance he saw that is "special" and can possibly fill a gap in his client list. (Unless the agent is merely doing a friend a favor in seeing you.)

Now he wants to size you up. Do you have craft? Intelligence? Knowledge? Common sense? Are you confident without being cocky? Can he send you out on an interview and know you won't make a fool of yourself? Will you come through with poise when the cameras roll or when you meet important people? Are you pleasant to be around? (The last we heard, "Grumpy" still doesn't have an agent.) And, most important of all, can he sell you — will he make money if he represents you?

If he hasn't seen your work and you have no videotape on yourself, he may also want you to do a "cold reading" or an "office scene" for him. (More about interviews, cold readings and office scenes in the next section; they're skills in themselves, and you'll be doing a lot of them for casting directors, producers and directors as well.)

Okay. The interview went smoothly. A few days or a week has passed, the agent has done his thinking and discussed you with his associates, and has decided he wants to take you on. Now the question is: Do you want *him?*

12 CHOOSING A THEATRICAL AGENT

Just because someone shows an interest in you doesn't mean he's necessarily the best person for you.

Jerry Cohn, Personal Manager

It's hard to relate to "Choose your agent carefully" when you're thinking "I'll be glad to, as soon as I can get one to talk to me." And, when an agent shows some interest, it's even harder not to leap into his arms screaming *"Take me!"*

If only one franchised agent is interested in you, sign with him. Still, find out who you're dealing with. A franchise tells you only that the agent is basically on the up and up. It doesn't say that he's any good or that he's right for you. Even if you were buying the last car on earth, you'd still want to know how it runs.

LOOKING HIM OVER

There's no Better Business Bureau for agents; but fellow actors, instructors, and other industry people can be of help. Should you meet a client, ask if he gets out on interviews; if he's treated courteously; if he has easy access to, and is happy with, the agent. Just bear in mind that every agent is hated and loved by someone.

The agent's enthusiasm

The key ingredient in choosing an agent is the excitement factor. His enthusiasm about your potential can cover a multitude of sins. If all his clients hate him, if he doesn't work for anybody else, if he's not very pleasant to be around, but if he's excited about you and works for you — you've got a good agent.

Conflicts/clients

Any actor signed with your agency who would continually go up for the same roles as you is a "conflict." You don't want your agent choosing between you and him for roles. As theatrical agent Joel Rudnick says, "That's a decision that should be made at the casting office, not at the agent's office." If you're a direct conflict with one of their clients, a

95

theatrical agent should turn you down.

A little research can save you grief. Find a copy of the *Academy Players Directory* and leaf through the section that displays your glorious mug. If you spot a conflict, mention it to the agent. That actor may have departed the agency. Or the agent may see you differently. Can you live with that? If not, don't sign — you have enough competition *outside* your agency!

Agency size

To start, you want a small- to mid-sized agency that is excited about and will work for you. Forget the William Morrises and CAA's. If your agent handles Tom Cruise, who makes millions per movie, and you, who makes scale, who's he going to work for? There's even an expression for this: "Buried in your own agency."

Number of clients

No single theatrical agent can adequately handle more than about 50 people. (If there are two theatrical agents in the agency, they can handle 100 actors; three, 150; and so on.) More than 50 clients means you're signing with a meat market that's hoping you get lucky finding work on your own, and then they'll cash in.

SAG says agents must present a "reasonably current" list of their clients to prospective clients on demand. But, to be diplomatic, pop over to SAG and ask to see the agency's client list. Count the names. (Only those signed theatrically. Some agencies have many different departments. You don't care how many people they've got signed, say, commercially. SAG uses a different code number for each category.)

One man, one job

If you come across a guy who works alone and claims he's a commercial, theatrical, voice-over, modeling, and kitchen-sink agent, pass on signing with him unless you want your career to go down the drain. No one individual can handle more than one category.

Not across the board

As mentioned above, many agencies have multiple departments with different people handling commercials, theatricals, etc. — and it's possible they may want to sign you in every category (called "across the board"). Well, that's fine, but things can get a bit sticky if you wind up happy with your theatrical agent and miserable with your commercial agent. If that's the only way the agency will sign, and you really want them, go ahead. But it's best to sign with *different* agencies for *each* category.

Clout

"If someone wants you, it doesn't matter who your agent is," says theatrical casting director Marci Liroff. That's absolutely true. But don't let anyone kid you — clout counts, baby. There *are* such things as "day player agencies" (small agencies a casting director calls when casting bit parts that are shot in one or two days). Most likely that'll be your first agency, and that's fine when starting out. You want to get some small parts under your belt. (It's rare to get bigger roles anyway.) But the agent should intend — and have the drive — to grow beyond this. If he won't, you won't.

Despite any denials you may hear, the size and clout of your agency has a direct effect on how the industry sees you. (An actress we know went up for a three-line bit part. While talking with the casting director, she mentioned that she had just left her "day player" agency for a slightly larger one. The casting director blanched and said, "Oh . . . Oh . . . You're with *them* now? Well, I can't read you for something this small." He then immediately handed her a *guest starring role* to read.) Not convinced? Ask any casting director to pick up the phone and call CAA for an actor to fill a two-line part.

One method of pinpointing clout is to think of all agencies as being "A," "B," "C," or "D" list agencies. An "A" list agency is a giant such as William Morris, CAA or ICM. They handle major directors, writers and, especially, stars (which is what gives them their clout). Whole movies can be, and are, "packaged" almost entirely from within that agency alone. A "B" list agency is almost as big, with mostly name actors and, possibly, directors and writers among their clients as well. A "C" will handle some guest stars and many supporting players. A "D" is your basic day player agency, top-heavy with newcomers.

It won't hurt to ask yourself periodically where you are (are you a "C" list actor yet?) and where your agency is. The twain should meet. But remember, agencies *can* grow with their actors. As theatrical agent Jim Gibson put it, "I'm not a farm club for William Morris."

Office/employees

You can learn a lot by keeping your eyes and ears open when you go for your interview. What does the office look like? Is it one room with paint peeling, giving the feeling the agent doesn't know where his next commission is coming from? What's the general atmosphere of the place? Dead?

Alive with activity? Are the people warm or cold? Polite? Rude? Happy? Miserable?

Does the receptionist seem to know what she's doing, and does she treat you with courtesy? How about the agent's stationery — does it show class? All these things are direct reflections on the boss and will tell you a great deal about how the agent views himself as a businessman and how you'll be treated as a client.

INTERVIEWING THE AGENT

Once the agent is finished interviewing you, gently "interview" him by asking . . .

How he sees you

You should both basically agree on how he'll be submitting you. If he's too far off the mark, look elsewhere — but be sure it's *him* who's off. "Be honest," says theatrical agent Pat Doty. "I can't work with people who perceive themselves as Elizabeth Taylor, and I'm seeing Ruth Gordon."

How often he wants to be contacted

One agent answered that question by saying, "My clients are only to call me between 9:10 and 9:30 A.M." Well now, wait a minute — who's working for whom? It's one thing for an agent to ask clients to call him, say, only in the morning; another to give a 20-minute time span. That answer told us he was not only a bureaucrat, but a bully.

Good agents want to hear from you. They welcome ideas. They won't want you to call every day, but will be open to suggestions. Got the feeling the agent "doesn't want to be bothered"? Don't "bother" him by signing.

How much independent seeking of work/auditions/contacts he expects you to do

When you're starting out, your agent will expect a lot. As you move on, perhaps a little less. But neither party should ever be expected to do it all. Some agents will tell you not to seek interviews on your own, as they feel this is "bad form." If so, go along for a few months. If the interviews are coming in, fine. If not, go back to work. You can starve playing by someone else's rules.

After the interview, it's time for a mull. Was the agent straight with you? Did you catch him in any lies? Did he ignore you? (At lunch with a prospective agent and his sub-agent, an actor we know listened as they spent the entire lunch talking about what a great deal they had just gotten for *another* actor.) You don't have to love your agent — perhaps not even like him — but at the very least there should be a little rapport. "It's critical that you have good chemistry with your agent," advises theatrical agent Joel Rudnick. "Your relationship with him or her is very important. If there's someone in town who has good clients and a nice office and irritates the hell out of you, you really should look elsewhere."

And *go with your gut* — agents do. Often, they'll accept or reject an actor strictly on gut instinct. If a small voice tells you something's right or wrong — something's right or wrong.

OTHER SUGGESTIONS

Agencies can get typecast too; some are known for handling character actors, others for "beautiful people," others for ethnic groups, etc. Other agencies mix their talent. It's best to be compatible with your agent's specialty because a casting director in a desperate hurry for your category of actor will call your agency first.

Verbal agreements

If your prospective agent tells you, "We won't have a contract, we'll just have a verbal agreement," bluntly, you don't have an agent. He's waiting: if you fall into a part, he'll be glad to take ten percent. As Samuel Goldwyn supposedly said, "A verbal agreement ain't worth the paper it's printed on."

But, if that's all you can get, take it — and keep looking for an agent willing to put it in writing. Meantime, write the agent a letter confirming your verbal agreement, send a copy to all the unions, and list him as your agent in the *Academy Players Directory*. This way, potential employers will be able to find your representative, and you'll appear more like a pro.

THE CONTRACTS

The two contracts you sign with a franchised theatrical agent (AFTRA contract and SAG TV/Theatrical contract) are standard contracts, hammered out between agents and the unions. There are no "surprise" clauses and both contain an "out" — a provision that *when you first sign with an agent you must get ten days of work in the first 151-day period, or you or your agent may terminate the contract.* Further, if you get *no work at all in the first 120 days* the contract may be terminated. (After the first 151 days all this changes to ten days of work in any 91-day period. For more on agency contracts, see Appendix 9.)

This came about because actors didn't want to be saddled with an agent for a year if the agent obviously was not working for them. There's nothing to stop you from signing with an agent you're not crazy about and continuing to look for someone who suits you better, safe in the knowledge that (unless you work, in which case there's no point in leaving) you'll be available in four or five months. It's not the most pleasant thing to do, but neither is looking for an agent when you don't have one.

So, when you're starting out, sign with any franchised agent who wants you — and, if you're unhappy, keep looking for another, better agent. A cardinal rule of Show Biz psychology is: it's easier to find an agent when you have an agent.

13 DEALING WITH/ MOTIVATING AN AGENT

*Q: When it comes down to it, does the actor
work for the agent, or does the agent work
for the actor?*

A: Well, ideally, both.

Interview with Sandra Siegal, Theatrical Agent

Overheard conversation:
First Actor: "What should I get my agent for Christmas?"
Second Actor: "A cattle prod."
All of us like to think of ourselves as special and tend to get a little bitter when we discover our agent actually has the audacity to sleep at night when we're not working. And when enough sleep-filled nights go by, we start thinking about cattle prods.

Well, that's not the solution — at least, not exactly.

Assume for a moment that your agent has 30 clients. Assume he works ten hours a day. If he treats *every* client equally, the most he can spend on your career — submitting, talking about, meeting with and negotiating for you — is *20 minutes per day*.

Naturally, the time he spends on your career on any given day will vary. But, if he takes more than 20 minutes, another client loses out completely. In other words, there will be many days when your agent won't be working for you *at all*.

No agent will *ever* work as hard for you as you'd like him to. He's not your savior. Theatrical agent Mort Schwartz sums it up: "The prime job of an agent is not to help an actor seek work. It is to negotiate contracts and to open doors."

If you're thinking of cattle prods, you'll be a lot happier if you *turn them on yourself*. "You *cannot* sit back and say 'My agent isn't doing anything for me,'" says theatrical agent David Westberg. "What are you doing for your agent? Are you getting out there? Are you hustling?"

WHAT YOUR AGENT LEGITIMATELY SHOULD EXPECT FROM YOU

- *To get work on your own*: Especially when you're new. Frankly, when starting out, think of your agent as the person you call after you've gotten the job — to negotiate the deal. That way you won't be disappointed when he doesn't call and pleasantly surprised when he comes up with an interview or two.

- *To be active and visible*: A life on the beach will net you two things: a tan and no work. Show your talents: do plays, showcases. Stay fresh: take all sorts of classes and seminars. Publicize your activities: if you're in something important enough, take out an ad in the trades (*Hollywood Reporter* and/or *Variety*). If it's a play, send out post-cards, résumés, and photos. Theatrical agent Vikki Bandlow says, "I get inspired by someone who's out there doing."

- *Be a fantastic auditioner*: Including cold readings, interviews, show-cases, etc. You're only entitled to do badly occasionally.

- *Be on time and don't miss interviews*: "There is nothing worse after you've built up an actor to a casting director for him not to be available for an interview," says agent Doris Ross. Your regular job isn't your agent's concern. He's not going to understand that your boss can't spare you from the typing pool.

- *Be "reachable"*: Use voice mail, beepers, message machines, etc. With today's electronics, your agent should be able to talk to you in person no later than 30 minutes after his first call. "The first time you don't check your machine, as God is my witness, is the day you get the call," says theatrical agent Mary Spencer. If you're out and don't have a beeper, call your machine or the receptionist at your agency, and check if you're "clear." And be sure to notify your agent when you go out of town. Theatrical agent Pat Doty sums up the feelings of all agents when she says, "When an agent is out there busting his tush to get you roles, you better damn well be where he can find you."

- *Keep your agent well-heeled in résumés and résumé shots*: Peri-odically check with him to be sure he won't suddenly get caught short.

- *Keep your Academy Players Directory listing current.*

- *Keep in touch*: On the average, no more than once a week; no less than once every two weeks. As personal manager Mel Becker says, "If every client called his agent once a day and spoke to him for five minutes, he'd spend all his time on the phone talking to clients and never get any work done."

- *Come up with ideas:* If a show is casting and you know the producer, remind your agent.

- *Pay him his commission.* (The agent would put this first, surprise, surprise.)

WHAT YOU CAN LEGITIMATELY EXPECT FROM YOUR AGENT

Here's a start from theatrical agent Pat Doty: "My feeling as an agent is that I'm responsible to you as a human being. I'm dealing in your life and your career and I better damn well do a good job for you if I possibly can." And, to be specific, you should expect . . .

- *To be submitted and talked about:* At the least! If he's not doing that, he doesn't deserve you.

- *To be told the truth:* A lot of smoke is blown at actors, not only about submissions (a very difficult thing to check), but in the entire actor-agent relationship.

- *To be submitted singly:* If an actor from your agency is auditioning for the same part, check to find out if he was *called in* by someone, or if your agent *submitted* him along with you. In the latter case, your agent isn't playing fair — not by a long shot.

- *To represent and negotiate for you not only well, but in good faith:* When submitting you, your agent is a salesman. But, when you get a part, he's got to grow fangs and battle for *every* dime and piece of billing he can get. But he can't negotiate in a vacuum. He knows, sooner or later, that he's going to be back knocking on the casting director's door with résumé shots in hand, acting like a salesman again.

   Further, you're not his only client. Therefore, Truth, Justice and the American Way end at the point where the agent is in danger of getting someone mad at him. He'll be circumspect about going out on a limb for you because, if the bough breaks, his entire tree of clients falls down too. Theatrical agent John Mekrut: "The agent-casting director relationship is funny; subtle; strange . . . you can push them, but you can't push them too far. That's who's going to buy your actors from you and you can't force them to slam the door in your face — which they'll do — ultimately to the detriment of all your clients."

Don't constantly ask your agent to stick his neck out for you. But he shouldn't be Chicken Little all the time either.

For example, continually asking your agent to go over a casting director's head to producers you know places the agent's entire client list in jeopardy with the casting director. But, if you know a producer will see you for a part and the casting director has refused to call you in, as long as you don't make a habit of it, you'd be right to press your agent to call the producer. If he refuses, he may be too worried about irking people. And this is no business for irk-shirkers.

- *He should keep an office that's decent and organized:*We're leery of an agent operating out of his home. Not professional. If he has pictures scattered all over the place, we'd worry whether we'd get lost in the stack. Yep, neatness counts. In his stationery, too. And in his submissions. Even in the way he dresses.

- *He should return your calls and inquiries:* (But not if you're constantly bugging him.) As one agent put it: "A lot of agents don't want to hear from their clients — ever. That's notorious in this town. Actors say, 'Well, they didn't call me back at William Morris; now they're not calling me back at ICM.'"

- *He should follow up on your suggestions:* Want to climb a wall? Suggest an approach to your career and have your agent greet it with an excited yawn.

- *He should be interested in and see your work:* In a play, movie or TV show? He should be in the audience. When you put together an expensive presentation tape, he should look at it.

MOTIVATING AN AGENT

Start by treating him like he's human — most likely he is. Once with him awhile, take him to lunch, dinner or just coffee and *don't* talk about your career. Try to make not so much a friend, as a *colleague* of him. "It's so important," urges theatrical agent Joel Rudnick, "It's hard to represent somebody you don't know. And knowing a person takes more than just a few meetings in an office." Be honest, but not brutally honest. Try to see his viewpoint. Make him laugh. Give him a hot tip on a good horse in the ninth.

Personal manager Cathryn Jaymes suggests: "Ask your agent 'What can I do to help you help me?'"

Another tip: whenever you visit your agent, wear different outfits. Various looks will generate various submissions.

And another: How about thanking your agent for getting you an interview? As one agent put it, "I almost never get thank-you notes from actors — when I do, I remember them."

However, you may hammer away and still not make a dent in your agent's steel mind. Sylvester Stallone on a TV talk show said that whenever he walked into his agent's office (prior to achieving fame) his agent would say, "Oh, we were just talking about you." He'd look down on his agent's desk and, sure enough, there was his picture — *with a coffee ring on his face!*

Your relationship with your agent will be as good or bad as the two of you are willing to make it. It's a kind of wacky marriage. Hopefully, it'll be made in heaven, not in Las Vegas.

Still, don't expect too much. Sure, technically he's your employee. The better agents take that to heart; others merely pay lip service to it. After all, when push comes to shove, you need your employee more than he needs his employer. But even the best agent can only spend those 20 minutes on your career. You can spend 24 hours.

14 CHANGING AGENTS

*Changing agents is like changing chairs on
the deck of the Titanic.*

Olde Hollywoode Saying

"Who's your agent this week?" is a common, if not very happy, joke in the industry. Some actors change agents like socks.

Agent-hopping is an exercise in futility, can speak poorly of the actor's judgement, and tends to frighten off prospective agents. After all, commitment is a two-way street. Establishing a relationship with an agent helps more than constantly changing cards in a Rolodex.

Agents know you can leave them at the drop of (a maximum of) 151 days, and this can create a lack of drive. When asked if it drove him crazy to work for a client, only to be suddenly fired, one agent's answer was very telling: "No. I expect it."

Still, actors do outgrow their agents (and vice versa), and agents can "cool off" on a client, or not bother from day one. So the trick is to know . . .

WHEN?

A tough call. Your agent needs time to get you moving, but it shouldn't take forever for him to start the car. We'll give a basic time limit, but take into consideration union strikes, hiatus (the slack season — roughly, April through June), bad economic times and factors particular to you. (Did it take you six months to get him decent photos to submit?) Also, if you're *certain* your agent hasn't been working for you, there's no need to wait for any time limit.

Give him about a year and then ask two questions: *how many interviews have you gotten,* and *how far up the ladder have you moved?*

If you haven't been out at least a few times, something's wrong. And, if it's been years and you are still going out on three-line bit parts, it may be that the agent doesn't have enough "clout."

Is he working?

He keeps telling you he's submitting you — but no interviews. Is that the truth or is he just "feeding you wolf cookies"? To check, give your agent photos in relatively small numbers, 25 to 50, and see how long it takes him to ask for more. If you gave him 50 photos a year ago and there are still 49 on the shelf, some of those "submissions" are phantom.

Is he REALLY working?

There are submissions . . . and then there are *submissions*. "You like to think they're all out there pitching to get you in, but they don't," says theatrical casting director Bob Harbin. "Many of them 'submit' you for a project — they put your picture in an envelope with 40 others, send it in, and hope they get a call. There are a lot of agents in town that I've never talked to. Not because I don't call them back, but because they never call me."

"When an agent says he's put you up for a role, "says casting director Simon Ayer, "Try and find out specifically what that means. Does that mean your agent sent your pictures along with 40 other pictures? Does that mean the agent called the casting director and said, 'What about so-and-so?' Does that mean the casting director didn't know you, but the agent talked to him enough about you to get you a chance to meet him? If you're just starting out and your agent puts you up for the lead in [a series], more than likely it ain't gonna happen. That's one thing that does annoy me about agents. They'll get a breakdown and they'll see [age] 35 to 40, 45 to 50, and you know the guy's gonna be [a well known TV star], and they submit somebody that was just in *The Owl and the Pussycat* in Glendale."

Can he dicker?

Over time, your agent should get you better billing and possibly more money.

Money

We used to say *"at first,"* you probably won't get paid much more than "scale plus ten" — union scale plus an additional ten percent, which serves as your agent's commission. Unfortunately, "at first" seems to be lasting a lot longer these days. More and more, agents for non-star actors are hearing, "The job pays scale plus ten, take it or leave it." How can an agent dicker with that?

Why is this happening? Number of reasons. To start, there's the producer who agrees to pay a star the equivalent of the national budget of Guam, figuring that it'll all balance out by paying other actors less. But perhaps the best reason was stated by Thomas Mills in his column in *Back Stage West*, "Tombudsman." In it, he noted that SAG was about to do a study on *why* producers are increasingly insisting on scale plus ten. "I can answer that," he wrote, "It's because they're cheap as hell."

Think he's kidding? Years ago we attended a seminar with a producer who unabashedly told us this story: Caterers to motion picture productions are most often paid by the plate. To figure out how much they are owed, they will make a note of how many paper plates they put out before the meal and, after the meal, will count how many paper plates are missing. Knowing this, our intrepid producer would find out what kind of paper plates the caterer was using. Then, he told us, he'd go out and buy the identical type at a store, and slip a few into the stack at every meal. And he wasn't kidding, either.

So don't be surprised if your agent calls you with the dreaded "scale plus ten" offer. And that, of course, makes figuring out whether your agent is a good dickerer or not harder than figuring out what your local councilman is actually saying.

In any case, when moving from one job to another, expect a *maximum* increase of about $50 to $100 per day and $100 to $300 per week. And bear in mind that studios and casting directors keep records of your salaries (called "your quote" — any casting director can find out your quote, even from a different studio).

Bottom line, (aah, there's a word producers like) over the years, your salary should increase. By how much and when is answered in another book — by Nostradamus.

Billing

. . . is dickered over as fiercely as money. (Better billing is often used in place of higher pay.) If your agent concentrates solely on dollars, he's paying more attention to his commission than your career and he's hurting you.

Does he really know the ropes?

"Come January, a smart agent will try to get an actor in to see me for a general interview because he knows the pilot season will soon be upon us," says one network casting director. (A pilot is the "selling" episode of a proposed new series. Pilots are actually made all year, but the "season" is February to mid-April.) If a network buys the pilot, airs it, and it's a hit, it means years of work, thousands to millions of dollars and possible stardom. Need we say it wouldn't be destructive if you are going up for a few each year?

But it's not just making contacts and selling you. It's his knowledge of contracts, union rules and regulations, and general rules of the game. For example, many agents (and actors) are woefully ignorant of what constitutes a "studio day" or what overtime actors are due under certain circumstances. We're not saying he should be a walking handbook of regulations, but he should know the basics.

As to contracts, he ought to be able to read and understand what he's asking his actors to sign or have someone he contacts for advice. "Frankly, more agents ought to get more guidance than they do," says entertainment attorney Michael C. Donaldson. Actors have literally signed away thousands of dollars because their agents didn't get that guidance.

HOW?

It's not a hot idea to storm out of your agent's office yelling "You're fired!" You might feel better for awhile, and it's certainly dramatic to slam the door and disappear in a cloud of dust — but, when the dust settles, you'll be the one left high and dry. Before you fire that @#!!?$*, have another agent waiting in the wings.

When interviewing with a prospective agent, if you feel the urge to badmouth your old agent, lie down till it passes. All the while you're talking about what a rotter your current agent has been, the new guy is going to be wondering what you'll be saying about *him* in the next few years.

Also, avoid saying you, not your agent, got all of your jobs, even if it's true. The prospective agent has no way of knowing that and might figure you're unwilling to give credit where it's due.

Actually, just say, "Well, my agent is wonderful for many of his clients, but with us, it just doesn't seem to be working out." And drop it. As theatrical agent Bernie Distler put it, "When an actor says 'My agent is terrible,' I think the actor is terrible."

When you're ready to change, write your old agent saying:

Dear _____ :
This is to inform you that your services as ___TYPE OF___ agent are no longer required by me as of this date.

Notice no fireworks? SAG suggests telling the agent specifically why you're firing him, but on this we disagree. (If you've got something nice to say, certainly include a private note.) Not being specific doesn't invalidate the firing, and dropping him is eloquent statement enough of your opinion of his performance.

Sign, date and mail the letter to your old agent, send copies to the unions and your new agent, and keep a copy for yourself. SAG also suggests including your Social Security and SAG membership numbers along with the name of your new agent, on the copy you send to SAG.

That's it. Just remember, a bad agent can set your career back; a good one can be a godsend. But no agent will ever be as good a salesman of you as *you*.

IV
SEEKING WORK

15 THE BUYERS OF TALENT

As far as actors are concerned, casting directors are the keys to the kingdom.

Noel Black, Director

Know a gaffer? Might help. Your dentist's cousin Zelda works in the mailroom at Universal? Ya never know.

Still, your most important contacts are the buyers of talent: network executives, producers, directors, and, especially . . .

CASTING DIRECTORS

They can be "independents," hired by the job, or studio or network employees. They may or may not be members of the Casting Society of America (CSA). They go to showcases, "Equity Waiver" theatres and nightclubs. They hold forth at general interviews and "pre-screening" cold readings. They peer at TV shows, view videotapes, and attend movies from Grades A through Z, all in order to do their one basic job: finding talent.

Using knowledge of the talent pool, they suggest actors to the producer/director/network executives, based on guidelines they're given, the script and agents' submissions. Actors considered "right" are called in.

They negotiate your salary and billing with your agent as the producer's representatives. Rarely do they hire or make final decisions on what to pay or how to bill you. They need the approval of the check writers.

"The only power that the casting director has is to give you the opportunity to come and play," says commercial casting director Beverly Long. "I mean, I invite you to the party. I send out the invitations."

Why not skip the middleman and go right to the host? First, you'll rarely meet a producer or director without being screened by a casting director. Second, "An officer of the DGA told me the majority of working TV directors do only two or three shows a year," says director Andrew McCullough. That means a casting director can cast a half-dozen projects in the time it takes a producer or director to shoot one.

To an actor, a casting director is a walking employment agency.

NOTE: For addresses, phone numbers, websites, prices, fees of items mentioned throughout the book, see Appendix.

GETTING INTERVIEWS/KEEPING IN TOUCH

We use "interview" as the industry does: an all-inclusive term for:

1. *Auditions:* You perform (usually a cold reading, see Chapter 17).

2. *"Look-sees":* You talk with a producer, director or casting director. You don't cold read, even though they're casting a specific project.

3. *General interviews:* Same as a look-see, but only to meet you for future reference. There's no specific project.

All casting directors hold auditions and look-sees; only some hold general interviews. (Many do showcases too — see Chapter 18.) No matter. The kind of interview counts only when you get one.

That's the key — getting interviews and keeping in touch. And it's tough. After all, your agent is your business partner. You can (and should) occasionally pick up the phone merely to remind him you're around. But try that with a casting director and he'll wrap the cord around your neck. Yet, as one producer put it, "This is an out-of-sight, out-of-mind business." How do you beat this game? Well, first, there's . . .

Your agent

That's his job — getting you interviews and reminding people you're alive. But don't bet on it.

Showcases

Currently *the* way to meet and perform for casting directors. (See Chapter 18.)

Theatre

Especially 99 Seat ("Equity Waiver") theatre. It's hard for a casting director not to be reminded of you if you're in a play he's watching. Plays beget parts.

Dropping by

In New York, regular rounds by aggressive actors are an accepted practice. In laid-back L.A., rounds must be made with discretion and subtlety — as though you are doing nothing so crass as *making rounds,* but just happened to be in the neighborhood and thought you'd say hello.

To show you how sticky the subject of rounds can be, here's a list of word-for-word answers we got from casting directors when we asked them "Should actors drop by?":

- "No."
- "I don't mind — if I know the actor."
- "I hate it! Don't drop by. The dialing finger is important."
- "Well . . . no. Except to drop off a résumé shot."
- "I feel terrific about it. But the studio doesn't."
- "Well, it's not too great."
- "Doesn't bother me."
- "N.G."
- "I don't mind, as long as they don't camp out."
- "It's the pits!"
- "It works 100 percent better. Not to try to get into the office for an appointment, but to drop a picture, because it's very hard to trust pictures . . . sometimes the 'feeling' of the picture isn't always the 'feeling' of the actor."
- "It's okay, as long as the visit is brief and the actor isn't persistent."

Paralyzing, isn't it? Here's what industrial film producer Don Ciminelli had to say: "There will be times when you'll feel like you're pushing, and maybe you are — but you will find people like me who will understand that that's what you *have* to do. Because if you call me at the right time you get to work for two weeks. You have to keep campaigning."

And personal manager Larry Fonseca: "The difference is, out here we're all 'laid back,' and in New York they go for the jugular vein. Be aggressive. Go for the jugular vein."

Anyway, to find casting directors, use the guides on sale at your local drama bookstore (*The Working Actor's Guide, Breakdown Services' C/D Directory*, etc.).

The offices of most theatrical casting directors are on studio lots, so unless you've got a friend who works there and can get you inside the gates, either wait until you have an audition/job on that lot or try chugging briskly past the guard with a knowing wave and all the chutzpah you can muster.

Once inside, it's visiting time. Since nobody keeps track of how long you stay, bring résumés and photos, and drop in on every casting director. Give the receptionist/casting coordinator/secretary your best "I was in the neighborhood" speech. If he wants to talk, make hay. If not, make tracks. But always ask to leave your résumé and photo. "You could be a little devious and attach a note with it that says, 'My agent asked me to drop this off,'" suggests an agent.

Remember, actually getting to see the casting director will be a bonus — your prime mission is to make that first contact or to jog memories. Stay pleasant, don't be pushy and don't keep turning up like a bad penny.

The mails

Besides résumés and pictures, there are thank-you notes, holiday and birthday greetings and, of course, postcards. Also announcements of your plays, movie and TV appearances. And yes, even an occasional note saying "hello" is okay, especially if it's witty. They don't always get read, but the right reminder at the right time might result in Bank Night. It only takes one.

Phoning

Mostly considered obnoxious, a call is okay if it's about something specific — a play, film or TV show. That's valid business. Expect to leave your message with the assistant.

Other methods

Anything from ads in the trades to asking a pal to say hello can help. For example, every studio has a commissary. Have lunch there when you can (not every week, though; that's too obvious).

A few casting directors now have their own websites on the Internet. If you've got a computer, you could e-mail them with notices about plays, showcases you're in, or some other event in your career. But be prudent. We haven't yet heard of casting directors screaming "Stop with the e-mail already!" (probably because not enough actors have computers), but e-mailing a casting director, saying nothing more than, "Hi, I'm still cyber-alive," will start those screams coming.

Try to keep in touch with every casting director you know, and add several new ones to your list, about every three to six months. If you do, you'll work. Casting directors *are* the keys to the kingdom.

PRODUCERS/DIRECTORS

Both hire, so once you've worked for either, you'll want to nurture that contact. Use all those "reminders of your existence," and try to spark at least casual friendships. As television stage manager James Hamilton says, "If people like and trust you it's only natural that they'll want to work with you."

Unfortunately, only Jello moves more than producers and directors, so keeping track of them can be tough. Check the production charts in the trades. Producers with "permanent" offices can be located in directories such as *The Hollywood Reporter Studio Blu-Book* or even the tele-phone book. For directors, also try *Film Directors — A Complete Guide* or the Directors Guild of America's own directory of members. You can pick up the latter at the DGA offices, or, for a few dollars more, have them mail you one.

It's iffy but possible to contact a director through his agent. Without a prior okay, calling a director at home is *more* than iffy. It'll get you an audition — at Murder, Incorporated.

While business contacts are the meat and potatoes of getting work, actors have gotten parts through friendships arising from chance meetings at anything from a Lakers game to a fundraiser for The Flat Earth Society. Skip the re-runs of *Gilligan's Island* and get out there.

But — and it's a big one: if you drop in on the offices of producers and directors you *don't* know, your "rounds" are time-wasting circles. Why? "I can tell you right up front — they *hate* it," says theatrical casting director Ron Stephenson. "It's dumb. If you know that producer as a friend, that's one thing, but please don't go around bugging producers. They really hate it." As one producer put it, "If I'm not casting, what have we got to talk about?" Sure, you might get lucky, but spending your time getting to casting directors pays off more often.

AND NOW A WORD ABOUT THE REAL SPONSOR

Networks get involved in casting, sometimes even to the level of bit parts. While they tend toward "names," newcomers often get their big break in pilots. In fact, that's a major part of a network casting director's job — scouting for new stars. The catch here is, as Susan Glicksman (former Director of Casting for the West Coast, ABC-TV) put it: "We're looking for really unique people — for stars of series. There are always roles for 35-year-old, really gorgeous guys . . . for a young, sexy girl who can do comedy."

Theatrical casting director Paul Bengston: "Television has a look. NBC has a look; ABC has a look; CBS has a look. And I'd advise actors to watch and see what that look is." Absolutely; but, what the heck, no matter what your "look," send your résumés and photos to all network casting directors. Who knows? They may even change "the look" this season.

WELCOME TO THE TEAM

Whenever you meet a producer, call an agent, write a casting director or interview with a director, try to take the long view. Welcome him into your club of contacts. Think of the future rather than that one job. It'll make you a relaxed pro, not an uptight amateur.

In short, you'll probably get to "go" sooner if you think in terms of later.

16 THE GENERAL INTERVIEW/ LOOK-SEE

Think of it as having a cup of coffee with a friend.

Terry Lichtman, Theatrical Agent

You've got five minutes. You've busted your buns to get there, 'cause that's where the jobs are. Now it's 300 seconds of dynamite or forget it.

Most actors understand this — when it comes to auditions. But they treat interviews like spinach — something to get past to the good stuff, the dessert: the "cold reading" (audition).

Sure, cold readings are vital, but if you think being a "good interview" isn't important, you don't understand this industry. Jobs often come directly and *solely* from interviews. Director Noel Black: "That small talk is very important; in some cases more important than the reading . . . A lot of directors don't even read people. They'll talk to an actor for five minutes and base their decision on whether to cast the actor on what they think of the actor's personality."

Fortunately, interviewing, like cold reading, is a skill that can be learned — with practice.

DOING A PERSONALITY INTERVIEW

Hell and bad interviews are paved with good intentions . . .

"They just want to meet and talk with you," says your agent.

"What the heck does that mean?" you ask yourself. "How do I behave? *What do they want?*"

An old high school lecture on "Proper Job Interview Technique" comes to mind, and, obediently, you take the pinstripe approach: you sit up straight, answer all questions succinctly, are *very* businesslike, get to the point, give all your credits, speak only when spoken to . . .

. . . And the other guy gets the part.

Want to be a good interview? Tear up those high school notes, drop any preconceptions you may have had, and start with an attitude that may startle you: no matter what, *never treat an interview as if you are applying for a job.*

The purpose of a show business interview is to meet the interviewer and introduce your look, type, voice and — especially — your *personality* to him. And to show that you won't be a pain in the knickers. That's all.

Forget going to interviews as a job applicant looking for work. Just go to meet and talk with the interviewer, using the techniques we'll describe below, with a friendly and relatively easygoing approach. (We'd like to change the name from general *interview* to general *conversation*.)

In short, don't do a "business" interview — do a "personality" interview — by applying the following five ideas:

1. Be interesting;
2. Be interested;
3. Have a conversation;
4. Control the interview;
5. Be (the better part of) yourself.

- *Be interesting:* When asked what she looked for in an actor, theatrical casting director Sally Dennison replied, "A sense of humor." Notice no talk of business, credits, and so on. Merely being polite will get you a nod of the head. Being fascinating will get callbacks and jobs. Don't confuse this with coming on like gangbusters. If you're naturally quiet, fine — be quietly interesting; as theatrical casting director Ron Stephenson says, "I don't think coming in and bubbling all over the place and bouncing off the walls is the answer."

  At the same time, as theatrical casting director Paul Bengston says, "If an actor just comes in and stares at me it puts me off because I don't know what to do. I really don't." Or, as producer Buddy Bregman puts it, "Don't clam up. The producer or director will think, if you don't have anything to say to him, you won't have anything to 'say' in the picture. If you're shy take a class or something, because shy people just aren't going to make it."

- *Be interested:* Don't talk to the *title* (casting director, producer, etc.), talk to the *person*. As television stage manager James Hamilton says, "If people see you only want something from them, it turns them off fast. They see it all the time and they get so tired of it."

- *Control the interview:* The interviewer may control the questions, but *you* control the answers.

- *Be (the better part of) yourself:* "On an interview, don't try to be something you're not," advises theatrical casting director Jerry Franks.

SEEKING WORK

If you're up for the role of a villain, and apply for the job by trying to behave like Boris Karloff, the interview will be a disaster. You'll come off phony and affected. If you're a brooding Nicholas Cage type, don't try to act like Robin Williams; if you're a bubbly Goldie Hawn type, don't try to be a fiery Jessica Lange — no matter what you think they want. "I think you get in to trouble when you try to second-guess what I'm looking for," says one casting director. "All you can do is to give us you and be true to that."

"But what's me?" we often hear. Stop worrying about it. You don't have to try to be yourself. You already *are*. The trouble only starts when you actively try to be anyone else.

However, notice we added "be the *better* part of yourself." If you're a miserable rotter, we'd suggest behaving as you did last August, on that one day you were fun to be around. Being a spoiled child because you've decided "that's me" is not being yourself, it's being self-indulgent — at your own expense.

Shortly, we'll show you how to put these ideas to work. First . . .

BEFORE THE INTERVIEW

There's no dress code for an interview. Clean and neat is good. And, as theatrical agent Miriam Baum says, "Lay low on the jewelry."

Also note: come-ons are turn-offs. If the interview is with an agent there's no reason for you to be wearing an outfit that makes people wonder if you're out trying to get in or vice-versa. Even if it's a look-see for the role of a hooker or gigolo stay within the bounds of good taste.

ARRIVAL

Always, always bring a résumé and photo with you, even if you're sure your agent has already sent them ahead. But offer them only if asked, so you won't seem too eager. (Keep them discreetly tucked in a purse or briefcase.) Don't bring your book (a book of photos, used by models). Booooooring. Besides, acting is not modeling. (You might bring your book to an interview with an agent, but only offer it if asked.)

Arrive early or forget it. "I never hire people who are late for readings," says director Andrew McCullough. "They often have brilliant excuses, but I'm afraid they'll be late to the set, so I don't hire them." Give yourself plenty of "get lost" and "get set" time. "Get lost" time is for getting stuck in traffic or running all over the lot, looking for the right office. (We've yet to understand the directions given us by those friendly, helpful guards at the gates. We're sure they write tax forms in their spare time.) "Get set" time is for catching breath and thinking about what you're going to do.

(By the way, if you drive onto the lot, here's some good advice from theatrical agent Pat Doty: "When you arrive at the studio and get out of that car, switch on 5,000 watts, 'cause when you're walking across the lots you never know who's going to see you. And keep up the energy and don't drop it until you have returned to the car.")

Once there, look for the "sign-in" sheet (almost always there in theatrical interviews/auditions; always there in commercials — see Chapter 23) which requests your name, Social Security number, agent, the time you were told to arrive (called "Actual Call") and the time you actually got there. (Special note: since your Social Security number should be kept as private as possible, SAG permits you to put your SAG number in its place.) Leave blank, for the moment, the box that says "Time Out"; put your initials in the next box and circle the number that corresponds with whether it is your first, second, third or fourth interview (third and fourth interviews are extremely rare in theatricals, but can occur in commercials). The final four items on the sign-in sheet are voluntary. They're there to help SAG/AFTRA keep track of what's happening in the industry. You're asked to check off: your sex, age, ethnicity and if you're "PWD" (a person with a disability). These sheets are sent to the unions, so if you don't want to inconvenience the casting director, don't forget to sign in *and* out.

Once this is done, don't make the mistake of going around glad-handing fellow actors. Focus your energy. Sit down and think about . . .

THE MOST-ASKED QUESTIONS AND HOW TO HANDLE THEM — AND YOURSELF

The following questions are only a shorthand method to get you to talk. They're formula stuff, more boring to the interviewer than you. And he'll ask more than one or two of them only if you make him feel like a dentist who has to pull things out of you. Thus, the more of these questions you're asked, *the worse the interview is going.*

"Tell me about yourself"

The dreaded question. And you can bet it will be asked. (Or a variation — "What've you been doing?", "What's been happening?", etc.) The usual bad reply: "What do you want to know?" (Terrible. Answering a question with a question is obnoxious.) Or the actor responds by becoming the fearsome Incredible Walking Résumé, reeling off credits to an increasingly glassy-eyed interviewer. Imagine listening to that litany actor after actor? If the interviewer wants to know your credits, he can read your résumé. If you're ever tempted to "talk business," remember producer William Kayden's statement, "I look for that undefinable quality called 'uniqueness.' I'm not interested in credits." Credit talk only makes you as serious as a tax auditor on a bad day. Director Noel Black: "Don't give your credits. A lot of time you'll look too eager, as if you're distressed merchandise."

So how do you answer the question? *Any way you want.* Translated, "Tell me about yourself" means: "Talk — and *please* be interesting."

That's why you need "get set" time — to think of something entertaining, interesting, memorable and/or funny. Then, you'll be ready for THAT question. You can talk about your recipe for nut soup, how you spent your childhood in a lighthouse, or even, as theatrical casting director Paul Bengston suggests, "Find something that happened that day." The point? The topic literally doesn't matter as long as *it's interesting and leads to conversation.* "We're interested in what you're interested in," says commercial casting director Pamela Campus, "And, if we're bored, we'll change the subject, don't worry."

Remember, it's a *personality* interview. Talk about something you're genuinely interested in and your personality automatically comes shining through. We've seen it. Try to be "businesslike," and you hide your personality. We've seen that too.

One other little bonus. With an interesting enough topic, there's a good chance the interviewer (if a casting director; an agent eventually needs to talk turkey) won't get around to any more of these by-rote questions. If so, you just had a super interview!

"What have you done recently?"

The one time you discuss your career. But it too requires planning. During your "get set" time, pick one or two of your best credits and find something specific and interesting to say about them. (Rambling on about finding motivations for Hamlet is dull; talking about how the technical crew conjured up Hamlet's Ghost could be fascinating.)

Notice we said your *best* credits — *not* your most recent. With no dates on your résumé, no one knows if your best credit isn't your most recent unless it's obviously dated (*Hill Street Blues,* for example).

Idle times come to all actors — times when recent credits are getting slightly dusty. When (not if) that happens to you, and the interview is with a casting director, producer or director, it's frankly time to bend the truth a little. We hate telling actors to fib, but saying you haven't done anything for six months (or longer) makes you look a little yellow around the gills. "In my opinion," advises director Noel Black, "It's a lot better to say you're in a play at some little theatre than to say 'I did something eight months ago.'"

On those occasions, pick a credit that's undated (maybe an out-of-town play) and say you just "recently" finished it. If, however, the interview is with an agent, tell the truth. Never lie to an agent. If you haven't done anything recently, whimper so.

"How old are you?"

Answer the question and drop it. "How old do I look?" or "Well, I can play between ages 20 and 30," or "How old do you want me to be?" etc., all sound like you're embarrassed. Should you lie about your age? Up to you, but pick one realistic number and stick to it. Don't go around giving different ages in order to qualify for particular parts. The age you say will be remembered — we promise.

Two other points. First, if you lie about your age remember (at least as it is now) your employer might see the awful truth on your I-9 form. Second, if you're under 18, don't age yourself up. When the truth comes out — and it will — the legal problems will be enormous. Besides, adding numbers to your age is foolish. Eventually it'll haunt you like Amityville.

"What brought you to L.A.?"

A good answer: something like "This is where the action/business/work is." A bad answer: "This is where my boyfriend lives."

"Do you have any film on yourself?"

They mean a videotaped record of a film or TV appearance. If you don't, simply say, "Not yet."

"Do you have an agent?"

With a casting director, producer or director: if you've got one, say so but don't proceed to bad-mouth him if you're unhappy. You may be talking to the agent's best friend, and (supposedly) only non-working actors are unhappy with their agents. Either say something nice or *nada*.

If you are interviewing with an agent, simply say you have no agent if that's the case. And try to avoid crying hysterically.

Questions about your résumé

Once again, that "get set" time is invaluable here. Use it to go over your résumé. Be prepared to say something positive and interesting about every item on it. And be sure you know who produced, directed and cast every production mentioned. We know one casting director who said she'd never cast any actor who didn't know this. That's extreme, but knowing who you worked for avoids a lot of stammering.

Can you (do a skill: ride a horse, affect an accent)?

Say "yes" only if you can do it. That builds trust. If asked about an accent, however, don't fall into the trap of replying in that accent. Looks too eager, and you'll invariably blow it.

Other questions can include:

- "Where are you from originally?"
- "What made you decide to become an actor?"
- "Who have you studied with?"
- "Are you studying with anyone now?"
- "Have you done any theatre in L.A.?"
- "Have you worked only on stage?"

Naturally, your answers to these depend on your personal circumstances. But be ready to handle them. Only Mortimer Snerd goes to an interview not knowing what he's going to say ("I don't know, yup, yup"). This doesn't mean having a set spiel, by the way; just know basically what you want to say.

Okay, now you're ready. When called, put out the smokes, get rid of the gum, and remember the interview starts when you walk in the door. That first impression is vital. With your hand on the doorknob, take a deep breath, mentally say "Action" — *and be ready for anything.* For example, most interviews are one-on-one (you and the casting director, director or producer), but be prepared to talk to a roomful of people if that's the case. Or, as theatrical agent Miriam Baum cautions: "Even when you go on a general interview, you'd better be ready to do a cold reading."

OTHER RULES OF THE GAME

Don't be negative

Laugh and the world laughs with you; cry and the other guy gets cast. Each negative remark lessens your chances; each positive word increases them. Be especially aware of how you talk about yourself. We've seen actors with credits as long as their arms talk as if they're total greenhorns. Question: "What have you done recently?" Answer, from an actor who has just finished a guest-starring role on a major TV show: "Oh . . . not much." Or "Well, I just did a small/nothing/tiny/silly little/non-existent role on Broadway." Think we're kidding? Those are word-for-word answers we've heard.

You'll be treated exactly as you tell people to treat you, and they'll look on your previous work exactly in the manner in which you explain it. We're not talking about "hype." We're talking about pride.

Don't be hostile

It's surprisingly common. If you've got a temporary mad on, go kick a garbage can. If it's permanent, go yell at a psychiatrist or take up linebacking for the Chicago Bears As theatrical casting director Susan Sukman observes, "Negative vibes will come out whether you know it or not."

Don't talk in a vacuum

It's a conversation, not a monologue. Some actors give the impression the interviewer could leave the room and they would just go on yapping. *Listen to what the interviewer says and ask questions.* For example: it's the start of the interview and your topic is skiing. As you talk, the interviewer says "Oh, I love to ski." The foolish actor drones on. The smart actor zooms in: "You do? Do you have a favorite spot?" Bang! A conversation. The more you involve the interviewer, the more involved he'll be with you.

Don't try to be Robin Williams

There's a difference between having a sense of humor and having an *act*. Also, never make yourself the butt of a joke; like Rodney Dangerfield, you'll get no respect. Be sure your sense of humor isn't negative, cruel or so off-the-wall that people will think you're weird. And don't get gladhandy or act like an Uncle Tom. All of these things hide you as much as sitting there like a sphinx. In fact, they're worse. At least sphinxes don't land on you like a ton of bricks.

Know when to leave

When you hear "Thank you for coming in," it's curtain. Skip the exit speech. Split.

SPECIAL NOTES

The techniques we've talked about will work with anyone, with the following minor differences:

If the interview is with an agent

There really are two possible kinds of interview, depending on:

1. Whether he only wants to talk business.
2. Whether he likes to schmooz first, with business later.

Since you can't know in advance which it's going to be, start with your topic. He'll either play along or abruptly change the topic to business. Either way, you'll be ready.

If the interview is with a producer/director (a "look-see")

Try making your topic *his project*. If you've read the script, ask a question about it. If not, you could always say, "I'm curious, how did you come across the script?" or "Will you be shooting on location?"

There's also a chance he may start talking about the project on his own. When that happens, bad interviewees sit stonefaced, as if to say, "But what about ME?" Good interviewees are fascinated. Not only are you conversing on a subject dear to his heart, but the talk is almost always interesting.

In short, show an interest in his project (but not an overt interest in putting yourself in it).

Also, as theatrical casting director Marci Liroff points out, "Some directors love you to say 'I liked your last movie'; others hate it." We'd advise not saying anything. Makes you look too much like a fan or that you're applying heavy butter.

A word about nerves

General interviews/look-sees can be rattling, but most industry people will go out of their way to relax you. Theatrical casting director Sharon Himes is an example: "When I see an actor is nervous, I'll tell him, 'I just did two loads of diapers this morning.'"

Granted, it's hard to be blasé, especially if you walk in, and there, seated on a sofa, is your all-time favorite star. Unfortunately, you just can't come off as a Nervous Nelly; they'll worry that if you can't handle the pressure of a simple interview, you sure won't be able to handle the pressure on a set. "If you go in very shy and inhibited and very insecure about what you're doing there in that office, they're not going to feel very respectful of your talent, unfortunately," says theatrical agent Maxine Arnold.

Remembering not to "apply for a job" can help. So can remembering to treat anyone you meet as a fellow professional, not as some god whom you can't wait to worship. Nobody hires fans.

Practice

If you can't afford a class, set up a tape recorder (or camcorder) and do a mock interview. Enlist a friend to ask the questions and listen to (or watch) the playback of your answers. Videotape can be invaluable — gets rid of tics.

And a word about listening

Oh don't be silly. Of *course*, when the interviewer opens his mouth you'll listen. Theatrical casting director Mike Fenton:

"We were casting a film with Claude LeLouch. LeLouch speaks English but he doesn't think he speaks it very well . . . We were having interviews. An actor would come in and sit in a chair, and I would say — per Mr. LeLouch's instructions — 'Mr. LeLouch is very pleased that you've come to see him today. He is hesitant about his English. He doesn't feel comfortable speaking it, so he probably will not say a word. But what he would like to know, first of all, is: What did you have for dinner last night?'

"Well, that stumped a lot of actors. I mean they were totally thrown. They didn't know what to do. And then, *there would be a further instruction*: 'Say it as if you were very angry' or 'Say it as if you were very joyous'; 'Say it in a sensual way'; 'Say it as if you were mad at the world.' So there were different instructions on how to say what you had for dinner last night. Well, it was bizarre. An overwhelming number of actors *never heard* the second instruction. They just went off saying what they had for dinner without adding to it the inflection he was looking for — so that at least 65 percent of the actors who came in for that motion picture never had a chance at it because they never heard what was said to them. They never heard the instructions. It's real important to listen."

'Nuff said.

AFTER THE INTERVIEW

Don't forget to sign out, and then on the way home ask yourself: How'd it go? What worked? What laid an egg? Did you control the interview? Did you do and say the things you wanted? How'd they react? Any negativity on your part? Did you fall into the trap of bad-mouthing yourself? Was it a conversation or an interrogation? A joy or a bore?

If it worked, know why. If it didn't, know that too, and treat it as a learning experience, not the end of the world — or your career. Which brings us to our last point.

You were great? Enjoy it. Fair? Okay, work on it, but remember, nobody does a *perfect* interview. Bombed? Try not to get down on yourself. As theatrical casting director Judith Holstra puts it, "You're not doing cancer research, y'know." No matter how badly it went . . .

. . . Life will go on, phones will continue to ring when you're in the bathtub, that flick you've wanted to see will still be playing at the Bijou, your income tax will still be due on April 15 — and other interviews will come your way. And Fido, God bless him, will wag his tail just as frantically when you walk in the door.

Ultimately, that's far more important.

17 THE (RARELY) COLD READING

The most distressing thing is when an actor feels the people he's going to read for are enemies. If I'm bringing you in, I'm rooting for you. The producer and director are wide open. They've got to have someone in their show and they want someone good. So you walk into a room full of people who are pulling for you. It's a room full of friendliness. We all want you to be terrific. So come on in and be wonderful.

Ron Stephenson, Theatrical Casting Director

"Oh, I'm terrible at auditions," blathers the famous actor. If you believe that, we've got a condo we'd like to sell you — on Venus.

In rare cases, an actor will be seen in one show and cast in another without ever auditioning. If that happens often enough, he becomes famous without ever having to read for a part. Still, how did he get the first part? By osmosis? And do you want to bet a career on that kind of luck?

Cold readings are the crux of an actor's career — make-it-or-break-it time. Read poorly often enough, and you'll find yourself back in Sweetwater, Nebraska, being a plumber like papa wanted in the first place. Read well often enough and you might become just famous enough to demur, "Oh, I audition terribly."

UNDERSTANDING COLD READINGS

The confusion starts with the name. Nobody "reads." It's an audition with script in hand. And only an idiot does it "cold."

But that's just the tip of an iceberg that sinks an awful lot of actors. Far too many otherwise competent people blow jobs — sometimes careers — because they don't know what's expected of them at a reading.

Start here: Cold reading is not an art. *It's a skill.*

You cannot go about it in the same way you perform a rehearsed role. Your preparation will be different, and your goals are different. Why?

1. Unless you got the script in advance you don't have the time, and even if you did . . .

129

2. You'll be acting with a script in your hand.

3. Nobody wants a full-blown performance anyway.

Don't take that to heart, *take it to bone*. First, though . . .

FOR WHOM THE PHONE RINGS

When your agent (or, in rare cases, a casting director) calls, get the particulars: when, where, and for whom, and repeat them back to make sure you've got them right.

Then find out as much about the character as possible. Your agent can read you the description from the Breakdown Service, or pass on any other particulars obtained from the casting director. (Sometimes nobody knows nuttin'.) This brings us to . . .

SHOWFAX

Scripts are *supposed* to be available 24 hours in advance of the reading. If so, try to get the pages you'll be reading — called "sides" — faxed to you from SHOWFAX. Your agent or personal manager may be able to do this for you; if not, you'll need to open an account with them via credit card. The fee is relatively small and if you don't own a fax machine any print shop can receive a fax for you. (SHOWFAX also has its own website.)

If you do get your sides in advance, work on the scene *exactly* as explained below, with the one exception of possibly memorizing the lines. If you memorize, *keep the script in hand* anyway — if, under the pressure, you forget a line and your sides are still in your briefcase you'll want to crawl in there with them.

CLOTHES MAKE THE . . .

Now, to the closet. On a theatrical cold reading, dress to *suggest* the part. If you're up for a construction worker try jeans and a workshirt. But don't wear a hard hat, carry a lunch pail or rent a pneumatic drill.

ARRIVAL/PREPARATORY WORK

If you got the script in advance, you did all the things at home we'll be talking about below. However, just to give yourself time to get settled, be at least 15 minutes early. If you're going to see the script for the first time at an office, be at least 30 minutes early — you've got some homework to do.

After signing in (see Chapter 16) first be sure you got/are getting the right script and the right part. We're not kidding. We've seen the deflation that comes with walking into the producer's office, ready to read "Spag," only to find you were supposed to do "Hetti." (We know they'll give you more time, but somehow it's just never the same.)

So, if you're not positive, check. In fact, if there's anything you don't understand, including the pronunciation of a single word, don't be a scared rabbit, talk to the casting coordinator. "That casting coordinator is a resource," says theatrical casting director Deborah Barylski. "If you have a question about the material, ask."

Now before you go to work, here's . . .

WHAT NOT TO DO

Don't memorize

Ever been to a first rehearsal "off book"? It's a disaster. Why? Because you can't act and worry about lines at the same time. Don't try to memorize in the hope you'll impress somebody. You won't. *Cold readings are not line memorization contests.* It's assumed you can memorize, and you're only setting yourself up to fail. "As a matter of fact," says casting director Susan Glicksman, "We discourage actors from memorizing lines because they get too involved with remembering the lines."

This advice holds even if you get the script in advance of the reading. In that case, be familiar with the script, but don't set a trap for yourself by putting the script down and going, as they say, "off book." (Some say memorizing guarantees you'll keep your nose out of the script. Gorilla pucky! Staring out with glassy eyes, trying to remember your next line just looks like there ought to be a "Vacancy" sign on your head.

If you have only a couple of lines; if you're one of those rare individuals with photographic memories; or if you get the script so far in advance you can't help but memorize it, go ahead. Otherwise, forget it.)

Skip "business"

Every time you decide to do something in a reading (a cross, a way of reading the line, etc.) you've got another job to do. The more jobs, the worse the reading will go. We call that "assigning yourself too many tasks." Lewis' Law: under the stress of a cold reading, the human mind can handle only so many tasks before it blows a gasket.

If you see *"demurely"* in parenthesis, that doesn't mean you have to interpret it that way (as long as you're not changing the writers' intent) and if the script says "He lights a cigarette," forget it. In fact, ignore all stage directions — including your own. Skip props, pantomime, or nifty ideas for blocking.

Remember, your strongest selling point is your eyes. So, if you want to be effective, sit. Uncomfortable sitting? Then stand. Still. Movement distracts.

(Speaking of all this, theatrical agent Joel Rudnick tells the following hilarious story: "Never use props at an audition. I mean you learn that in Acting 101. At our agency we had an actor who was going up for the role of a bad guy in a very important movie. And he decided that he would be shaving the other person in the scene. You know, holding the knife at the other person's throat. And he went out and bought a straight razor. And the person who was reading the part opposite him turned out to be the casting director. And it wasn't just a casting director, but the head of talent of a major studio — an executive. And I can still remember when he called us back to tell us how it had gone, the voice of the agent yelling into the phone, 'You what?!? You *what?*!? *YOU KNOW WHO THAT WAS?!? YOU-HELD-A-RAZOR-TO-HER-THROAT???!!!???*")

Don't get cute

First, rehearse and play what's on the page. Don't read a love scene and decide he secretly hates her. He doesn't. As theatrical casting director Judith Holstra put it, "Don't look for hidden meanings . . . they just ain't there, folks." Second, don't start "improving" the script by purposely changing the lines. The "help" won't be appreciated. "I put no limitations on an interpretation or how a scene should go," says director Leslie Martinson, "But never ever change the lines. That's a no-no. An *extreme* no-no."

Don't create a "character"

Whenever an actor asks theatrical casting director Judith Holstra, "How old is my character?" she replies, "How old are *you*?" In theatre, you merge and adapt yourself to the character; in film, you merge and adapt the character to you. In other words, *play yourself.* (That's a lot of people. "You" can be a doctor, lawyer or Indian chief. "You" can be angry, loving, murderous, shy.) Forget limps, aging yourself up or down, nifty speech patterns, accents, etc., unless the role specifically calls for that. "I look for naturalness, not 'acting.' Don't hide behind a character," says director Gary Nelson. "When an actor comes in and acts and talks one way and then, when he picks up a script, acts and talks differently, I get scared."

Immunize against the "I'm not right for this" syndrome

Like silly mistakes? Here's a lulu: You're a brunette, who's, well . . . pretty, and you look around, seeing nothing but gorgeous blondes. What do you do? You become your own (negative) casting director. You decide you're not right for the part, and give up before you start.

Well, Dummy, as theatrical casting director Bobby Hoffman says, "A part isn't born till an actor gives birth to it," and you have no way of knowing how they see the part. Maybe they're vacillating between a Denzel Washington type and a Will Smith type. Maybe they're positive they want the next Marilyn Monroe until just lil' ole kinda-pretty you walks in, blows them away with your reading and they, in Hollywood terms, "change the concept." Or maybe they only cast you in a different and bigger part.

If you've been called in, *assume you're right for it* — *period.* (Besides, the worst thing that can happen is you get called in later for another part.)

Don't overwork the scene

There's an expression: "Being too good at a reading." That's when an actor comes in with a full-blown performance. A reading is not a house, it's a blueprint for a house. It's a way of saying, "Okay, guys, here's an idea — but, if you don't like it, it can change." Don't try to do too much with it. (Actors especially get into trouble with bit parts. They try to make "Telegram, ma'am" into a devastatingly dramatic, Oscar-winning Moment. As casting director Barbara Remsen put it, "Don't make two lines more than they are.")

Don't "work on" being nervous

Telling you "Don't be nervous" is like saying, "Try not to breathe." Besides, a certain degree of nervousness is good. Gets your energy up. (There's an old radio saying: "When you're not nervous, it's time to get nervous.") But deal with the nerves — don't fixate on them. Don't sit there thinking, "I'm scared . . . I'm *scared* . . . GOD, AM I SCARED!!" Don't give nerves the "mental time." Channel your mind away from them by concentrating on what you're trying to do with the reading. Rehearse. Go over objectives. Re-read the script for new insights. When nerves attack, fight back by . . .

WORKING ON THE SCENE — IT'S YOUR STAGE

Before going to work, we want to pass on to you the best seven words we've ever heard about cold readings. They came from director Noel Black and should color your entire outlook: *"It's your stage — do what you want."*

Okay, find a place to rehearse, even if you have to leave the building. If your rehearsal area — which includes the sidewalk, if that's all you can find — is out of calling range, tell the assistant where you'll be and periodically pop in to let them know you're still nearby.

If they call you in early and you haven't finished rehearsing, ask for more time. Never read before you're ready. (Unless you arrived late — tough luck, bro'.)

On the other hand, if you finish and they're not ready for you, sit quietly and keep you mind on your reading. Don't clown around with your fellow actors. Save your energy. You're there to get a job, not to make friends.

Now, to work — step by step:

- *Read your script:* Sound obvious? Hand an actor a script and he acts like a thoroughbred chomping at the bit. Bang! He starts saying the lines, bolting the starting gate before he even knows what race he's in. And where does he wind up? Dead last. So we'll repeat, READ it. As if you were reading a book. Ask yourself:

1. *What type of show is this?* (Soap opera means an intimate, underplayed delivery. Sitcom means a bright, zesty reading with lots of energy. A standard TV show or film is more energetic than soap opera, but not as zesty as comedy; be energetically real.)

2. *What's going on?* What are these people talking about? Anything you're not clear on? Again, ASK.

- *Memorize the first and last lines:* That insures being out of the script at the very beginning and the very end of your reading. Makes a strong first and last impression.

- *Say your lines out loud:* That's why you need a rehearsal area — a place where you can talk out loud without disturbing some secretary's typing. Inevitably, the first time you say a line it doesn't come out "right." The way it comes out may even throw you. Have that shock come when you're by yourself and can fix it.

- *Get your eyes out of the script:* The sure way not to get cast is to read with your nose stuck in the script. If they can't see you — especially your eyes — forget it.

  Look up and out to an imaginary actor. Work especially on being out of the script when he would be speaking. Watch out for the "reading trap": looking down, reading the other person's lines as he speaks.

  If you're worried about losing your place, run your thumb down the page as you go along, but, with a little work and trust in yourself, you'll find your eyes automatically will go to the right place. Anyway, no one is going to jump down your throat if you get lost for a second and take an extra beat to locate your line.

- *Pick a "direction":* That's a way to play it — which consists of two things:
  1. Specifically, how does the character feel?
  2. Specifically, what does he want?

Period. Nothing else. And don't worry about being "wrong." As long as you play what's on the page, you're right. Better an interesting reading than a safe one — even if it misses the mark. That can be corrected. Being tepid is too boring to fix. "Too many people try to please instead of doing what they want to do," says director Andrew McCullough. "There's something impressive about an actor who comes in and says 'This is the way I want to play it.'"

- *Practice going out on a limb:* Once you make your two choices, *commit to them.* If you've decided your character is angry, be angry, not just irked. If "She" wants to keep "Him" there, fight to keep him there. Take chances. Go for it — *really* go for it. Director Harvey Laidman: "I look for intelligence, good choices. Even if you're wrong, be interesting. I'm looking for people to keep me awake."

- *Work on playing to, listening and reacting to an imaginary partner:* A solid direction makes the reading interesting. Adding listening and reacting will get you *cast.* "You have to remember that sometimes the camera's on you when you're not doing lines," says producer William Kayden. "Reactive readings are very important." (Nobody means "mugging" — exaggerated facial expressions — or "indicating" — making sure your audience "gets it." Think it and feel it — they'll *see* it.)

  Doing this with no one there to look at might feel odd, but it'll get your mind on listening and reacting — and that's vital. When we asked theatrical casting director Doris Sabbagh what she looked for in actors, she answered typically: "Listeners. Don't stand there waiting for your next line."

  That's it. Nothing more. You don't have the time. Even if you did, anything else would gum up the works.

  If you want the part: *eyes up, "feel," "want,"* and above all, *listen.*

INTO THE BREACH

"I was involved in casting for a major studio with the executives, etc., and the person who generally got the pilot or that role on an episodic show was the guy who came in and sold us *before* he started reading. You've got the job when you walk in the door — if you walk in *right*," says theatrical casting director Paul Bengston. "I look for three things," says theatrical casting director Deborah Barylski. "First, when you walk in the room, what do I get from you as a person. Second, what do I get from you as an actor during the reading. And third, do I like you as a person."

So, when you're called, take that proverbial deep breath, put on your pleasant face, walk in oozing confidence, and . . .

. . . *Expect the unexpected.* There may be a roomful of people or one lone, slightly embarrassed-looking director. You may have to sit in a chair smack in the middle of the room or on a sofa in the far corner. Two seconds into the room someone may say, "Ready?" or you might hear, "Let's not read, let's just talk." The atmosphere may be funereal or "Hey, Joe, you got gum?"

No matter — don't alter your reading because of the atmosphere. Remember, as theatrical agent Pat Doty puts it, "The minute they say 'Are you ready?', you're in command. Take command."

THE READING: ANSWERS TO TYPICAL QUESTIONS

Should I try to get more information before reading?

We've come around to "No." Creates more problems than it solves. Sometimes, though, the producer/director/casting director will launch into a dissertation. Let 'em talk. The more said, the more you know. If what you're hearing is completely different from the way you rehearsed it, switch gears and get as close to that as possible. Yep, you've got to be a chameleon in this business.

Should I ask "How do you want this done?"

"That's amateur night," says director Ralph Senensky. Why? Is it wrong for a chef to ask if you want your eggs scrambled or sunny-side up? Four (typical) views:

Commercial casting Director Pamela Campus: "For years I thought, 'Gee, I'll just tell every actor who comes in, 'this is what we want, and this is how we want it.' And the actors would look at me as if to say, 'Oh, O.K.' And then they'd still deliver it their way. I learned the hard way. You let them deliver and see what they do, and you either like it or you don't. And if you don't like it, but you think they have potential, then you offer a suggestion — once. And if they're really good, they'll get it."

Producer William Kayden: "What we want is what you give us. We don't want to sit around and intellectualize the role."

Director Leslie Martinson: "I never pre-channel an actor's thinking. [Besides] we're hearing the lines for the first time too."

Director Noel Black: "Some great actor may come in and have an inspiration, and for me to tell him something might be unfair . . . insulting."

Should I say anything about the script?

Not worth it. Compliments are nice but tend in this situation to turn your nose brown. Anything negative will end it for you. If they didn't write it, they chose it. "In all the years I've worked," says one veteran director, "I've only had one producer *ever* say to me, 'This is a piece of crap. Do the best you can. Dazzle them with footwork.'" Remember that and dazzle them with footwork.

Should I ask to sit or stand?

Nope. Sit or stand *without asking permission* (assuming you're not directed to do otherwise). You're not a child, you're a pro. "Come in and take charge of the room," says theatrical casting director Deborah Barylski. "Not in a jerky way, but as a professional. That's where your power is. Take it."

How long before I start?

A beat. During which, you collect yourself and get in the scene. Nobody ever got cast by breaking the record for the fastest start. But, remember, we said a beat. Don't stand off in a corner "preparing" for five minutes. That's artsy-craftsy, wastes people's time and will lose it for you right there. "When someone does that in my office," said one personal manager, I'll give them about five seconds and then I'll say 'Next!'"

Who do I play to?

To the person reading opposite you. Don't include the others — they want to watch. Just make sure they can. Position yourself so they can see your face. And get the hair out of your eyes.

What if the other person is bad?

Play it as if he's Anthony Hopkins. If the other person (often the casting director) can't act his way out of a paper script, and you commit to what you rehearsed, it really won't matter — provided you go at your own pace. If you feel rushed or can't hear your cues, ask him (nicely) to slow down, speak up, or whatever.

What if I get lost, blow or accidently change a line?

Nobody cares. They know the difference between that and an "improvement." But you care. So, until the very end, if something goes awry: start over. Nobody will get mad. Trying to muddle on with your mind still going over that mistake will destroy your reading. "Stop if you're doing badly," says producer Philip Mandelker. "After all, you've only got one chance. If you can, try to do it humorously. What have you got to lose?"

What if I'm not sure it worked?

Try saying something like "Was that the general ballpark?" (Not "Was I good?") And don't be negative. They may have loved it. If you (or they) are unhappy, ask to do it again — once. You can't keep doing it over and over. Two tries and rack your cue. "When a reading is over, it's over," says producer Michael Rhodes.

Did they hate it if they directed me?

"Even if the reading was right on the money I'm almost always going to give you a second direction, just to see how quickly you adjust and whether you resist the direction," says theatrical casting director Deborah Barylski. That happens a lot — but only if they like you. So, don't get upset, rejoice! They almost never stop an actor who can't act. They let him read straight through and say goodbye. "One of the things I always do when I read actors is to direct them," says director Andrew McCullough. "Even if I like what you're doing I will ask you to do something else."

Why? Are they just playing games?

Director/cinematographer Bruce Logan answers: "I never read an actor once, because I want to know if I can change what they did or if they can only give me one thing. Usually, what they brought in is a lot better than what I give them, but it's just a way of finding out how flexible they are."

What if they just cut me off?

Not a bad sign either. It probably means they liked you and your reading and they don't need to hear any more. (This is decidedly different from a New York stage audition, where being cut off is almost always curtains.)

What if I'm asked to read a different scene or character?

Ask for time. Never read anything cold — it's the surest road to failure. You *must* work on it. And unless they get sticky about it — which we seriously doubt — leave the room. This shouldn't upset anybody, if for no other reason than it's a sign of your professionalism. That's not a bromide. It's the absolute truth.

Should I ask if I got the part?
Only if you don't want it.

What if I was terrible because my salamander died?
Make no apologies or excuses. No matter how justified, excuses always sound like excuses. Besides, you probably don't need an apology: most actors feel they did far worse than was the case. Say thanks and go.

Isn't "they're on your side" just a lot of bull?
Honestly, no. They really do want you to be successful. Theatrical casting director Tony Shepherd put it all into perspective: "We all want you to be good, if for no other reason than once we get the role cast, we all get to go home."

AFTER THE AUDITION

Sign out, and call your agent on the way home. Unless you're positive the audition was a disaster, simply say it all "went well." Don't worry your agent with a lot of yammer about all the mistakes you think you made.

Then, if you're upset, go home and kick a door. And forget it. Your reading is only a part of the casting process. You may have read beautifully but be too tall or too short; the role may have been all but cast before you read; the producer's wife may want the part; the part may be cut; the budget may demand an actor who will work for less. "Quite often it has to do with pairings," says commercial producer Bob Wollin. "The best people aren't always cast."

"If you don't get it, it could be for a million different reasons, sometimes very subtle," says director/cinematographer Bruce Logan. "For example, I'll say I like what this actress is doing and I like what that actress is doing, but the character is supposed to be genetically related to this other actor whom I've already cast, and the first actress doesn't look like his daughter."

Not enough for you? How about this one from theatrical agent David Westberg: "It may be a 'pay-back show.' When they get down to the end of the season, and there are 21 or 22 episodes of a show in the can, with only one or two episodes left, there are favors all over this town that are owed to friends, relatives, the brother-in-law of the guy who put up the money to back the show . . . It's the pay-back show where all those roles go to pay back favors done throughout the year."

It's hard to generalize, but, in television, you often know within days if you "got it." However, that painful time span can vary from five minutes to five months depending on the project.

Don't expect your agent to call when you don't get a part. Nobody has the time. The casting director only calls the agent if you're cast or (rarely) if you were absolutely embarrassing. If the role is special, you can ask your agent to inquire, but don't make this request every time you read. If you miss this "bus," eventually there'll be another.

THE BARE FACTS ABOUT NUDITY AND AUDITIONS

It's not our job to advise you on whether or not to do nudity in films (except to warn that doing hard-core porn is hard-core stupid). A few words, however, about the sleaze muffins you may encounter and how you can protect yourself. First, understand that no agent on the up-and-up should ever ask you to disrobe or do an "improv" or reading that involves physical contact with him (recently a franchised agent was sentenced to jail for these kind of shenanigans). Next, if a film is non-union, be very careful. Don't go alone to the audition, and the people you are auditioning for should keep their hands to themselves. If the film is union, you are supposed to be notified *before* the audition that the role will require nudity. You also are permitted to bring a person of your choice with you to the audition, and you don't have to completely disrobe. "Total nudity," says SAG, "Shall not be required . . . the performer shall be permitted to wear 'pasties' and a G-string or its equivalent." (Question of the decade: What's its equivalent?)

CALLBACKS/SCREEN TESTS

If your reading was for the producer or director and was only a few lines or speeches, you won't be called back. But don't be surprised if you're called back half a dozen times for a major part or a continuing role in a series. (Callbacks, even for one word, are very common in commercials.)

If you read for a casting director (as a screening process) he'll either call you back or take you to meet the producer/director on the spot.

Regardless, remember: you did something right. Do the second reading just like you did the first. Don't outsmart yourself by changing things (that's called "improving your way right out of a part"). We'd even wear the same clothes.

Unless you're up for a major role, you'll almost never be asked to do a screen test. If you are, though, check the material in Chapter 20, "On the

Set," and again, make as few changes as possible.

FINALLY . . .

We promise you'll never learn to cold read just by studying a chapter in a book. You're going to have to practice, at best in a good class, at least with fellow actors at home. And the time to start is *not* when you get "the call."

And never forget that everyone involved in casting is on your side. "The greatest moment for us," says theatrical casting director Jane Feinberg, "is when the director says 'Him.'"

18 SHOWCASES AND OFFICE SCENES

I had two people in to do one, and they set
up a place setting, and candles, and real
food . . . and by the time they were through
setting up I was so bored . . .

Susan Glicksman, Theatrical Casting Director

THE KINDS OF SHOWCASES

Today, when someone says he just did a "showcase," he might mean any of three different things:

1. *99 Seat ("Equity Waiver") theatre:* Often referred to as a "showcase production," or a "showcase," this is a play produced in a theatre that seats 99 people or less. The only money involved may be pocket-change salaries. (For more, see Chapter 25.)

2. *The prepared scene showcase:* You and a partner prepare a scene and perform it in front of an audience of one or more casting directors, agents, producers or directors — and you pay for the privilege.

3. *The cold reading workshop:* The most prevalent and perhaps most potent wrinkle, it's *the* way to be seen in Hollywood. It's a standard cold reading, usually done for a casting director or agent, and — yes — you pay for these too.

SHOWCASES — SHOULD YOU DO THEM?

That involves two questions — readiness and ethics.

• *Readiness:* "The readiness is all," says William Shakespeare. The purpose of a showcase is not to show how bad you are. If you're not a good actor, don't do a prepared scene showcase. And if your cold reading technique is anything less than terrific, don't do a cold reading showcase. Not only will the competition kill you, but agents and casting directors have very good memories.

NOTE: For some showcases, see Appendix 5.

- *Ethics*: Actor Steve Ray (who has done well over 100 of these) summed up showcases like this: "I can think of no other way to describe a showcase other than an audition that you pay to do. That's really what it comes down to, no matter how many nice little colors the casting directors or the people who run them try to put on them, it's basically an audition that you pay for."

Should you pay to be seen? Fact of the matter is a lot of people are making a lot of money running these things or doing what they ought to be doing as part of their job: seeing who's out there. (According to *The Los Angeles Times*, in one year one casting director made $16,000 in fees attending showcases.) But: showcases work. Actors do get roles from doing showcases. *Lots* of roles. Actress Terri Semper says, "I look at each showcase as a small investment in my future. Many times actors get called in for an audition up to a year or more after they've done a showcase. It's a great opportunity to publicize yourself."

And actor/teacher Mike Muscat (who has also done hundreds of showcases) sums it up: "Small theatre just doesn't pay off as fast as showcases. It takes three months to get a show up once you cast, and unless you get in a play in which all the elements mesh — unless it's one of the hottest plays in town — it's hard to get industry people to the show. I hate to pay to be auditioned, but it's the lesser of two evils: I pay my fee, and I know just who I'm going to see and what shows he casts."

Finally, there's the point made by actor Patrick Higgins: "I like showcasing because it's a great way to *practice auditioning*. Then, when the real thing comes along, I feel far less pressure. I'm fresh and ready, and, because I've been practicing, the audition almost becomes business-as-usual."

SHOWCASES — WHEN YOU DO THEM

A few hints:

Pick your shot carefully

Doing showcases willy-nilly wastes time and money. If you don't have an agent, do one for an agent. If you have representation, do one for a casting director who casts shows you have a chance to do. "When you're picking showcases, go to the ones that can do you the most good," says one casting director. "For example, if you're starting out, try a soap opera casting director. Or, say it might be better to do a showcase for the casting director who does a large cast series simply because there are more small parts that they need to cast."

Each showcase gives a list in advance of the casting director or agent in attendance for each session. (Some places have more than one room, and will offer more than one showcase per night.)

Forget learning anything

Some places call their showcases "classes" or "workshops," but no matter the label, learning ain't why you're there. You're there to be seen. Yes, we've heard of people lucking out by getting someone who knows acting and can teach. But frankly, a lot of industry people think a "superobjective" is an objective that's just peachy. "My experience," says theatrical agent Joel Rudnick, "Has been that most casting directors don't know what they're doing. Casting directors should teach casting directing, not cold reading. Actors should teach acting. Not agents, not casting directors, but people who have done it themselves."

Don't let somebody with a title next to his name ruin years of solid training. When you're critiqued, you may need to purposely ignore what you're told. (Some of the things actors are told during these showcases range from the silly to the absolutely bizarre. One example: With his voice dripping in venom, one agent told two excellent actors, "You're *obviously* of the 'less is more' school. Well, let me tell you, *stillness is for stars*.")

Don't volunteer

In our chapter on cold reading, we say to give yourself at least 20 minutes to go over the script. In many of these showcases, the person will hand out a script and give the first couple up five minutes to go over it. *Five.*

Insane? You bet. (One casting director said he just wants "to see what the actors will do with it." So did Pavlov.) Remember, directors and producers in a real casting session could care less if you've had five minutes or five days with the script. They just want to see a good reading. Nobody hands out gold stars to the actor who gets it down fastest. They hand out *parts* to the actors who do it *best*. Trying to do a cold reading for anyone in five minutes is just plain dumb. The casting director may think of it as a bogus casting session, but it isn't to you. What he winds up thinking of you is very, very real. So, if you can take longer by hanging back, hang *way* back.

If no one is given more than five minutes, read the script over once, decide what strikes you the most about the scene based on that first reading and then *go for it!* Don't second-guess yourself. Trust your instincts and go out on a limb. Better to be interesting and totally off than to be "correct" and dull. Bear in mind a five-minute reading is pure and simple a form of gambling. Enjoy the roll of the dice. Your odds of doing well if you trust yourself are far greater than hitting sevens at Las Vegas.

Follow-up/be patient

Once you've met the person, go after him. Don't expect him to run all over town looking for you. And be patient. The showcase you do next week may not pay off until next year. As Mike Muscat put it, "Follow-ups are crucially important. So many actors do 30 showcases, don't follow-up, don't get anything and then are ready to quit. I did 50 before I got cast, 150 before I really started working — but now I figure I've made 20 to 30 times the amount of money I put into showcases."

PREPARED SCENE SHOWCASES AND OFFICE SCENES

A "prepared" or "office" scene is exactly that — a scene; rarely monologues — they want to see you relating to your fellow actor performed by two actors, preferably each of the opposite sex.

The rules of the game for prepared and office scenes are virtually identical. Really, the only difference will be where you are performing it. You'll perform the former on a stage and the casting director or agent will come to see you. For the latter, you'll go to their offices.

THE CARDINAL RULE

Maximum: five minutes. Strong preference: three minutes.

Sound like acting for a stopwatch? When you work in TV, that's exactly what you do anyway. Don't try to cheat the time limit. We know of actors who were cut off in the middle of a scene long before, as they put it, "we even got to the good part."

If the scene doesn't fit into that three-minute time span, cut it or find another scene. When you begin working on the material, read it aloud with your partner and time it. Since blocking and business adds time, when it's ready to be seen, time it again. Longer than four to five minutes? Pull a "T-Rex": chop without mercy. If you err, be short. As theatrical agent Miriam Baum put it, "Too short is fine — if you make an impression."

CHOOSING A SCENE

The source doesn't matter. You can cull your scenes from television and movie scripts, plays and books. (You can even write your own — *if* you can write and are shrewd enough to keep your authorship to yourself so your audience doesn't judge that instead.)

If you've got a VCR, videotape television shows and films regularly — especially ones that are not all that famous and/or seen by the general public. (Your local video store is a treasure house of obscure movies.) Or try soap opera: the intimacy and intense actor-to-actor relationships make them perfect.

Beyond that . . .

- *Cast yourself close to the grain*: Don't stretch. Perform roles you would play. Forget accents, roles calling for you to be older or younger than you are, and character pieces — they're not looking for a new Dracula. Says actor Steve Ray, "One thing I hear all the time from casting directors is 'The person miscast himself.' Pick something that you would get cast in."

- *"Who's that other guy?"*: If an agent has you in to do an office scene, choose one that shows you off — not your partner. (If it's a showcase — where both actors are paying equally — both parts naturally will have equal weight.)

- *Res ipso loquitor*: That's a Latin expression, used in law, meaning "the thing speaks for itself." Make sure the scene is self-explanatory. "Intros" are boring and they won't help.

- *Make sure it "translates" well:* You're going to be doing the scene in someone's (probably cramped) office. The more activity, the "bigger" you have to be to make the scene work, the worse your choice. The aim of the scene, remember, is to show you relating and reacting to your fellow actor; a lot of running around defeats that. And scenes requiring emotional fireworks can be embarrassing around typewriters at nine A.M. (You can be slightly bigger in a showcase — you'll be on stage.) The best scenes are usually two people sitting, talking and reacting in a relatively quiet way.

- *Forget English Lit 101*: Shakespeare, Ionesco, Pinter and the other masters may speak well of your knowledge of theatre, but not of your knowledge of what's needed on television.

- *Find something fresh*: As one casting director put it, "If I see one more version of a scene from *Barefoot in the Park,* I'll scream."

- *"Who's doing Brando in this one?"*: The only person who gets anywhere doing famous scenes, pitting himself against legendary performances, is Rich Little.

- *A good laugh . . .* : Some food for thought from Steve Ray: "There's a theory that anybody can do drama but not everyone can do comedy — comedy is special. So, if you do a comedy well, they will assume you can do drama. But if you do a drama they will not assume you can do comedy."

  He has a point. So, if you're good at it, give serious consideration to comedy — but only if you're good at it. "I prefer comedy," says theatrical casting director Paul Bengston. "I'm there for a long day's work and I don't want to cry. Also, comedy sticks in the mind."

- *Don't have set- and prop-itis:* When choosing (or working on) a scene be sure your concentration is on acting. If it'll take longer than 30 seconds to set up, it's wrong. The best scenes require nothing in terms of props or set. And choose one that keeps blocking and business to a minimum.

Bottom line, the scene should only ask you to do four things: *sit, talk, listen,* and *react.*

CHOOSING A PARTNER

If you're not in an acting class, or have no actor friends who are "right," you can tack up a notice in one of the many workshops around town. Or ask an instructor for a recommendation. Or simply place an ad in *Back Stage West/Drama-Logue.*

Just be sure your partner understands it's *your* scene if it's an office scene and a *shared* scene if it's a showcase — not a chance for him to upstage you. And don't choose a partner who is a bad actor in the hope that he'll make you look good. He won't. On the other hand, thinking of choosing a partner vastly better than you? Razor blades are quicker.

Above all, be careful. "Most actors choose friends," says Steve Ray. "Your friends are not always the best people to do a scene with."

And, once again and most important of all, don't ever, EVER do a showcase or office scene if you're not ready.

V
WORKING

19 MAKING A DEAL

Your money indicates your value. You don't want a hungry agent who just wants to make a deal.

Jack Rose, President, Jack Rose Agency

With respect to Charles Dickens, the period between your audition and the closing of a deal is "the best of times and the worst of times." You know they want you, but how much? And your participation is usually limited to saying yes or no to a deal that has been worked out between your agent and the casting director.

Just remember: billing is at least as important as salary. From the top down:

- *Star*: Name usually above the title.

- *Also Starring*: Name after the title.

- *Guest Starring*: Most often used in TV. Name usually will appear before the story, after the above.

- *Co-Starring*: Name after the above, usually at the beginning, sometimes at the end, of the show.

- *Featured; also called "end titles" in film*: Name appears at end of story, in the "crawl" — the names move upwards from bottom of screen.

- *Separate card*: Name appears by itself on the screen regardless of type of billing. Naturally, "Star" and "Also Starring" are almost always separate card. "Guest Star" and "Co-Star" separate card billing may require some dickering. "Featured" is almost never put on separate card.

There are all sorts of variations ("Extra-Special Super Whoopy-Doopy Guest Star," etc.) including type sizes, name in a special box, and so forth. Your concern will be to move up from "Featured" to "Co-Star" to "Guest Star." Beyond that, you no longer need this book.

NOTE: For fees and other contract regulations, see Appendix 7.

Regarding money, you'll be hired on a daily basis (called "day player"); on a special three-day contract (television only); or on a weekly basis (called "freelance"). Most likely, if you're working for "scale" (minimum union salary), an additional ten percent for your agent, called "scale plus ten," will be added to your paycheck. As you move up, your salary will increase. But be careful. As theatrical casting director Ron Stephenson puts it, "An actor should get a raise periodically, but an agent shouldn't price an actor out of the business." And bear in mind producer William Kayden's comment: "Usually that part is budgeted. Sometimes we'll 'steal' money from another role, but generally, if you can't get one actor for your price, you get another." Sticky, isn't it?

If you're hired as a day player to work for three days on, say, *Space Sluts in the Slammer* (that's a real movie, by the way!) and production is going slowly and the producer sees he's going to need you to work longer (say, six days), he can convert you from day player to weekly contract player (called "weekly conversion") to save money. Assume you're making $900 per day. Six days would total $5,400. He can convert you to a week at, say, $5,000. (The reverse is not true. If you're contracted for a week and work only one day, he's still on the hook for a week's salary.) The conversion is not retroactive and goes into effect only from the day you're notified. Also, if the conversion would reduce your salary to below your daily rate times five, it must be negotiated.

According to SAG, you've got a firm engagement if: the studio or producer gives you written acceptance; you're given a contract signed by the producer; you're given a script with intent to hire you; you're fitted (other than wardrobe tests); or when you're called and agree to report.

However, once your agent calls the casting director to confirm you said yes, for all practical purposes, you've got a deal. The speed of this industry requires a telephone conversation to be considered a contract; sometimes you'll be working the next day.

If there's no time to assemble a full-fledged contract, as further protection you're supposed to get a "booking slip." It's messengered to you along with the script, or sent to your agent, or given to you on the set, and is a memorandum briefly outlining your length of employment, what you'll be paid, how you'll be billed, and your start date. Don't bet your inheritance you'll get it.

If you're hired but not given a specific date, and another job offer comes along (jobs come in clusters — for reasons, see your local guru), you or your agent must give the producer 24 hours' notice. If he gets back to you and gives you a specific start date, that date and job become binding to you both. If he doesn't get back to you, you're free to accept the other job.

To further clarify the negotiating process, here's what agent Jack Rose had to say. Pay special attention to what he says at the end:

"There are many types of negotiations, so I'm going to give you a very simple one . . . They call for an actor to work for a period of time to do a film. They tell us how many days they want the actor, and how much they want to pay. At that point, we say, 'Well, that's not enough money.'

They say, 'Of course that's enough money.' And then we say, 'Well, on the last film the actor got X numbers of dollars per week.' Now, some casting directors already have that information in front of them, so you can't lie to them. Once you lie to those people forget it; forget about dealing with these people again. And you know which ones work that way, so you say, 'Yes, *but* the actor has another project that we're probably going to have to sign him for, unless you offer him more money.' Or, 'You want him for a week; your film's going for three weeks, let's make it a two-week guarantee.' And you come to some kind of compromise that way.

"Then you get into billing — if they're going to give billing or not and the position of the billing. Those are the simple terms of a basic negotiation . . . Unless your agent is a good negotiator, you're going to wind up making very little money, and just working as a day player."

20 ON THE SET

Q: How much direction do actors get on a set?

A: Well, let's be honest — you're not going to get a whole lot.

Interview with Harvey Laidman, Director

Big cities, move over. There's no lonelier time or place than a first day on a set. It's kind of a combination opening night/first day on a ("regular") job. If you feel a sense of alienation, you're not alone. You'll sense a curious arm's-length between you and everyone else on the set — until you work. Then you become one of the family.

PRE-SET DOINGS

Costumes/scripts

Once you're hired, the producer will have a complete script (assuming there *is* one) delivered to your door by messenger, or you'll be asked to pick one up.

Next comes the call from the costumer. When he calls depends on how soon you'll be working.

Now prepare yourself for an unglamorous shock: If the show is modern dress, you'll be asked to raid your closet and provide your own wardrobe. Yep — just like back in South Patooie Community Theatre. You'll be paid a fee, though.

On the phone, the costumer and you will decide on what you will wear on the show, and you will be expected to bring your "costume(s)" with you to the first day of work. (If you don't want to drive the sound man crazy, avoid polyester and leather. They're too noisy.)

Even if you provide your own wardrobe, however, the costumer will want to know your sizes in case the clothes you show up with aren't "right."

- *Sizes men should know:* Shoe, hat, glove, shirt (small, medium, large, extra large), sleeve length, collar size, pants (waist and length), jacket and/or coat.

- *Sizes women should know:* Shoe, hat, glove, blouse, dress, pants, jacket and/or coat.

NOTE: For on-set work rules, regulations, fees, etc., see Appendix 7.

If the show is a period piece, you'll need a fitting. After getting your sizes, the costumer will set a day and time for you to come to the studio. (You may or may not be paid for this. See Appendix 7.)

PREPARING

First, when rehearsing, stay with the basic interpretation you had when you auditioned. That's what got you hired.

Next, understand that anything can happen, and that it's a lead-pipe cinch your scene won't take place the way you envision it. Positive you'll be behind a desk? There won't be a desk in sight. Rehearse the scene in as many ways as possible: standing (looking left, then right); walking; and yes, even behind a desk.

Know your lines, but be ready to see them (drastically) changed. And don't bet on getting the right cues. Besides error, many actors — especially stars — can't resist "improving" the writing.

As "opening day" approaches, your agent or the second assistant director (A.D.) will phone to give you your "call" — the day and time you're expected on the set. You'll get as much sleep as a rat on catnip.

ARRIVAL

Don't run up to the producer or director chirping "I'm here!" They've got other things on their minds. Report to the second A.D. He'll show you to your dressing room (it should be private) and give you your contract or booking slip. Bear in mind it's his job to have you ready to go. If he makes a mistake he's going to have you ready too early. There's a lot of "hurry up and wait" on movie sets.

Settle into your dressing room, perhaps get a cup of that brown iodine they pass off as coffee, get into costume and then report to the makeup artist. (Unless you're highly experienced, leave makeup to the experts. Street makeup is one thing; stage makeup is another; camera makeup is yet another.)

With those chores squared away, sit down in your dressing room and prepare to wait . . . and wait . . . and wait . . .

THE CONTRACT

While waiting, read your contract. Check to be sure your name is spelled correctly, that your Social Security number, address, phone number, and salary are correct, that your billing and any other special deal is as agreed. If everything is okay, be sure to sign all copies (usually three). Then fill out your tax forms. And then . . . more waiting.

SAVING ENERGY/BEING READY

Eight hours rehearsing is less tiring than four hours sitting around on a set. You're bored. You're antsy. You're *very* bored. You're *very* antsy. You just can't relax. Try. Don't go running around. Lie down in your dressing room; read, do crossword puzzles, vegetate. You may wait 30 minutes or eight hours. Save it for "Action."

About 732 years later, the second A.D. will come a-knocking at your dressing room door, saying "We're ready for you." It's rehearsal time.

When you arrive on the set itself, the second A.D. will introduce you to your fellow actors; you'll "re-meet" the director, and, if he's there, the producer.

What you do next will depend on the project . . .

FEATURE FILMS/FILMS FOR TV

Films for television include almost any drama made for TV except a "multiple-camera show" (see below). Feature films are movies. For you, the only real working difference between these two will be the number of takes you do. Feature film directors tend to shoot scenes over and over until they're happy with what they've got. TV Films — figure three takes and out.

We'll assume you've landed your first job on the hit new series about Beverly Hills dentists: *L.A. Jaw.* What will "the shoot" be like? It'll all start with what is laughingly referred to as . . .

THE REHEARSAL

You'll go through the entire scene. Your fellow actor — if he's the star — may be carrying a script, mumbling his lines as he goes. Sooner or later you'll realize that unless you want to look like a statue, you'd better move. So you do — totally on your own. And when you stop, somebody rushes in and puts a piece of masking tape at your feet. The scene ends. The second A.D. comes onto the set, says "Thank you," and yells, "Second team please!" That's it. "Rehearsal" is over.

In a state of shock you go and sit. Where's all the talk about motivations and stuff? Where's the struggle to get it right? What's going on here?

A typical shoot.

Want direction? Go back to the stage. In TV and film, you're expected to come up with the ideas. Blocking will be vague, usually of the "play it over there" variety. And forget discussions about character motivation.

Directors expect you to be ready to perform when you arrive on the set. (As one director expressed it, "I don't have time to play schoolmaster.")

Some directors feel giving direction to actors is "insulting." Others are camera nuts who wouldn't know how to direct an actor if their lives depended on it. But all are fighting one relentless enemy — the clock.

A director shooting a one-hour TV show has a week to ten days to get it all "in the can." Why? Time is money. If he "goes over" without a darn good reason, *he's* either gone over or just plain gone. So, if at all possible, he'll want to rehearse the scene once, light it, and shoot it in *one take*. (Yes, feature film directors have longer schedules, but still, as director Noel Black says, "You'd better assume you're going to do your great work on take one.")

Okay, while you've been sitting there, people have been moving back and forth, lighting and "dressing" the set (putting in props, drapes, books in bookshelves, etc.).

Now, it's time for . . .

THE SHOOT

You stand where you started when you rehearsed. (Called "first position." "Second position" is your next "stopping point"; "third position" your next and so on.) Often they'll strap a hidden microphone on you — this is "being miked" — and the following (in order) will occur:

- *"Roll camera!"* or *"Turn over!"*: Is called out by the first A.D. Either term means the cameraman is to start running the film through the camera. (When it does, you'll then hear: "We're rolling!")

- *"Speed!"*: Is called out by the sound man to let the director know his tape recorder is running and recording properly.

- *"Marker"*: Standing a few feet away, the man with the legendary clapboard (called "the sticks") will snap it (sometimes in your face if they're doing a close-up) to synchronize sound with picture.

(Somebody always then quietly says, "Settle, please." Who *is* that guy??)

- *"Action!"*: Is said by the director. That's your cue to start.

And what are you shooting? A take called . . .

THE "MASTER" SHOT — WHAT TO CONCENTRATE ON

The "master" is the "scene setting" shot. It tells the audience where the scene is taking place, and who's in it. It's always the first take, includes all the actors involved, and lasts for the entire scene. It's also almost always the first part of the scene you see in the actual final movie, and the director may cut back and forth to the master as the scene goes on.

When shooting the master (or any shot) concentrate on . . .

- *Marks*: Remember those pieces of masking tape they put at your feet? Not decoration. When you move, the cameraman has to know in advance where you'll be stopping so he'll stop with you. Those stopping/standing points are "marked," and it's your job to hit those marks — *dead on*. "Marks are of the essence," says director/cinematographer Bruce Logan. "If you don't hit them, you won't be in the light; you won't be in focus; and you won't be in the shot."

    Mostly, masking tape is used; sometimes chalk. With either, they want your toes directly on the mark. (If you're standing on grass they'll use a wooden "T." Each foot is on either side of the stem, with the toes immediately behind the bar of the "T.")

    "Marks are critical," says commercial producer Bob Wollin. "You're dealing with very sophisticated lenses." Miss a mark and the cameraman will have to stop the shoot — he's aiming for one spot and you're in another. Keep missing? 'Bye now.

    Unfortunately, if you're inexperienced at hitting marks they'll really get in the way of your acting. If you can't afford a film technique class, practice with masking tape at home. Pros hit their marks, amateurs don't — and they're not paying you to be an amateur. From an article in *PEOPLE Weekly*:

    " . . . Robert Conrad is taping a scene for his new CBS adventure series, *High Mountain Rangers*. The afternoon is cold and the crew is tired when, suddenly, a scream loud enough to roust a bear out of hibernation rings through the wintry air. It is Conrad, and he is enraged. 'We had a chopper in the scene, and there was a storm, but the skiers on the back side of the mountain could still hear him,' marvels Joan Conrad, the show's producer and the star's daughter. The reason for his fury? 'One of the actors,' says Joan, '*missed his mark*.'" [Italics ours.]

- *Matching*: Remember last night when you were watching *Attack of the Slima Beans?* An actor lit a cigarette. The camera cut away from him for a moment. When it returned, no cigarette. That's an extreme example of a bad match.

Whose fault? The actor's. Yep, matching is *your* responsibility. There is a script supervisor and/or a continuity person to check on the general continuity of a scene, but you're still expected to match. "Continuity mistakes from an actor are really unforgivable," says cinematographer Howard Wexler.

If you shout "Get out!", pointing on the word "out" in one shot, point on that same word every shot. Match all movement (when and how you rise, sit down, turn, gesture, pick something up, etc.), and also be certain to look the same (costume, hair, general makeup). You should also match the emotional intensity of the scene from one shot to the next. If you're furious in one shot, and merely angry in another, you're not matching.

Unless the mistake is blatant (like the cigarette mentioned above), it's possible no one will tell you you're not matching. But it will be spotted later. Where? You got it. "If it's not matched, it won't go together and it will wind up on the cutting-room floor," says director/cinematographer Bruce Logan.

They'll use other shots of the scene and you'll lose screen time (most likely close-ups). Ouch.

- *"Cheating towards the camera"*: Always be aware of where the camera is located, and position yourself accordingly; it's your audience. If the camera can't see it — face, prop or whatever — it doesn't exist. "Actors," says director/cinematographer Bruce Logan, "Make two mistakes: not being aware of the camera; and being overly aware of the camera."

- *Overlap(ping)*: In theatre, cues need to be fast and stepping on another actor's line can often add excitement. But film actors shouldn't do this. It makes editing the scene difficult. Often, if you overlap, the take will have to be re-shot. Exceptions are allowed (a "violent" argument or Altmanesque film), but in general, let your fellow actor finish his line before you speak.

- *Scaling down your acting*: In a feature film, everything you do will be "blown up" about 35 times. The TV screen may be smaller, but it hates overacting. Be careful not to be too "big." "Step back" from the camera. Don't "show" the camera what you're thinking or doing; allow the camera to "discover" it.

- *Stillness:* That is, feeling comfortable moving less, and more economically. Director Leslie Martinson: "Actors will sometimes move for the sake of moving, which is deadly. If you have a head-to-head scene, play it. Many times the actor will say, 'I'm glued here,' and I say, 'Where would you like to move in the middle of a line like that?'"

- *Staying in it:* For as long as the camera is running. You can't break concentration for a second. As TV newsman Dan Rather phrased it in the title of his book: the camera never blinks.

  And you absitively, posolutely cannot break character until you hear . . .

- *"Cut!":* This is when you stop acting — not a moment before. There will be times you'll feel the camera has been on you forever, but never break character until the director says "Cut." He will need this extra footage later when editing.

  If he didn't like it, or he wants to see what else he can get, he'll re-shoot it — as many times as he can — which in TV isn't a lot.

  If he liked (or because of time had to settle for) that take, he'll say, "Print," or "Print that." Essentially, he's saying, "Okay. Good. Save that shot. That's one I'll (probably) use."

  When you hear the director say "Print," that's the shot you'll need to match — all through the many and various kinds of additional shots of the scene that will be taken.

OTHER SHOTS — "COVERAGE"

A cardinal rule: Time is money, but film is cheap. In other words, a director will try to "cover" a scene using as many different shots as the clock will allow. His least concern is "wasting film."

Here's a brief list of the most common shots that'll involve you. Remember, each one requires the camera to be placed differently, the lighting to be changed, etc. (called "a new deal.") That's why filming is so time-consuming.

- *Two-shots/three-shots, etc:* A two-shot has two actors in it; a three-shot, three actors, and so on.

- *Long shot:* Takes in your whole body.

- *Medium shot:* From the waist up.

- *Close-up:* (Usually) head and shoulders.

- *Choker close-up:* The top of your head to your chin.

- *Extreme close-up:* Anything from an eyeball to a pore.

Since you can't always tell by the location of the camera which is being shot, *"Where are you cutting me?"* is the question of the day, for two reasons:

1. *To scale to the shot:* The closer in they go, the smaller you must get — both in movement and acting.

2. *To always have things "in frame":* Important props such as letters, books, etc. must be held at the right height to be seen.

SEMPER READY

Does all this sound tough? You betcha. To illustrate how tough, here's an example of what can happen to you on *one line:*

You've shot the master and they're ready to shoot your close-up. As the final seconds tick off, the cameraman says, "Listen, you're slightly off your mark and, when you say that line, cheat over a little into the light." You nod. (Now you're thinking, "Let's see: mark, cheat over, I'm angry in this scene . . . ")

The sound man approaches. "Listen," he says, "try not to drop your voice so low on that line; I'm not getting you." "Right," you reply. (Now it's "Mark, cheat over, voice up, angry . . . ")

The director passes by and says, "Don't do that line quite so angry." "Gotcha, " you say. ("Mark, cheat over, voice up, less intensity . . . ")

The makeup artist slips in and pads the perspiration off with a Kleenex as the cameraman adds, "And be sure to hold that cup up high enough so we can see it." "Uh huh," you reply. ("Mark, cheat over, voice up, less intensity, hold up cup . . . ")

The assistant director says "Stand by."

Your costume begins to itch.

You hear "Roll camera," "Speed," a man snaps a clapboard in your face, saying "Marker," the director says "Action" . . .

. . . And the star changes your cue.

The next time you're watching television and you think the actors are "phoning it in," remember this example. And get training. Lots of it.

And one other word about keeping up your energy. If you're working on a feature film, and the director keeps re-shooting the scene, after the fifteenth take it's easy to stop caring about what you're doing. Care.

Inevitably, the take you got sloppy on will be the one they use — because the rain was just perfect.

THE LINGO

As you're shooting, here's some other terms you'll be hearing:

- *Wild track*: To prevent calling you back another day because of sound problems, you'll occasionally do a "wild track." You'll stand at the microphone saying your line(s) as the sound man tapes it/them.

- *Looping*: Is done in one of two ways. Let's say you're looping one line. You hear that line on a "looped" tape that plays over and over like a short version of your home answering machine. You listen to the way you said it during filming, then try to duplicate the line reading so your words will match the way your lips move.

    The other method is done in a projection room, with the scene shown on a screen. Wearing a headset, you'll hear four "beeps." You start after the fourth, matching your words to the movement of your mouth as you see it on the screen.

- *Key light*: That's your own personal "spotlight." (Daytime, outdoors, it's the sun.) If you don't know where you're key light is, ask, and try to make sure you're in it when shooting.

- *Hot set:* When shooting is suspended the set will be labeled "hot." This means nothing is to be moved, so that everything will match when shooting resumes.

- *Honeywagon:* The trailer(s) containing dressing rooms.

- *Call sheet:* Given out toward the end of the day, it's the list of actors, their calls, and other crew and items needed the next day.

(MULTIPLE) THREE OR FOUR-CAMERA SHOWS

At the beginning of many half-hour sitcoms the announcer says, "Taped in Hollywood before a live audience." That's a multiple-camera show.

Usually with sit-coms (as opposed to soap opera — see below) four cameras are used simultaneously and the show is taped in sequence, just like a one-act play. There's no stopping to change camera setups (that's why they use four), and breaks occur only when actors move from set to set. Made a mistake? Keep going unless it's drastic.

Like a play, rehearsals start with a read-through, with the cast seated at a table, and proceed to blocking and business. The rehearsal period is usually four days, followed by taping on the fifth. On the day or night of performance, you'll probably do the entire show twice, in front of two different audiences.

With the exception of the re-writes that constantly come up, stage actors love this. It's as close to doing a one-act play as you can get without actually doing one. Directors work more with you and the audience adds to that ole theatre feeling. Also, the level of your performance is close to that of a comedy or musical done in a small or medium-sized theatre.

SOAP OPERA

These, too, are multiple-camera shows, but they use three cameras and are usually rehearsed in the morning and shot in the afternoon of the same day. Short of summer stock, there's no better training ground for learning lines, business, and delivery of a believable performance in a short period of time. "Soap operas are one of the best ways to learn your craft," says producer William Kayden. "They're marvelous training."

Once again, even though there's no audience, you only stop to move from set to set. The standard rule is: keep going. And the acting level is extremely understated. The audience should feel as though they're observing you in your living room through a keyhole. That's why one producer cautions: "Soaps are wonderful training because you are forced to very quickly make transitions, build up to a certain emotional result, etc. But, I don't think, if you possibly can avoid it, that you should stay on a soap too long because there is the danger of becoming too facile."

BLUE SCREEN PROCESS

America is being invaded by all sorts of squiggly creatures from around the galaxy (not to mention assorted dinosaurs from the time period next door) and it's becoming increasingly possible that you'll be asked to "work with" them.

How? Through a method of filming generically called "blue screen process." Fundamentally, you'll be placed in front of a blue (possibly green) screen (or in an entirely blue *room*) and asked to imagine and react to what you're — er — *not* seeing. Gorgo the Spit Creature will be added later via computerization. (In fact, in New Media formats you might even have to imagine one creature after another — for more, see Chapter 24.)

This kind of work requires you to be technically proficient in dealing with marks and staying in frame while all the time being free and honest in your reactions to things that simply aren't there. (Jodie Foster's scene on the beach toward the end of *Contact* was done in blue screen. And, when she was in the ship, she was looking at nothing when she ecstatically exclaimed, "It's *beautiful!*")

Pierre R. Debs, Business Rep for SAG's Industrial/Educational Interactive Media Contracts, compares the technical changes in movies today with the change-over from silents to talkies. "The Internet is becoming a major player and technology's changing every day. In this high tech age, it's becoming more important for actors to pull off a 'digital performance'." This is where training in improv, maybe mime, and a good film acting class that requires you to be honest can come in mighty handy.

THE WE-HATE-TO-MENTION-IT DEPARTMENT

We wish we could promise you a grand ole time on every set, but, if the truth be known, there will be times you'll think you walked into a scene out of Dante's *Inferno* — and, if you're not careful, you could get burnt.

Understand first of all that a caste system does exist on a set — unspoken, but there in spades. At the bottom of the heap are the extras; at the top, the stars. Extras are served last at lunch. Day players would be wise not to sit in the star's chair. Stars get the best dressing rooms; other actors get smaller but still private rooms; extras of the same sex dress in one room together. "I've worked on sets where a principal comes up and we'll start talking," says one SAG actor who also does extra work, "And as soon as they find out I'm an extra there's a whole change in attitude. And they make you feel kind of . . . really crummy. And it's not just them — it's everybody." You'll see plenty of top dog/underdog manifestations of human behavior, and you'd be smart to take note of how much of it is taking place on any given set.

On some sets, this behavior is kept to a minimum, with everyone sharing in a joyful, generous camaraderie. On others, it's best to keep to yourself and not try to become "one of the boys," as you'll be at grave risk of being humiliated.

If your spouse joins you on location (there's usually no objection), be circumspect about inviting your sweetie to the set itself. On a good set, visitors are treated with the utmost respect and charm. On a bad set, they're made to feel like they just walked in on a very private conversation.

Even on a good set, be discreet. Don't run up to the star to introduce yourself or — great holy amateur night! — to ask for an autograph. Have the second A.D. introduce you at the right time. Don't even start a conversation with a star; let him take the lead.

Sound like Chicken Little? Two stories:

On one set, a *veteran* actor (a you-know-his-face-but-not-his-name type) sat next to a major star. Silence. Hours of it. Finally, the actor turned to the star and ventured, "Hi, I'm _____. I just can't sit next to someone and not talk to them." The star slowly turned to the actor and replied, "I can."

A highly-talented actress got a part on a show when the star was having a contract dispute with the producer. At the start of rehearsal the actress said her first line, and immediately, the star threw up his hands, saying, "I'm not going to work with such an incompetent actress!" and he walked off the set. Naturally, her stomach knotted up as tight as a fist. Fortunately, the director knew her and took the time to tell her not to worry, the star was just using her as an excuse not to work.

Using her.

"I think there ought to be a class at every institution about temperamentalism," says theatrical agent Joel Rudnick. "I call it 'star-itis.' It's an occupational disease that people get that can exist on the star level and on the amateur level. And it's important to know about it for two reasons: first, to know how to work with people like that, and second to know how to deal with it when it happens to you."

We're not saying that your on-set experiences need be bad. Just be on your guard. As producer Michael Rhodes jokingly put it, "You already know you have to be crazy to be in this business, so, on the set, treat everybody as if they're potential ax murderers, and you'll be all right."

WRAP

If you're working the next day, the second A.D. will hand you your "call sheet." If you're not working the next day, but are still on salary, next to your name will be the word "Hold."

When you're ready to leave the set, the second A.D. will ask you to sign out. Note carefully the arrival and departure times he has recorded. This is what they will base any overtime on. Be sure the times are accurate and in ink.

Don't expect anyone to come rushing up to you telling you how wonderful you were, especially not the producer or director. They may have loved your work, but right now their minds are on the next scene.

Then you're on your way back to your hotel, or home. You won't be very good company that night. You'll feel as though you've just come back from another world — and you have.

VI
COMMERCIALS

21 COMMERCIALS: THE WONDERFUL WORLD OF HAPPY

What do they want? What plays in Disneyland.

Pamela Campus, Commercial Casting Director

THE COMMERCIAL TYPE

"We're not in the entertainment industry. We're in the business of selling widgets. And, if you sell a lot of widgets other people will hire you to sell a lot of their widgets," says voice-over casting director Bob Lloyd.

Want to know how much work you can expect to get in commercials? Or how to look? Or how you should act? Sit down in front of a TV set. Mostly, you'll see "white bread" — an industry expression describing actors (of whatever race) with rather bland, wholesome, all-American looks. You'll see "P&G housewives with perk" — another industry expression meaning idealized Midwestern mother types oozing perkiness and cheer. (P&G stands for Proctor and Gamble — purportedly the inventors of what is now a standard look.) You'll see warm, loving dads with short hair and conservative clothing, adorably cute children, teens who never saw a pimple (unless they're selling zits removers), grandmothers still dressed like they did back in 1926. Clean streets. Musical comedy. Happy endings. Energy. Brightness. Warmth . . .

"Most calls, they want Midwestern," says agent Karen DiCenzo. In short, you gotta think Iowa.

You'll have to look harder for character faces, and many nights may go by between "ethnic" faces or actors with accents . . . unless you're tuned to an "ethnic" station, where "ethnics" will predominate. Only a limited number of high-fashion products will use women in low-cut, sexy dresses, heavy rouge, or orange eyeshadow. Men will almost never sport mustaches or beards.

In short, you'll see the look the makers of commercials want. The closer you come to that, the more you'll work.

Which brings us to . . .

ARE COMMERCIALS WORTH IT?

Are they worth shaving off that beard you love so much, or changing your hairstyle and makeup from "Zoweena of Hollywood" to "Mary Smith from Peoria" just to please some faceless corporate executive who's decided (based on millions of dollars of research) that his customers relate to "Middle America"? Should you hassle finding an agent or go to the expense of taking commercial workshops in order to be proficient in an area that makes the *product* the star? (The script designation for a product is the word "hero"!) Is attending commercial workshops, learning to convince America it can't live without Uncle Georgie's Better Mousetraps worth the time of a serious actor? Three points . . .

Money

Don't want to do them? Okay. Go into your wallet and throw out every third dollar. According to SAG, one third of the income of actors comes directly from commercials. A commercial is almost always shot in one day and can pay thousands of dollars in residuals. Not too shabby for eight hours' work. Beats slinging hash in a diner.

Career

We could fill these pages with the names of stars discovered doing commercials, as commercial casting director Pamela Campus testifies: "A few years ago I walked through Columbia Pictures Studios, and I saw up on their wall all these pictures of [TV stars] . . . people I had hired five years ago. And I said to myself, 'Wait a minute, I'm training these people for sitcoms, mini-series and television.' Let me tell you something. The top people you see in commercials today, especially if they're comedic, will be the top people you later see in a series. If you stand out in a commercial, usually you'll be picked up in a series. I've seen it."

Entrée

If you're a middle-aged housewife from Peoria who's thinking of fast bucks or doing commercials on a lark, we'd advise skipping it. Getting an agent will be rough, and even if you luck into a commercial or two, the sparse work won't be worth it. Regular work in commercials requires you to be experienced and highly trained. Sorry.

However, if you're a newcomer with some theatre and/or commercial training, commercials (along with industrials and low-budget films) can be the way to that first break. Casting for commercials is far more cut-and-dried than theatricals. When you're called in for an audition, they know exactly what look they want — fit that and you've got a good shot. As one agent put it, "Commercial agents sometimes sign non-SAG people because they know that if the advertising agency loves your face and loves the way you sell their product, they have enough clout — money — to get you into SAG via Taft-Hartley." (See Chapter 7.)

Further, as theatrical agent Mary Spencer points out, "Many times, if you're new, you can get into an agency 'across the board.' If you have a great commercial look, and are saleable, they'll take you on in all fields."

Just remember: newcomers yes, untrained, no.

Are they worth it? If you're not convinced, better stay out. If you're contemptuous of commercials it'll show, you'll annoy people, and wind up not working anyway.

If you want to do them:

- Get *commercial* training.

- Make yourself as "white bread" as possible.

- Find the one person you simply can't do without: a commercial agent.

22 COMMERCIAL AGENTS

You can eat your way to a fortune in this industry.

John Fisher, Commercial Agent

Two kinds of people spend their lives on the phone — bookies and commercial agents. Here's why:

When casting, commercial casting directors usually will "put out the call" in one of two ways. Just as with theatricals, the notice can be put out on the Breakdown Service (for more on the breakdowns and how they're used, see Chapter 10). Or, if the casting director doesn't want to be inundated with submissions from agents, he may simply call the agencies he trusts. He'll ask for specific actors or just say, "Send me ten daddies and eight mommies." In cases when the casting director isn't quite sure what he/the advertiser/the producer wants, he may explain the part and ask for suggestions.

In any case, once the casting director tells the agent which mommies and daddies he wants, the agent then phones those lucky people to give them information regarding the audition.

If you're the right mommy and you get the part, the casting director will phone your agent to tell him when you'll be shooting. There are no salary or billing negotiations (unless you're a celebrity — more on why later.) The agent then calls you to tell you when and where to report. A fairly set routine? Couldn't get much setter. In the fast, furious world of commercials, you're either right for the part or you're not. Your agent doesn't often sell you — your pictures (and, later, you) do. "We're really order takers," says one commercial agent. Naturally, if the agent is smart, he'll make friends of all commercial casting directors. He wants them to trust and call him first.

The upshot of all this is that you shouldn't expect quite the kind of personal attention from your commercial agent that you should be getting from your theatrical agent. Your commercial agent serves as a kind of clearinghouse of commercial types before you're cast, a messenger of information when you're cast, and a guardian of your financial interests (straight pay and residuals) after you're cast.

NOTE: For more on commercial agency contracts see Appendix 8.

Furthermore, in Los Angeles you can't survive in commercials without an agent because there's little opportunity to submit yourself directly for a commercial. Most casting directors freelance; besides, commercial casting is a speedy business, often going from first audition to "in the can" within a week. You can search the trades from now till Elsie the Cow comes home and never know what's casting. Voice-over agent Don Pitts: "In New York you can make the rounds to the ad agencies and production houses. Out here, there's nobody there to talk to, and, at the ad agencies, nobody wants to talk to you. You really have to rely on your agent."

SEEKING/CHOOSING AN AGENT

Since you won't need quite the personal attention so necessary in theatricals, there's nothing wrong with your commercial agency having a client list that numbers in the hundreds. In fact, the larger the better. Big agencies tend to be more trusted by casting directors and, consequently, receive the bulk of the calls. "The others get the crumbs," said one commercial casting director.

Since even large agencies seem to change with the seasons, check any of the periodic guides to agencies available and you'll get a good idea of who's "big" this vernal equinox.

How do you interest a commercial agent? Compared to finding a theatrical agent, it's refreshingly simple. Just send a *good* commercial headshot (with résumé and covering letter). Recommendations can help, but one good pic will do the trick — if the agency is looking for your type.

When called in, use all the techniques found in "The General Interview/Look-See" and add a good helping of "perk."

DEALING WITH/MOTIVATING THE COMMERCIAL AGENT

Taking your agent to lunch and making a colleague of him is a given — even in commercials. Beyond that . . .

What he'll expect of you

Obviously, he won't expect you to get commercials on your own. He won't care that much if you do plays and showcases except as a way for you to keep fresh and promote your general value as an actor. (And don't expect him to come and see you — that's like asking a baseball manager to come watch you play quarterback.)

And he won't expect you to be calling him with suggestions regarding submissions.

He will expect you: to keep him well-heeled in pictures; to be a fantastic auditioner; to be on time and not to miss interviews; to pay him his commission; and to keep track of your residuals and, especially, your conflicts (see Chapter 23).

Above all, be reachable! Commercial auditions pop up fast. Do all in your power to be sure your agent can reach you on a moment's notice. (Here's where a beeper can come in mighty handy. The result of one good beep might buy you a lot of stock in ATT.) On the other hand, there's the nightmare scenario: You're out to lunch. You call your commercial agent at noon. You're "clear." Ten minutes later, he gets a call telling him they need you *now*. You don't call back until two P.M. You're *really* out to lunch.

He may not mention it, but he'll probably want you to take as many workshops taught by commercial casting directors as possible. The reason? Contacts.

What you should expect of him

Assuming you've given him good pictures, and you're "white bread," you should go out on commercial auditions far more often than for movies and TV shows. It may take a little while, but once you get rolling, expect to go out at least twice a week.

"The most I ever went out on," says one good commercial type, "was ten in two days." Lower that number if: you're not "white bread," your agency is small, you haven't got good pictures, or you suddenly "cool off" (hang in there; things will eventually pick up again).

Beyond this, your agent should keep track of your residuals and conflicts, and, possibly, help you with ideas for your photographs.

CHANGING COMMERCIAL AGENTS

You change commercial agents in the same way as theatrical agents (See Chapters 12 and 14), but there's one important difference. In a theatrical contract, if you don't get ten days' work in that first 151-day period, or ten days' work in any 91-day period after that first five months, you may fire your agent. Since most commercials are shot in one day, that's asking your commercial agent to come up with ten different commercials every three months. So a dollar figure is substituted: if you don't earn *$3,500 or more* during the first 151 days, you may fire your commercial agent. (Also, if 120 days go by and you haven't made any money at all, you may fire the agent.) After the first five months, you may fire your agent any time you don't earn $3,500 during any 91-day period.

If you have signed with an agency "across the board" (for both commercials and theatricals), the television/theatrical contract takes precedence, i.e., ten days' work in the first 151 days, ten days' work during any 91-day period after that. (For more on agency contracts, see Appendix 9.)

23 FROM AUDITION TO PAYOFF

*We actors often tend to over-analyze
things . . . I don't want to complicate it. When
it comes to commercials, it's selling. There's
no other way to put it. It's selling the product.*

John Edwards, Actor

Depressed? Skip the pills and go out on a commercial audition. There you'll find a roomful of people who are up, bright and happy. (If they want to work, they'd better be.) Just being around all that enthusiasm will brighten your day. "In commercials," says commercial casting director Beverly Long, "You have to be willing to make a fool of yourself. To jump in and say, 'Oh, I get it. This is all a game. Okay, I can be a fool too and have a good time doing it." Or, as commercial casting director Estelle Tepper says, "Just go out and have some fun."

And sell.

BEFORE THE INTERVIEW

Unlike movie/TV auditions, where you "dress to suggest," in commercials, dress as close to the part as you can without visiting a costumer. Cowboy hats, jeans and boots are perfect for a Western commercial, but not six-shooters and spurs — that's *too* eager. As one commercial actor put it, "I once went up for a commercial in which there was a writer. I've never seen such a profusion of pipes in one room in all my life."

When your agent calls with the usual when, where, and for whom information, press him to be specific about how you should look. "Don't let him blow you off," urges Beverly Long. "Just say, 'I'm really not clear about that. Could you call them and find out what I'm supposed to wear and then call me back?' They [sponsors, etc.] can't see beyond what you are wearing. If you come in for a truck driver in a suit and tie, that's it. Goodbye. You're history." And bear in mind actor Joe Bays advice: "The most abused word in commercials is 'casual'. It can mean anything from a sport jacket and tie to shorts and a tank top. Ask your agent who you are or what you are doing in the commercial to give you a clearer idea on how to dress."

NOTE: For more on commercial regulations, holding fees, exclusivity, residuals, etc., see Appendix 8.

Many commercial actors keep these "audition clothes" in their car, along with a box of probable props (boots, sneakers, eyeglasses, and — yes — pipes, etc.), in case they're out of the house when the call comes in. Their portable equipment also includes photos, résumés and a clipboard (you'll learn why later). And they keep their cars gassed up. Casting director Kathy Smith advises, "Always have at least one casual and one 'up-scale' outfit in your closet. When the call comes in, that's no time to try to run to the dry cleaners." And Beverly Long adds, "All the guys should have a sweatshirt in the back of their car because a sweatshirt goes with a lot of things — a jock, a guy playing softball, an auto mechanic, a jogger. Or a plaid shirt. Or a tie in the glove compartment just for emergencies."

Once again, arrive early to the audition with photograph in hand. Then find the table with the "sign-in" sheet (see Chapter 16) and bear in mind that in commercials it's very possible to be called in three to four times. (They must pay you for the third and fourth.)

In addition to your picture, they'll often want to take a photo of you with an instant camera.

What you do next depends on the kind of audition you'll be doing, but it's almost certain you'll be videotaped. After screening out inappropriate candidates, the casting director sends these tapes to the advertiser, often in another city. He chooses what actors he wants to cast or call back. "Remember," says Beverly Long, "There are fast-forward buttons on those videotape machines. You don't want to be a 'fast forward.'"

PREPARATION

Preparing for the general interview audition

You'll rarely do a general interview with a commercial casting director. In commercials, a "general interview" is a form of audition. If you're faced with this, you'll need to be proficient in the techniques described in our chapter on "The General Interview/Look-See," especially regarding the art of choosing a topic. And be more upbeat than *Little Mary Sunshine*.

The improvisation audition

There's no script — you're given a situation and asked to improvise it. And that's where the problems start. The unions are concerned because there's nothing to stop the commercial-maker from stealing a good idea from you. Therefore, if you do an "improv audition" you're supposed to be paid a "creative fee." Since it's typical to audition over 100 actors for *each role* in a commercial, that means producers would be writing hundreds of checks for "creative fees." So you'll see that fee about as often as you dance with a dinosaur. Instead, improv auditions are simply held without paying the actors, most of whom know nothing of the fee anyway. Then a little birdie informs the unions. Then that same little birdie flies back to the producer and tells him the unions are about to clamp down. End of improv auditions. Eventually the atmosphere relaxes a bit and improv auditions, to mix a whole bunch of metaphors, start rising from the ashes like Phoenixes. Then the little birdie flies again and . . . In any case, if you're asked and choose to do one, the best approach is to be alert and alive, have fun, not stand there like a lump. Classes in improvisation and pantomime can be a big help here.

The scene audition

There's a script and you'll need time to work on it. First, ask yourself: what's the tone of the scene? Intimate? Yahoo? Slice of life? If the script itself isn't in storyboard form (a shot-by-shot illustration of the commercial), ask the casting director if there's a storyboard nearby to look at. The more you know about how to approach the commercial, the better.

If you're going to audition with a partner, ask who the actor will be and work with him. The scene may call for you to be a part of a large group, or to be mommy, daddy, sister or brother in a "family unit" that includes a child. Don't be swamped by the others, especially the young-un'. Make a friend of the little bugger, then control him.

If you've got only a line or two in the scene, go ahead and memorize. Otherwise, just learn the first and last lines.

As you work on it, bear in mind that even the most realistic slice-of-life commercial should be kept relatively light. If you're doing a commercial for Dr. Zhivago's Wonder Elixir and your character has a headache, be mildly in pain — not ambulance agony.

Sometimes the dialogue will rival Oscar Wilde in its wittiness, other times the dialogue will be so stilted it would choke Oscar Meyer. No matter, it's your job to make those words "work" — just as a good actor does with any script. (More and more you'll hear commercial casting directors talk about wanting *actors*, not merely faces.)

The spokesman audition

The most difficult. It's just you and the camera. You'd better be well-trained before you go out on one of these. And be vocally trained, and know how to enunciate (comin' and goin' will not get you workin').

You're given 23 seconds of copy and, if hired, will have to be able to take tenths of a second off your reading, stretch a word here, emphasize a word there, all the while looking into the camera (without blinking) being absolutely warm and genuine. Without solid training, we doubt you'll be able to hold up to the stress. Be ready or pass.

Spokesman commercials — indeed, all commercials — present a *problem*, followed by a *solution*, followed by a *resolution*. In pencil (so you can erase it later), break down the copy into these three sections. Your approach to each will be slightly different. You *present* the problem, *emphasize* the solution, *sum up* with the resolution.

Often, these sections are preceded by "transition words": "so," "but," etc. Punch these words slightly harder, take a beat, then continue — that lets the viewer in on the fact that the solution/resolution is coming.

Also look for "billboard words" — words to be emphasized. These can include: "only," "delicious," "bigger," "better," "safer," "new," "superb," etc., as well as a price — if that's there, the advertiser thinks it's a selling point. Ask yourself, "If I owned this product, what part of the copy would I want to stress?" "The successful performer," says voice-over agent Don Pitts, "will go through the copy sentence by sentence and look for the key words — look for the 'hooks' in the copy. That's what separates the successful performer from the one who's just good."

Next, say the speech out loud, working to create the "golden triangle" of spokesman commercials: you to the viewer to the product. A common error beginners make is to treat the copy like a speech to an audience. It isn't. It's a *conversation* between you and one other person, seated in his living room, and you talk to him about the product. "Don't make them feel that you're trying to sell something," says Don Pitts. "Rather, make them feel that you're sharing some information with a friend."

For maximum effect, be sure you're out of the script at the beginning and end. Memorize (only) the first and last lines. Give some authority to your voice; make the viewer feel you know what you're talking about. But don't be a bully. And don't point. Make all gestures, even facial gestures, "soft" and restrained. Do it standing. And *love your product.*

Finally, find a way to "tag" your reading. Smile, nod knowingly, do something that puts an ending on the ending. Acting shtick is usually stomach-turning, but in commercials it works. We saw an actress wink at the end of her reading — *wink!* — and it played.

Above all, you'd be wise to heed Beverly Long's advice for any kind of commercial audition: "A lot of actors miss out because they don't understand commercials. They think, 'Oh, I might screw up all the rest of the copy, but that last line will be brilliant.' Or, 'They'll be able to see that all I need is time. I can get all this down by next Thursday. I'm going to be great when they give me the part.' Wrong. They are only going to hire the person who does *exactly* what they want *at the audition*. Not tomorrow, and not next week, but *this instant.*"

THE AUDITION

When you walk in, you may see one lone person standing behind a videotape camera or any combination of producer, director, advertising agency representative, product rep, or casting director.

First, you'll be given a mark on which you stand or sit (if possible, stand — it's easier to be energetic). Next, they'll ask you to "slate"— give your name — into the lens. Treat the "slate" as part of your scene. As Beverly Long puts it, "From the moment you hit the door, by God, you'd better sparkle — including the way you say your name."

You may see an "idiot card" next to, above or immediately beneath the camera lens. Don't use it — you'll look like you're reading. If you have a lot of lines, put the copy on that clipboard we mentioned and hold it up at eye level, just out of camera range. Glance at the copy as needed. (You could hold the copy without the clipboard, but even the slightest case of nerves will cause the paper to shake, rattle and roll.)

If anyone says anything, *listen.* As commercial casting director Pamela Campus says, "Listen for the key word whenever you're being given direction. For example, someone says to you 'You're looking out the window. It's raining. It's a Sunday afternoon and it's cozy and intimate with your spouse.' 'Cozy' and 'intimate' are your key words." A common complaint is that actors don't listen. "You don't have to have a lot to say. More important is to listen to what's said to you." says commercial producer Bob Wollin.

If you don't like your reading, you can ask to do it again. But don't be surprised if they say no. As mentioned, they're often seeing more than 100 people. Also, don't assume a "no" answer means they didn't like what you did — they may have loved it.

Whatever you do, don't make negative comments on your reading — especially on camera. Before anyone says "cut," we've seen beaming actors suddenly break, grimace and say "Aaargh." That's the last thing anyone watching those tapes will see — the actor with a contorted, ugly face, being negative. Aaaargh.

AFTER THE AUDITION

Be sure to sign out. If you are kept longer than an hour, you're supposed to be paid. But as one commercial casting director says, "If it's only five or ten minutes, to keep relations with the casting director, I'd advise you to be kind and sign out under that one hour." It's that old penny-wise, pound-foolish thing again.

Then go home, feed your goldfish, and don't give the audition another thought. The advertiser and the producer are back at the studio, arguing over the length of your eyebrows. We're *not* kidding.

After screening the original tape, the advertiser will want to call back (often several times) the people he likes. If that's you, remember you didn't get there by doing something wrong. Match your original reading as close as memory allows — unless instructed otherwise — and wear exactly what you wore the first time. "If the ribbon was on the right side of your hair the first time, I'd advise it not be on the left the second time," says Pamela Campus.

A FINAL WORD ABOUT AUDITIONING

It's one thing to read about doing commercial auditions, another to do them. There's also the added problem of dealing with the camera. We've seen that little collection of wires make jelly of even the most experienced.

So, if you want to do commercials, take commercial workshops. Be sure the class uses videotape, that you get plenty of turns on camera, and that it's taught by someone (usually a casting director) who works in the field — that's who's best equipped to teach you how to be a "P&G housewife with perk." "Every one of my clients had taken at least one commercial workshop with a commercial casting director," says casting director and former commercial agent Kathy Smith. "Schools can teach but commercial casting directors can relate experiences." Sometimes it's good to take a class just to find out how the casting director works.

And watch commercials — lots of them. Look for your type: how your type is used, the kinds of things you might be asked to do. Also study in general the "spokesman" style, what trends are current, how various products are advertised. Those "messages from our sponsor" are your own personal school bells.

THE DEAL

You're paid union scale for the day (called your "session fee"). "Scale" commercials make up the bulk of all commercials produced. Unless you're a celebrity, stuntman, or established model, you'll rarely get more than scale.

WAITING TO SHOOT

You'll get a wardrobe call, and most likely have to go to a fitting. Since most commercials are shot off the lots, you'll also be given a map to the location. And don't change a thing about your appearance. That dynamite suntan can wait.

ON THE SET

The only real difference will probably be the number of takes and the number of possible "advisers" hovering around the director.

Anyone from the account executive to the product owner himself may be intently watching. After each take, you'll see numerous huddles. Everybody worries a lot. Somebody doesn't like the way your hair looks. Somebody notices the product was at the wrong angle. Somebody thinks the direction is getting too serious. And, yes, somebody doesn't like the way you said, "Goshums Martha, this stuff is great." Try not to let all this throw you, or take any of it personally, even if some joker says something incredibly tactless (such as "That was lousy!"). Could be he's not a show-biz type and isn't used to working with actors. Throughout the day, have a "Hey, no sweat" attitude.

Since they've got you for eight hours and have only 30 seconds of film to put together, you'll probably say "So eat Munchies!" enough times to dream about those little crackers for weeks. (We know an actor who had to dive into a swimming pool 200 times in one day.) As commercial producer Bob Wollin put it, "Even if the very first take is good, they may pick at it for hours."

Afterwards, go home and, again, forget it. Don't hold your breath waiting for all those residuals to come rolling in. Even if everything went beautifully, they may never use the commercial.

EXCLUSIVITY/CONFLICTS

What is the advertiser buying for what he pays you, besides your services as an actor on the day of shooting?

As your contract states, he's buying the right to keep you "exclusive" to his product — *whether or not he ever airs the commercial.*

Do a commercial for Maxwell House Coffee, and you can't do another for a competing product such as Yuban. That's called a "conflict."

If you do the second commercial, both companies will become perturbed — but Maxwell House can become perturbed enough to sue your agent and you, and force the two of you to rob your piggy banks to pay for a new commercial sans your presence. Figure, oh, about $250,000 or so. Plus the loss of your agent. Plus trouble with the unions.

Never try to get away with doing a conflict, even if your commercial for the competing product is only being shown in Dry Prong, Nebraska. Keep careful records. If your agent calls with an audition for a conflicting product, remind him and pass. Voice-over agent Don Pitts says, "It's very important to keep records of conflicts, and not to assume it's the agent's responsibility."

If it's a gray area (is a cereal commercial a conflict with a bread commercial?) and if you're both not sure, have him call the casting director. Don't fool around with nitroglycerin or conflicts.

How long does this exclusivity last? As long as the advertiser sends you a repayment of what he paid you for your session (called a "holding fee") every 13 weeks, it can continue for 21 months — called the "maximum use period." Again, the advertiser doesn't have to air the commercial.

Four months to 60 days prior to the end of the 21 months, you/your agent must notify the advertiser that your commercial is coming up for renegotiation. Fail to do this and, if the advertiser wants, he can start a brand new 21- month period. If you do notify the advertiser and he wants to continue to use the commercial, he negotiates a new deal with your agent. You're not obligated to agree. If you say no, his rights to that commercial end at 21 months.

USE FEES (COMMONLY CALLED "RESIDUALS")

"Don't ask me about residuals," says a commercial agent, "I've been in the business for 13 years and I still don't understand them."

Yep, they're complicated. Mighty. To avoid turning your brain into Grey Poupon, we'll only take a look at the basics.

First, understand that what you're paid for the use of a commercial has long ago been dickered over down to the last nickel. And it's based on a combination of two factors:

- Where it's shown
- How it's used — what *kind* of commercial it is.

Where it's shown: In a sense, you don't do commercials — you do "units." Obviously, a commercial can air in one or many cities, so each city is assigned a number of *units* depending on its population. (Houston has more units than, say, Sacramento.) When your commercial airs — in one city or many — the units for those cities are added together and . . .

. . . We're halfway there. Next, we have to know *how the commercial was used* — that is, the *kind* of commercial it is. This will govern not only how much you're paid for those units, but whether you're paid for those units in a flat fee (once every 13 weeks) or each time the commercial airs.

The kinds of commercials:

Network commercials

If you're lucky, here's the down payment on that Porsche, because you're paid every time this kind of commercial airs, based on a sliding scale (see Appendix 8). We can't give you dollar amounts, because we don't know how often your commercial will air. But we can tell you it can mean big bucks.

Wild spots

Remember watching *Witch Women of Azuza* on your local late show and, in between evil spells, you kept seeing the same commercial (an evil spell in itself)?

That's probably a wild spot. You're paid *a* flat fee, and the advertiser can show the commercial as many times as he likes, without paying you anything more. He does, however, have to pay that fee *every* 13 weeks. There's a bit of controversy over these commercials, specifically because the advertiser can air them time and time again without additional compensation to you.

Cable commercials

Think there's controversy over wild spots? Weird sight of the times: Actors standing outside of the SAG offices, picketing their own union. That's what happened when SAG announced the latest agreement they had negotiated with producers for commercials that are run on cable. You'll be paid a flat fee (a pittance) *per day* for the use of the commercial. In other words, the producer can run the commercial 50 times on Tuesday and he only has to pay you once. If he runs it another 50 times on Wednesday, he only has to pay you once again. (For the amount, hold your breath and see Appendix 8.)

Dealer commercials

A local Toyota dealer, say, wants to run a national Toyota commercial, at his own expense. In this case you'll get a flat fee and he'll get *unlimited* use of the commercial for *six months*. Don't get too distressed, since few dealers can afford to run a commercial over and over again.

Seasonal commercials

Santa Claus selling "Ralph's Reindeer Vitamin Supplements" is a "seasonal." Again, you'll be paid a flat fee, but the advertiser can use the commercial for only *13 to 15 weeks*. (Santa Claus in May wouldn't work anyway.) The advertiser can, however, bring back that commercial for another run a year later provided he pays you one holding fee after the first 15 weeks. (He's not obligated to use the commercial again, and you get to keep the holding fee regardless.)

Test commercials

Sometimes an advertiser wants to see if a given commercial will work, so he airs it only in a limited market in order to see what reaction it gets. That's a "test." Since by definition the commercial will run in a few cities at most, thus earning you only a few units, there's obviously very little money in test commercials — unless the advertiser gets great response and decides to go national with it. Then the commercial is converted to "program usage." (This is called a "roll-out," perhaps because, as far as you're concerned, it means "roll out the money.") Nice — if it ever happens.

There are also "in-house" test commercials that are shown to focus groups and only reach the air-waves if they are deemed to be successful.

AGENTS' COMMISSIONS

Your agent gets ten percent of every dime you make, regardless of the kind of commercial you do, what use fees you are paid, and including your session and holding fees, for the first 21 months. After that, he'll have to re-negotiate for at least scale-plus-ten if he wants to make any more money on that commercial.

EXCLUSIVITY REVISITED

First, don't confuse "use fees" with "holding fees." Use fees are separate sums paid to you *when the commercial airs*; holding fees are paid to keep you exclusive *whether or not a commercial is aired.* It is indeed possible that you'll get 21 months' worth of holding fees and never see a use fee because the commercial-maker never airs the commercial.

Second, the advertiser will deduct what holding fees he's paid you from what he owes you in use fees if the commercial does air. (Note: There are limitations on what he may deduct; see Appendix 8.)

Third, the initial session fee he paid you (that also serves as your first holding fee) also "pays for" the *first* time he airs the commercial — *only* the first time. Your use fees start when he airs the commercial the *second* time.

Fourth, as long as the producer sends you your holding fee every 13 weeks, you are held exclusive to him for all of the above kinds of commercials, with the exception *only* of a seasonal. You are *not* exclusive when you do a seasonal. You may do a commercial for a competing product, but you'll need to notify the second advertiser that you've got a seasonal either running or on hold for next year.

Fifth, and most important, you should look at commercials not only as income producers, but as possible blocks to future income. Do a test, for example, and you're cut off from auditioning for all other competing products for as long as you remain exclusive. Maybe no national commercials with competing products will come along during that time for which you would be "right," but maybe one (or many) will — especially if you're a good commercial type. Decisions, decisions.

KEEPING TRACK

How does anyone know if your commercial runs at 4:30 p.m. in Padooka? Do the unions hire little gnomes to sit in front of TV sets all over the country to be sure you get all your units? Who keeps track of all this?

Believe it or not, the very people who pay you. Specifically, the advertising agency, on a more or less "honor system." And it works. *Almost* all the time. (Since the agency gets a commission from the advertiser every time his commercial is run, it's to the agency's benefit to keep accurate records.)

Still, foul-ups do occur. It wouldn't hurt to contact your friends around the country and ask them to keep a watchful eye out. (It's not all that much of an imposition; people love to spot friends when they appear on the tube. It's exciting to know somebody who's actually "making it" in Hollywood.)

You might even keep a "commercial notification file" of your friends around the USA and, whenever you do a commercial, send them self-addressed postcards asking them to fill in:

"I saw you on a PRODUCT commercial on DAY , DATE , at the approximate time of TIME ."

If you find you haven't been paid for those units you or your agent can contact the advertiser or the union. Once you've got a starting point — that is, a date and city — it can be checked. Every station, by federal law, must keep a log book of everything they show on that station 24 hours a day.

The cost of the stamps and postcards could ultimately net you some very decent "found" units, and therefore, use payments you didn't even know were owed you. It's happened before.

VII
OTHER KINDS OF WORK

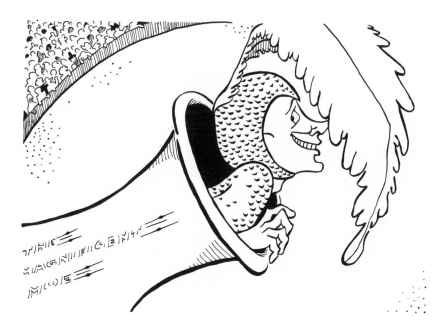

24 SALAD BAR

The people who work consistently at Hanna-Barbera work consistently because they work consistently.

Andrea Romano, Voice-Over Casting Director

There's a lot of other acting and related work out there that you might want to take a bite at. Some of these jobs can be filling to the wallet, others are only for those in need of some acting exercise.

So, belly up to the bar and think about . . .

UNION LOW BUDGET/INDEPENDENT FILMS

Since the producer of *Rampaging Math Majors* can rarely afford top stars, he's going to be far more open to taking a chance on a newcomer — even in a major part. So get out there and rampage.

Obviously, the trades are a source for what's casting, and you can find many producers and directors of independents by using the directories we've talked about. But, if you really want to get out there, mingle and network with people involved in independent filmmaking, give thought to joining . . .

- *Independent Feature Project/West (IFP)*: Included in what you get for your membership fee are screenings and seminars (some free to members) and "schmoozes" where members come together and talk movie-making. There's also a "skills bank" into which members can put their résumés for perusal by producers and directors looking for talent. IFP also sends out a monthly newsletter to members. "One of the best investments I've made to date is my membership," says actress Cynthia Ann Crawford. "You get to mix with people in all facets and levels in the business. People everyone has heard of and people everyone will be hearing of — producers, directors, writers, fellow actors . . . and they all love show business."

  The only excuse for failing to see what a gold mine this organization can be to you is cataracts.

NOTE: For addresses, phone numbers, websites, prices, fees of items mentioned throughout the book, see Appendix.

NON-UNION FILMS

Union members aren't supposed to do these — you're not protected. The producer can promise the moon and deliver a black hole. He can sign a contract in blood, but, as former industrial producer Don Ciminelli says, "All the paper in the world isn't going to get you paid if the guy doesn't intend to pay you."

If you're going to do one anyway, try to check up on the producer. Certainly ask him politely what he's done in the past and how you'll get paid.

If you're going out of town, get the plane tickets in advance — in *both* directions. And don't forget per diems and hotel rooms. You don't want to arrive in Oshkosh, and hear, "Got your room yet?"

Some actors come out of these deals happy as milk-fed cats. We've also heard horror stories. Be very, very careful — even when you go to the audition. Theatrical agent Miriam Baum says, "If I don't know the people, I tell my clients to bring an extra person with them."

NON-BROADCAST MEDIA

Basically, this is material that won't be broadcast on radio, TV, or shown in a movie theatre. It includes traditional industrial, corporate and educational films and video; CD-Rom games and Internet soap opera; CD-Roms for use in industrial/educational instruction; and "point-of-sale" videos/CD's in showrooms and trade shows ("Corporate Charlie," onscreen, saying, "Welcome to the wonderful world of widgets!!! For a quick history of widgets, touch the blue dot . . . ")

And, as far as you're concerned, non-broadcast media can be (often overlooked) ways to make money as an actor. *Somebody's* got to be Zonk the Monster Zapper in that CD-Rom game. *Somebody's* got to play Lorna Lovelorn in that new computer soap, *Interactive Arms*. *Somebody* has to explain lugnuts to Joe the Intern Mechanic. And *somebody's* got to look seriously entranced with widgets. Might as well be you.

Now much of this kind of work is non-union and much of the union work pays scale — but, as actor Thomas Mills said (speaking specifically about doing CD-Roms), "Don't look down at them. They're a great place to experiment, to get some tape, and to get paid for it."

Also, a non-broadcast job can be your first break and, if it's union, can end up being the way you get your SAG card. Bottom line, as former industrial film producer Don Ciminelli said, "You're polishing your craft at somebody else's expense." Beats selling widgets *door-to-door*.

- *Computer Games:* Producers have learned that using stars for these doesn't pay off because the medium is (at least for now) "game driven," not "star driven." Enter non-star you, probably dressed in your basic Captain Gordo of the Galaxy outfit standing on a mark in front of a blue or green screen. You'll be empty-handed, and will be looking at — nothing. Then they'll record you doing . . .

  Scenario #59: Gordo leaves the beautiful Demi of the Moors and walks towards "the Castle of Caligari." He stops. There's "the Dandruff Dragon"! It fires flakes at Gordo. Gordo ducks! He wipes off a "flake" or it will smother him. Gordo pulls out his "flugel-gun" and blasts it! Got him! He puts his "flugel" away. Cut.

  Scenario #60: Since Gordo in this version hasn't yet been to see the Wizard of Flugels to get flugels for his flugel-gun, he's got no ammo and is defenseless. Gordo walks towards "the Castle." He stops. There's "the Dragon"! Since he's defenseless, he . . .

  This multiple-scenario work is called "branching," and in a CD-Rom game the tree can have a whole lot of branches. Scripts for games can be hundreds, even thousands, of pages long (if you think the script is long, you should see the workday). If you can improvise well and come up with a ton of honest reactions, you'll get known in this part of the industry and there will be a lot of Dandruff Dragons in your future — all the while your fellow actors are waiting on *real* dragons at restaurants.

- *Educational material:* Remember snoring in rhythm with an ancient projector while your teacher showed *How the Dewey Decimal System Can Change Your Life?* That's an educational film. Today, films and videos are still made, but a lot of educational material has become interactive. In any case, whether the medium is traditional film or high-tech, actors may be part of the lesson plan.

- *Corporate image/training:* A car manufacturer wants to excite its salesmen about the new Whizzo. A film, video or CD-Rom is made, showing how the gearshift also does floors.

  Hordes of rabid housewives are shown, taking numbers just to sit at the wheel. The film is not intended for, and will never be seen by, John Q. Public. Neither will J.Q.P. see the training CD-Rom that teaches, interactively, a "new hire" how to operate the machinery. And J.Q.P. is definitely not invited to that company trade show at which the actor will be asked to say, with deep conviction, "Gee, Orville, that new Argonaut Zephyr system gives much better DPI when interfaced with the Slugpace 500."

Opportunities abound for newcomers in educational and industrial image/training films, videos, CD-Roms and trade shows because they want "low profile" people (Kevin Bacon playing a dental equipment salesman would be distracting in a corporate CD-Rom). But "low profile" doesn't mean amateur. The producers will want you to get it right and get it fast. If you're good, you can become an in-demand specialist, someone people have on their short-list Rolodex.

- *To learn the multimedia basics*: Take classes at community colleges, UCLA Extension, AFI, The Learning Annex, etc. Pick up the *Hollywood New Media Directory* at a drama bookstore; you'll get a list of new media content providers, on-line services, new media agents, unions, and associations. Definitions of terms, too. And Linda Buzzell's book, *How to Make It in Hollywood*, has a good overview of the subject.

- *To work in non-broadcast media*: Check the trades; producers often advertise for actors. Look for an agent who works industrials and/or new media. Drop off your picture and resume to every industrial film house you can find. Try to wangle appointments with someone at each, and keep in touch. Check out a few "new media" associations.

It's a huge new Information Superhighway out there — so hit the road, Jack.

STUDENT FILMS

Unpaid? Only in money. You'll get experience in front of a camera, film on yourself, and make contacts for the future. George Lucas, Steven Spielberg and Francis Ford Coppola — just to name three — were once student filmmakers. "Student films," says theatrical casting director Paul Bengston, "Are summer stock for Hollywood."

To find what's casting, check *Back Stage West/Drama-Logue*. Students (usually from the University of Southern California [USC], the University of California, Los Angeles [UCLA], Los Angeles City College, Loyola Marymount, Art Center College of Design and Columbia College) often advertise. Also, nose around bulletin boards of college film and drama departments, acting schools and the unions.

Both union and non-union people may do student films, making competition for parts keen, so don't think all you have to do is show up.

If cast, expect a daytime shoot (especially weekends) and don't be surprised if you're asked to tote a light or move a prop. (Also, ask to watch the editing, looping, and presentation of the film to the class. You'll learn plenty.)

And brother, you'll need patience. Everybody's learning. Your "director" may not know camera right from camera wrong. Things will go slooooooooooooooooooooooooooooooooooooooow.

Since you're working for free, the "deal" should include your own copy of the film (or at least the student should let you make a copy). But don't sit back and wait for him to get it to you. Keep at him. Some students would flunk Responsibility 101.

- *SAG/AFI films:* An AFI film is to student films what a Mercedes is to automobiles. To have a shot at being cast, you must be a paid-up member both of SAG and its "Conservatory" program. Then you'll be eligible not only for SAG/AFI casting but a host of other free programs developed for SAG members only (see Chapter 30).

  After joining SAG Conservatory, you can have your photos placed in a book of photographs kept at the prestigious American Film Institute, where filmmakers (called "fellows") from all over the world study. When an AFI fellow is casting (usually a 30-minute tape) he pretty much restricts his casting to Conservatory members. He thumbs through these books, and chooses the actors he wants to have in for an audition.

  But a student director is like anyone else — he likes to work with people he knows. So, to increase your chances of being auditioned, it wouldn't hurt to volunteer to work in the SAG/AFI office once or twice a week. "Fellows" are constantly in and out of the SAG/AFI office, and once they get to know you . . .

EXTRA WORK

"Anyone who says 'Don't do extra work' is crazy," says one casting director. We agree — up to the point mentioned by television stage manager James Hamilton: "When you're first learning it's a great way to get on a set. *But I wouldn't do it too often.*" (Italics ours.) If you've never been on a set, doing extra work is a great way to go to "film school" for a day or so and get paid for doing it. And, with SAG having jurisdiction over extra work on film, you can possibly get your SAG card directly from doing extra work (see Chapter 7). But pursue extra work on a continual basis? Not if you want to act.

Too time-consuming, for one thing. The hours spent registering with the casting agencies, calling them for work, etc., are time taken away from your acting career. Even days spent on a set are wasted except for the paycheck and general knowledge. Networking is difficult and probably not too smart, because, in contrast to New York, where actors go back and forth from acting to extra work with little career damage, in L.A. you're in danger of getting labeled as an extra. That'll do for your career what a heavyweight boxer can do for your stomach.

"When you do extra work, stay in the background," suggests one actor. "Don't be in too much of a hurry to get your face on the screen or to meet the director. If so, they'll think, 'Why should I hire and pay him as an actor if I can get him for what I pay an extra? And, if he's a serious actor, why isn't he pursuing his acting career?'" Now that SAG has union extras under its wing, more professional actors are taking extra jobs to help pay the rent (as has been the case in New York for years), but this "superior-than-thou" attitude really hasn't changed. Never forget that extras will always be at the bottom of the pecking order.

Still want to do it? Okay. Union work pays slightly more, and if it's SAG work you might get a SAG card out of it, so try to register with any or all casting agencies that handle union extra work. To find them, pick up a list of union casting agencies at SAG. (Unfortunately, these places tend to come and go faster than ink can dry. One constant is Central Casting — yep, there really is a Central Casting — which handles union work, and its division Cenex, which handles non-union work.)

Depending on the place, you may be permitted to register even if you're non-union. Most will charge only a small fee for photographs. If you're a paid-up member of AFTRA, send or drop off your photo and résumé to that union's extra file. Producers and casting directors of AFTRA shows constantly call AFTRA looking for extras. (Remember, though, AFTRA extra work will not qualify you to join SAG.)

If you're *not* a member of any union and are really hot to do extra work, proceed on to the non-union agencies. Some will charge you a registration fee, others won't. Only you can decide if paying their fee is worth it. You're not going to be buying lobster thermador on what you make on a union job, and you're pushing it buying hamburgers on non-union wages.

Whether any casting agency will want you to bring or mail a photo and résumé depends on the agency. Some say to call first, but you'll have as much luck getting through as you do calling a cable company. Just go and tell them you've gotten nothing but busy signals.

The methods of registering and interviewing you also vary, as do the chances of your application being accepted. "According to need" (theirs) was what we heard most often. Two hints: the more special skills you list on your résumé (provided you can do them) and the larger your wardrobe, the better. So, when you go to one of these agencies, dress to the nines. Of course, it's one thing to register with these places, another to get work. You'll need to call them every day, at least every half-hour or so. (Central Casting has its own "hotlines" divided up between men and women.)

If you can, get to know someone associated with a production, especially the assistant director if it's a movie, the stage manager if it's a taped TV show. They're the ones in charge of extras on the set, and they inform the casting agencies what extras are needed. A request from them is like grease to a wheel.

"You'll see wives, girlfriends, fathers of everyone from the cameraman to the make-up artist being extras," says one extra. "There's a lot of politics involved. An electrician says, 'Hey, how about my brother?' to the assistant director, and bingo."

If you're asked to do something like rollerskate, ride a bike, play football, etc., that's a "special ability," and you'll get paid slightly more. And, on a SAG job, if you're asked to shout, "Hang him!" you'll be upgraded to a "day player" on the spot (see Chapter 7).

Finally, if you're thinking extra work is an easy way to make a living, remember that the competition, especially for union work, has gotten tougher. While SAG's figures show a dramatic increase in union extra work, there are a heck of a lot more SAG actors out there scrambling for those jobs.

And, if you're not union, you're not the only actor in town who's heard that he can get into SAG doing union extra work. Today it's almost as hard to get Taft-Hartleyed into union extra work as it is to get a union speaking part.

Just listen to what Roy Wallack, past president of the now defunct Screen Extras Guild, had to say (and this was *before* actors could get in to SAG via extra work): "Working as an extra is very tough. Actors have agents, but extras don't. It's work getting work. I would say, of 100 people who start out doing extra work, at the end of a year you'll probably have ten or fifteen left. It's really a rough, rough type of business."

VOICE-OVERS

Of all the performing fields, this is the toughest to break into. "The voice business," says "The Voicecaster" Bob Lloyd (see below), "is the most lucrative part of show business, and, because of that, it is also the most competitive. You can count on two or three hands the number of new people each year who make a living at it."

In addition, because of the downscaling of salaries (see Chapter 14), more "middle-class" actors are now pursuing voice-overs just to keep food on the table. And, on top of that, more companies are opting for name actors to do their voice copy, if for no other reason that the president of Universal Underwear Co. can go to a cocktail party and say he's got Sally Superstar hawking his long johns.

However, if you keep hearing that your voice could make Scrooge buy mistletoe, and you want to take a crack at the Voice Biz, first understand, just as every other field, that this is no place for part-time fun and games. Bob Lloyd adds, "My biggest concern with people who are trying to get into it, is that they treat it as an adjunct to everything else. And there's nothing wrong with that, but it's probably pretty much in direct proportion to the rewards you will get from it. Being in the voice business requires a dedication and a work ethic that is perhaps even more difficult than being in the face business. If I had any counsel to give to anyone who wants to get into the voice business, they better damn well figure out how they can put in at least 12 to 20 hours a week working at it."

In any case, your first step is to get yourself into a good voice-over workshop. Regardless of how trained you are as an actor, you need specific training in voice-over technique. Then, when you're ready, the next stop is a recording studio to put together a good demo tape. Note, we said *when you're ready.* "Don't take a voice-over class that promises you a demo tape in six weeks," says voice-over coach Louise Chamis. "That's like promising you a spot in *A Chorus Line* after six weeks of tap dance lessons." On your tape, you'll want about three or four "commercials." Use anything from magazine copy to TV or radio ads and gear your choices to the impression your voice gives the listener (called how you "come in"). Can you come in "motherly"? Do a baby powder commercial. Can you sound sexy? Try a perfume spot. Is your voice light and bright? Soda might be a good choice. (Many V/O teachers will go to your session with you to help "direct.")

We didn't mention character voices (old man, wicked witch, etc.) because agents mainly want to hear how well you *vary in your own voice.* They only want to hear character voices at the end of your tape, and you'd better have what the industry calls "good separation": clear distinctions between characters (your Pluto shouldn't sound like your Yogi Bear). If you can do 20 well-separated characters, choose your best six, write a few lines of dialogue for each, and place them at the end of the tape. Just be certain the entire tape is no longer than three minutes, with the first two-and-a-half minutes or so demonstrating variations in your voice. "The people who make the most money in this business are those with one voice, but are able to have 13 variations of that voice (intimate, bright, etc.)," says voice-over agent Don Pitts.

And be sure your tape is not only professionally done, but that you are a pro. If you need more training in voice-overs, get it before you start sending out anything. Arlin Miller, voice-over teacher, sums it up: "You're only going to get one shot in this town. Make it your best shot. Don't rush it. Wait until you can give them something dynamite to hear, because that's what it's going to take. It's going to really have to blow them away. *Good's not good enough.*"

Send a copy of your tape to the voice-over agents at those agencies that handle the area.

If the agent likes what he hears, he'll call you in and have you do some copy live so he'll know it didn't take you six months to put together a decent tape.

Once you're signed, your agent will call you in periodically, along with his other voice-over clients who have the required sound for a particular commercial, to tape your auditions. He sends these for consideration to whomever is doing the commercial. He'll probably also give you a list of production companies, etc. — not only in Los Angeles but all over the country — and ask you to drop off or mail your tape to them. (These can number in the hundreds.)

If hired, you'll do a session and be paid residuals according to the SAG or AFTRA rules covering off-camera and/or radio announcers and actors.

Related job possibilities lie in the various forms of putting additional sound to a movie or television show. These include "looping," "foley," etc. "Looping" (also known as Automated Dialogue Replacement or ADR) is adding anything from lines to "atmosphere noise" — non-scripted background dialogue, grunts, laughs, etc. "Foley" means sound effects — people walking, matches being struck, etc. They can provide additional income (usually union scale for a day).

- *Looping*: An ever-growing area from which some actors are actually making a living. The reason has to do with what is known as "runaway production": films that are shot outside of L.A. There are many reasons for runaway production, but they all boil down to saving the producer money. For example, if you're hired as an actor in L.A. and need to fly to, say Georgia, the producer must pay your plane fare, your hotel room, etc. (see Appendix 7).

For major roles, the producer may be willing to do this, but for a minor two-line part, he can hire an actor in Georgia (usually for scale). Then, if the Georgia actor is bad, he can call in an actor in L.A. to loop in the lines during post-production and still save money.

Since more producers are doing this (that's why they call it "runaway production") there's more and more looping work out there.

Your chances to get this kind of work are greatly improved if you speak a foreign language (looping for foreign markets), or can do accents, especially those of your own ethnic group. Also, can you sound like John Travolta? Meg Ryan? Harrison Ford? If so, you're a "sound alike" and can be hired as a "temp dub" to loop in a line when the producer can't (or doesn't want to) obtain the services of a given star.

And to work more consistently, the best thing to do is to get known in the voice-over community. If so, you might be allowed to join any one of more than 35 different "loop" groups (such as "Superloopers") around town. (You'll need to be a good improvisor too.) They're not big on publicizing themselves or in a hurry to get more members, but once they know and trust you, there's a shot.

You can find these groups by dropping by to all the post-production facilities around town (see *The Studio Blu-Book* or any of the directories previously mentioned). Also, SAG has published a short list of these groups in their newsletter. Some post-production companies hire directly, so make the rounds.

- *Foley*: An extremely closed area. Your best shot is to try to attach yourself to experienced people, called "walkers," and become an "assistant walker." To find them, check the sound people at the various studios.

- *"The Voicecaster"*: Specifically, as referred to above, Bob Lloyd. He's apparently the only full-time voice-over casting director in the country. (There is a voice-over casting outfit in Toronto, Canada, called "Voicecasters." Others, such as on-camera casting directors, occasionally do voice-over casting, but that's all Mr. Lloyd does and he does it all the time.)

Getting him to give you a listen involves no more than bringing him a professionally-recorded tape. In this case, however, it's less important how long your tape is. You'll want to put every different kind of voice you can do — as long as those voices are, as Mr. Lloyd put it, "competitive" — that is, if they can compete with the already established pros. "My needs are different," he says. "I want to know as much about you (i.e., your voice/s) as possible. So your tape can be three times as long as the typical voice-over tape as long as it keeps telling me different things." (But use common sense — nobody will listen to ten hours of you warbling "Man, that's coffee!" in 400 different voices.)

If he likes what he hears, Mr. Lloyd will retain your tape and put your name in his computer with a description of all the good voices you do. When people from all over the country call him asking for, say, a guy who does a great Jimmy Cagney or a gal who can really sound like a Valley Girl, he pulls those names from his computer and, if you're among them, he may call you in.

- *Cartoon voice-overs:* "Voice-overs is the most exclusive area in the entertainment industry, and, with the possible exception of jingle-singing, cartoons are the most exclusive in the voice-over field," says Andrea Romano, former casting director for Hanna-Barbera. However, it's also true that people in this end of the industry aren't all that different from anyone else. They just change the words from "Send me someone new" to "Send me some new voices." So, if you want to take a crack at it, first get some training. Then, perhaps with the help of your coach, put together a cassette which, in this case, should primarily be cartoon voices (a small portion of the tape can be in your own voice). And above all keep it short. "A minute-and-a-half to three minutes," advises cartoon voice-over coach Bob Bergen. "You want to leave the listener asking for more." And, "The more versatility the better," says Andrea Romano. "And the funnier the better. And watch Saturday morning cartoons. You'll get a good idea of what's selling. And do a little exercise: turn the sound down and make up voices."

  Once you've got a good tape you'll need plenty of copies ("It's your calling card," says Bob Bergen) to send to all the animation places in town (Disney, Hanna-Barbera, etc.), to out-of town animation houses (such as those in Canada), and possibly even to toy manufacturers. Again, your coach can give you some advice about where to send it.

MODELING

Kinds of modeling work:

- *High-fashion/runway*: Better be a knockout who's very photogenic. With the "greying of America," age for women has become slightly more flexible, with some models still working at the ripe old age of 45. Still, the bulk of the work goes to young women (16 to 21). For men there is now virtually no age restriction, but, again, more jobs go to the young (18 to 22). Women also need to be at least 5'9" and wear a size 6 or 8 dress. Men must be about 6' and wear a size 40 regular suit. "A good barometer," says actress Donna Allen, who models and teaches modeling, "is the cover of *Cosmopolitan*. You'll notice there's a healthy, athletic look — anorexic is out. Today females are permitted to have breasts and hips — as long as they're in proportion."

- *Print*: Includes anything printed for advertising purposes — billboards, magazine ads, etc. The bulk of the work goes to high-fashion models, but you can possibly make a few dollars regardless of your "look," size, weight or age.

- *Commercial*: Non-speaking modeling "roles" on commercials. You can be anything from cute to pretty. Even older and more "real" types occasionally get work.

- *Parts of the body*: Got luscious legs? Handsome hands? Fantastic feet? Totally titillating teeth? Lush, languorous lips?

- *Industrial*: Includes demonstrating products at trade shows, fairs, department stores, supermarkets, and so forth. If you can be cheery, perky, and get along well with people you'll have a shot. If you're a young, beautiful, sexy lady to boot, your chances are better. There's little work for men. None for grumps.

If you really want to pursue any of these fields seriously, go to New York. That's where the modeling action really is.

Wherever you are, the way to start is to send your headshot — even a snapshot will do in this case — to agencies that do modeling and/or print work. (Just look for an "M" next to their name on the SAG agency list.)

While all models have "books" (portfolios of photos), there's no need to throw money at photographers to get one. "I can tell if you're modeling material from a polaroid snapshot," says one modeling agent. Or, as agent Karen DiCenzo says, "I don't think it's right for a person who wants to be a model to go out and spend $500 on a book, because they might not be the right material to be a model." If the agent thinks you're promising, he'll send you to various "test photographers" he knows, and they'll shoot you for free. Then you can complete your book gradually, from your assignments.

Enrolling in a modeling school isn't a requirement either. If you're model material you'll get a lot of "on-the-job" training.

Obviously, the kind of money you'll make will depend on the kind of work you do and how well you become known. For a "star model," the sky's the limit.

In the end though, modeling is still a young person's game. And, as Karen DiCenzo puts it, "In most cases, models turn into actors. Actors rarely turn into models."

NIGHTCLUB WORK (AND RELATED)

You'll do far better getting your feet wet in an out-of-the-way bar in Podunk than beginning this part of your career in Hollywood.

There are places, however, where performers can hone their skills in front of an audience, two of the best known being The Comedy Store and The Improvisation. For leads to a new or newly-hot place, check *Back Stage West/Drama-Logue* and the "Calendar" section of the Sunday *L.A. Times* and talk to fellow hopefuls standing around waiting to go on. Each place has its own particular rules as to how you go about getting onto its stage, but basically, first you perform on an "off night" and, if you're good, you move up to a more desirable night and time. Then, depending on the policy of the house, you'll be paid or continue to perform for free.

Certainly these places give performers — especially comics — a show-case. Certainly people have been discovered. And certainly they're demo-cratic, in that the best people move up. However, you'll be performing either for nothing or for a very small salary.

Yer don't get yer money and yer makes yer choice.

For paying work, places like Disneyland and Knott's Berry Farm often advertise open calls in the trades.

For versatile performers, including magicians, singers, etc., a good variety agent or personal manger wouldn't hurt. Also, consider joining AGVA (See Chapter 7). Besides health insurance and other benefits, being a member means there's at least one place someone looking for your kind of talent can call. The phones at AGVA ring off the wall and some of those calls come from the studios.

STUNTWORK

"I don't try to act — don't you try to do stunts," says one stuntman. Absolutely. Offered an additional thousand dollars to do a stunt? Terrific. It'll make a great down payment on a wheelchair.

If you're thinking of a career in stunts, it's at least as difficult to become a "star" stuntman (in the sense of earning big money) as it is to become a "star" actor, and there are additional "dues" to be paid in the form of broken bones, bruises and cuts — and that's if you're *lucky*.

In any case, you'll need to get your SAG card (all stuntmen must be SAG), and put together a composite with a résumé that lists all the physically-oriented things you can do. Then make the rounds of the studios, production houses, and especially any producers, directors and stunt coordinators, and hope they'll take a shot on a newcomer.

You can take a stunt workshop, but it isn't vital.

If hired, you'll be paid standard SAG wages for actors, plus a sum for the particular stunt. This usually is negotiated by you and the producer or director right there on the set, and you're paid each time you do it, whether the camera jams or the director "just wants another one." "Stunts such as high falls are often negotiated by the foot," says agent Karen DiCenzo.

And two last words of caution. First, carry insurance — lots of it. (That is, if you can get it.) Second, as an ad once run by a group of stuntmen in the trades said, "No shot is worth a life."

PORNOGRAPHY

Questions of morality aside, if the film is "hard core," it's a career killer. As soon as you become known for grunting your way through the hard stuff, you'll become virtually unemployable for legit films, TV and commercials. Even if you should do one only in a moment of desperation, that film will later cause you ten times more career grief than any amount you were paid. Even "soft core" is iffy.

Pass.

25 THEATRE

I am not going to hire anyone for a sitcom
who has not performed in public.

Andrew McCullough, Director

Two actors in a bar. First actor says, "Which city has more professional theatre, New York or L.A.?" Second actor sneers, "Obviously, New York." First actor *(triumphantly)*: "You owe me a drink!"

Because of the number of theatres operating under the 99 Seat Plan Equity contract, Los Angeles arguably produces more professional theatre than any other American city. But Hollywood is still Hollywood, not Broadway West. Its eye still focuses mainly into the lens of the camera. Actors find it hard to make a career out of paying theatre, but the right stage role can launch an on-camera career.

EQUITY WORK

First stop is the Equity offices in Hollywood, where you can pick up lists of Equity-franchised agents, LORT and other Equity-contract theatres including dinner theatres, stock, theatre for young audiences, and 99 Seat Plan ("Equity Waiver") theatres.

The major touring companies head for the big theatres like the Ahmanson and the Dorothy Chandler Pavillion downtown, the Schubert in Century City, the Pantages, the James A. Doolittle Theatre or the Henry Fonda Theatre in Hollywood. Casting is mainly done in New York, with opportunities for local actors usually limited to "Second Viking, Stage Left." Occasionally secondary parts, even leads, open up. Actors with legit agents have an edge.

In downtown Los Angeles you'll find the Mark Taper Forum, a nationally-respected theatre of the League of Resident Theatres (LORT) variety. In nearby Pasadena, there's the Pasadena Playhouse. Take an hour's drive down the coast; you'll reach South Coast Repertory in Costa Mesa. Get a cup of coffee, drive another hour south to San Diego, and you'll discover a surprising amount of theatre, including the La Jolla Playhouse, Old Globe Theatre, and San Diego Rep. Turn your headlights north and you'll find San Francisco's American Conservatory Theatre (ACT), only one of a

---

NOTE: For a sampling of theatres in L.A. see Theatre Map. For Equity
theatre addresses, phone numbers see Appendix 5.

number of Equity theatres in the Bay area.

There are no Equity dinner theatres in Los Angeles, although there are several non-Equity. South of the city there is the Lawrence Welk Resort Theatre, Escondido. Equity stock theatres include the La Mirada Theatre (Southern California) and the Sacramento Music Circus (Northern California).

These are just a few of the theatres out there. *Back Stage West/ Drama-Logue* publishes special issues which include comprehensive lists of Southern California theatres. There are also directories sold in drama bookstores.

Check with individual theatres for casting policies. Most have general auditions once or twice a year. Almost all maintain casting files, so send photos and résumés and request interviews.

99 SEAT PLAN ("EQUITY WAIVER") THEATRE

"Equity Waiver" theatre was born because union actors, who aren't permitted to do community theatre (see Chapter 7), needed to showcase themselves to the film industry, sharpen their skills in front of audiences, and feed their souls. In 1972, Equity agreed to waive all rules and permit union people to work unpaid as long as the theatre was capable of seating less than 100.

Things stayed that way until 1988 when, in response to complaints about abuses, Equity created the Los Angeles 99 Seat Theatre Plan, regulations on the Waiver houses regarding actors' payments, casting procedures, rehearsal conditions, etc. Today they're officially named "99 Seat Plan" or "99 Seat" theatres (but "Equity Waiver," now a misnomer, is still widely used in casual conversation). You're paid a pittance, but pay isn't really the point of the exercise.

Until recent years, "Equity Waiver" theatre drew industry people like flies. It's harder now, because many casting directors and agents give these hours to the cold reading showcases where they'll be paid for their time. And too many bad small theatre productions have made audiences more wary and selective. It's still a worthwhile investment of time, however, so you'll want to think about . . .

THE WHY AND HOW OF DOING THEATRE

Like classes, be clear on your purpose. Are you doing theatre to get experience, to make contacts, to flex your acting muscles, for the sheer joy of it, or to be seen?

- *For the experience*: You're wide open. If you're non-union you can do community theatre and not be disappointed when the only industry person in the audience is an out-of-work lighting technician. (In fact, if you're really inexperienced, that'll be a blessing.) If you're a pro who just wants to shake off some dust, you can do Shakespeare, Pinter, Albee, whatever, at any "Waiver" theatre anywhere, without experiencing the futility of trying to get agents to drive all the way to Glendale. So relax and enjoy it.

  One suggestion from theatrical agent David Westberg: "Make a list of 20 shows that you're right for and you'd like to take a bite at and watch for them."

- *To be seen*: Now you've got to be careful — starting with your choice of play and location. If you want industry people in the audience, you'll have to limit yourself to professional, most likely 99 Seat, theatre. And, regarding the latter, you'll do best following the "play shopping" criteria theatrical casting director Susan Glicksman outlines for herself: "I look for something new. I don't want to see any more *Barefoot in the Parks* or *Lovers and Other Strangers*. I look for something local, preferably a large cast, 12 to 15 people — I don't want to see a two-person show. No Shakespeare."

Next, make hay with the opportunity — both before and after the show. Work to get industry people there (using post-cards, ads, etc. — see Chapter 27), and follow up after they've come. And, if you're smart, you'll pay careful attention to what entertainment attorney Michael C. Donaldson says: "After an 'Equity Waiver' show you can just see who is going to have a career, and who is always going to be doing 'Equity Waiver.' Some actors gravitate to their unemployed actor friends. Others go over and meet the agents, producers or directors who were in the audience."

Finally, you'll also have to be a bit of a critic. As rehearsals progress, ask yourself "Do I really want to ask somebody to sit through three hours of this?"

If the play, actors, director — or you — is bad, get out of it (or at least don't invite people to see it). Yes, you have a responsibility to the production, but you have an even greater one to yourself. Invite people to see you in a play and you're putting your career on the line. Agents, casting directors, producers and directors have long memories and, as producer Buddy Bregman says, "If it's a bad production it'll permeate the person's psyche and the fallout will drop on your head — even if you were brilliant."

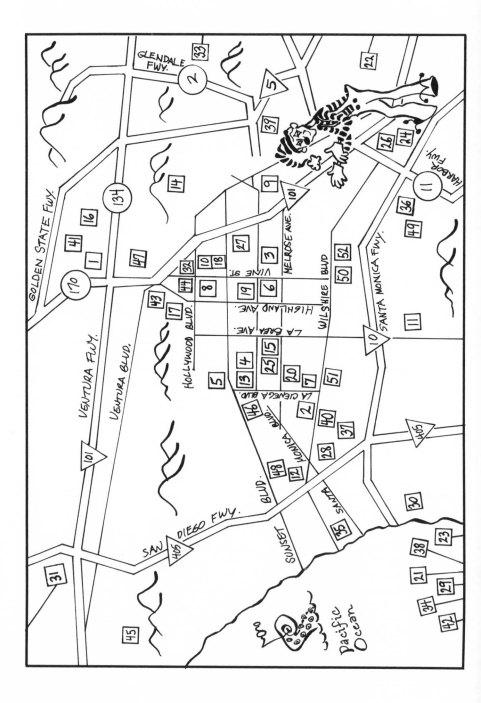

Los Angeles Area Theatre Map Key

A sampling of Los Angeles Area theatres and auditoriums. 99 Seat theatres are indicated by *.

1. Actors Alley*, 5269 Lankershim Bl., N. Hollywood 91601
2. Canon Theatre, 205 N. Canon Dr., Beverly Hills 90210
3. Cast Theatre*, 804 N. El Centro Ave., Los Angeles 90038
4. The Coast Playhouse*, 8325 Santa Monica Bl., W. Hwd. 90069
5. The Comedy Store, 8433 Sunset Bl., W. Hwd. 90069
6. The Complex*, 6476 Santa Monica Bl., L.A. 90038
7. Coronet Theatre/Playwrights' Kitchen Ensemble, 366 N. La Cienega, L.A. 90048
8. James A. Doolittle Theatre, 1615 N. Vine St., L.A. 90028
9. East West Players*, 4424 Santa Monica Bl., L.A. 90029
10. Henry Fonda Theatre, 6126 Hollywood Bl., L.A. 90028
11. The Forum, 3900 W. Manchester, Inglewood 90306
12. Geffen Playhouse, 10886 Le Conte Ave., L.A. 90024
13. Globe Playhouse/Shakespeare Society of America*, 1107 N. Kings Rd., W. Hwd. 90069
14. Greek Theatre, Griffith Park, 2700 N. Vermont Ave., L.A. 90027
15. Groundling Theatre/The Groundlings*, 7307 Melrose Ave., W. Hwd. 90046
16. Group Repertory Theatre*, 10900 Burbank Bl., N. Hwd. 91601
17. Hollywood Bowl, 2301 N. Highland Ave., L.A. 90078
18. Hollywood Palladium, 6215 Sunset Bl., L.A. 90028
19. Hudson Theatre*, 6539 Santa Monica Bl., L.A. 90038
20. The Improvisation, 8162 Melrose Ave., L.A. 90046
21. La Jolla Playhouse, 2910 La Jolla Village Dr., La Jolla 92037
22. La Mirada Theatre for the Performing Arts, 14900 La Mirada Bl., La Mirada 90638
23. Long Beach Entertainment & Convention Center/ Terrace Theatre, 300 E. Ocean Bl., Long Beach 90802
24. Los Angeles Theatre Center, 514 S. Spring St., L.A. 90013
25. Matrix Theatre*, 7657 Melrose Ave., W. Hwd. 90046
26. Music Center of Los Angeles County (Ahmanson Theatre/Dorothy Chandler Pavillion/ Mark Taper Forum), 135 N. Grand Ave., L.A. 90012
27. Nosotros*, 1314 N. Wilton Pl., L.A. 90028
28. Odyssey Theatre Ensemble*, 2055 S. Sepulveda Bl., L.A. 90025
29. Old Globe Theatre, Balboa Park, San Diego
30. Pacific Resident Theatre Ensemble*, 705 1/2 Venice Bl., Venice 90034
31. PCPA Theatrefest, 800 S. College, Santa Maria 93454/ P.O. Box 1700, Santa Maria 93456
32. Pantages Theatre, 6233 Hollywood Bl., L.A. 90028
33. Pasadena Playhouse, 39 S. El Molino Ave., Pasadena 91101
34. San Diego Repertory Theatre, 79 Horton Plaza, S.D. 92101
35. Santa Monica Playhouse*, 1211 Fourth St., Santa Monica 90401
36. Shrine Auditorium & Exposition Center, 665 W. Jefferson Bl., L.A. 90007
37. Shubert Theatre, 2020 Ave. of the Stars, L.A. 90067
38. South Coast Repertory Theatre, 655 Town Center Dr., Costa Mesa 92626
39. Studio Theatre Playhouse/The Colony*, 1944 Riverside Dr., L.A. 90039
40. Theatre 40*, 241 Moreno Dr., B.H. 90212
41. Theatre Exchange*, 11855 Hart St., N. Hwd. 91605
42. Theatre in Old Town, 4040 Twiggs St., S.D. 92110
43. Theatre West, 3333 Cahuenga Bl. W., L.A. 90068
44. Theatre/Theater*, 1713 N. Cahuenga Bl., L.A. 90028
45. Will Geer Theatricum Botanicum, 1419 N. Topanga Canyon Bl., Topanga 90290
46. Tiffany Theatre*, 8532 Sunset Bl., W. Hwd. 90069
47. Universal Amphitheatre, 100 Universal City Plaza, Universal City 91608
48. UCLA, 405 Hilgard, L.A. 90024
49. USC, University Park, L.A. 90089
50. Wilshire Ebell Theatre, 4401 W. 8th St., L.A. 90005
51. Wilshire Theatre, 8440 Wilshire Bl., B.H. 90211
52. Wiltern Theatre, 3790 Wilshire Bl., L.A. 90010

CHOOSING/GETTING IN A THEATRE

- *Choosing*: Reputations wax and wane as people exit and enter, so attend productions and decide if you like what you see. And read the critics; you can learn a lot about how often, how prominently and how favorably theatres are reviewed.

- *Getting in*: It can be as hard to get a part at a quality small theatre as to capture the lead in Andrew Lloyd Webber's next Broadway epic.

   Besides competing with scores of other actors at auditions, roles are often cast "in-house" long before a casting notice is put out.

   So, if you really want "in," volunteer for tech work. "Actors I can get, but good tech people are hard to find," says one director. Become "one of the boys" first. Then when you show up at an audition they'll be more receptive to you than the stranger who walks in cold. One warning about doing tech: be good, but not *too* good. You don't want miss out on roles because somebody doesn't want to lose a good technician!

A WORD ABOUT BURN-OUT

Can you do too much "Equity Waiver" theatre? Not if you need training and/or experience. But if you're a well-trained actor who's doing it mainly to be seen, be careful lest you get burned out and bitter. Wise words from theatrical agent David Westberg in the Equity Waiver days, but still valid today, when "pin money" pay can be almost as wearing as none at all:

"Equity Waiver is the best way to get an agent or be seen by a casting director. Believe me, we go all the time. But I think to go out and do Equity Waiver play after play after play is meaningless; something's not working. It's like *Lysistrata*. Why give away the only thing you have to sell — your talent? You can give it away for a certain time or a specific reason, but, after that, don't give it away anymore, because the more you give it away, the less people will be inclined to pay for it."

If you're dragging yourself to yet another read-through, getting angry because the stagehands can write better than the playwright can read, or if you have a vague feeling you're being unappreciated by, well, *everybody* . . . you're "play-ed out." For the sake of your fellow actors, your director, the playwright, your audiences, and, most important, your sanity, take a break. When you remember why you love it, you'll be back.

26 ACTING CLASSES

It doesn't get any better not doing it.

Michael Rhodes, Producer

Producer/director Buddy Bregman says, "The only way you can 'stretch' is in a class. You can't 'stretch' on a commercial." Or on a beach.

Maybe it's the air. Or the lack of pulsating, shoulder-to-shoulder humanity. Whatever, as one producer put it, "It never ceases to amaze me how lazy the actors are in L.A."

In New York, you'll find actors hurrying to a different class every night — and apologizing for taking Sundays off. Don't let "laid-back L.A." affect your drive. "Keep active," advises theatrical agent Colee Viedelle. "Our finest surgeons continue to study."

That sentiment was echoed by every single person we interviewed. It's a rare actor who doesn't go stale if he doesn't work at his craft. And that audition call will always come when you're at your stalest. "Acting is like any sport," says theatrical casting director Deborah Barylski. "If you don't keep working, you lose it."

Best training? Theatre. One show will teach you more than six months of training at any acting school. The audience instructs best. "Theatre shows me that the actor has discipline," says director/cinematographer Bruce Logan.

However, theatre alone isn't the answer. You can't learn cold reading, film technique, commercial technique, etc., on a stage. The specialized arts — dance, singing, dialects, mime — also require teachers. "Acting is like being a doctor or a lawyer or anything else; it takes an investment of time and money," says theatrical agent Mary Spencer. "As far as I'm concerned," says voice-over casting director Andrea Romano, "You can't take enough good workshops."

And, perhaps most important, in Hollywood, where memories are long, *a class is the only place where you can go to be bad.*

USING CLASSES PROPERLY

Lesson #1 (The hardest): You learn when you're bad. Always being the Meryl Streep of Acting 101 only teaches you you're not being challenged

---

NOTE: *For a list of some acting schools, teachers, coaches, and their phone numbers, see Appendix 5.*

enough. "Bombing out" in class can be terrific.

However, it's not a good idea to "explode" in front of Steven Spielberg. Showcases and classes offering "industry nights" where agents, casting directors, producers, and the like are invited to see what you can do, can be valuable, but as an adjunct to — not a substitute for — the class you take to learn. In other words, first ask yourself why you are taking the class.

To be seen? Fine. Be sure you're ready, play your acting cards very close to the vest, and consider learning anything a bonus.

To grow? Equally fine. But then be certain industry people *don't* attend so you can go out on a limb and stretch your acting to the bombing point.

Don't try to mix the two types of classes together. That's very serious oil and water.

WHICH CLASS FIRST?

What a toughie! And so relative to your circumstances.

New to L.A.? Find a class on the business of the business.

New to acting? Get into a good beginning acting class.

All other classes pale in significance. "New talent should always be in acting classes. If they're not, I don't even want to talk to them," says personal manager Melissa Tormé-March.

No matter where you are as an actor, a good cold reading workshop is a must. If you're a good commercial type, a commercial workshop is a priority.

Beyond that, play to your weaknesses. (A typical mistake: You're great at comedy. What do you take? That's right, a comedy workshop!) Done a lot of stage? Make a beeline to a film technique class. Done nothing but commercials? Find an acting class that emphasizes truthfulness and forces you to abandon your bag of tricks. Can't even make Neil Simon funny? Look for a comedy workshop. You're a character actor or ethnic type? Go for dialects and accents. Used to relying on exacting stage directors? Improvisation will loosen you up for directors who only say "Play it over there."

And never stop. As theatrical casting director Mike Fenton put it: "Do not vegetate . . . if all you're going to do is sit on your butt, then continue to be a waiter because that is all you will ever do. You must eat, you must be employed . . . drive a cab — but leave yourself time to study."

FINDING A CLASS

That's easy. Besides the teachers we list in Appendix 5, there are plenty of fine teachers, many of whom advertise in the trades. There are also guides to acting coaches available at any drama bookshop. On top of that, *Back Stage West/Drama-Logue* prints guides to teachers in specific issues and keeps those issues around for sale until a new one is printed. And, of course, there are your fellow actors.

Like photographers, it's not a question of finding a class; it's a question of . . .

CHOOSING A CLASS

First, don't get caught up in the "reputation game." A famous Hollywood acting school isn't necessarily any better than a teacher quietly plying his trade in Van Nuys — or vice versa. You learn from teachers — not reputations, institutions, buildings, fancy brochures or neon signs. By the time a school becomes famous, the people who brought it fame are often long gone.

And don't buy price. Someone charging three times more isn't necessarily three times better.

Some suggestions . . .

Does the teacher make promises?

Teachers occasionally help talented students get agents and jobs — but someone who promises this to a stranger is proffering bait; bite, and you're the fish. A good teacher promises one thing only: to train you.

What's the teacher's background?

"The only teachers you should study with are people who have been or are in the industry," says agent Doris Ross. Be sure the teacher knows his stuff. Find out what he's done; where he's gotten his knowledge.

Will he let you audit?

There are perfectly reputable teachers who won't. "You either want to study with me or not," says one. Why? "Lookey-loos." Here's what one well-known acting teacher had to say: "I used to permit audits. Not anymore. I got real tired of dealing with actors who either couldn't make up their minds or who are avoiding the issue by constantly shopping. They're too scared to actually get up and do it, so they constantly shop around, kidding themselves into believing they are working on their craft."

However, our thinking is you shouldn't buy *anything* without looking it over, much less an acting class. By their very nature, these can get pretty darn personal. So, our advice: audit about three classes in the area you're looking for (i.e. cold reading, comedy, etc.) and then, unless you really didn't like any of them, choose one. No class is going to be perfect. You're not joining the Army — if you're unhappy you can always leave.

To that point, the teacher who won't let you audit should at least be willing to give you an easy out if you're not happy with him. His refund policy should be very clear and flexible.

How large?

Fifteen to 18 max. If all you're doing is paying to watch others act, why not stay home and watch TV? it's a helluva lot cheaper. You should be acting in at least three out of four classes.

What's the general level?

Work with people who are at your level, perhaps a little better. "I've got a B.A. in drama," says one actress, "And I got into this class filled with beginners. Talk about frustrating! It drove me crazy to act next to them."

Is videotape employed?

Many excellent classes don't use videotape, but it is enormously helpful to see what you are doing. Also, Hollywood is film-oriented; you should know how you come across on camera.

What goes on?

Ask yourself:

- Is this training practical or artsy-craftsy? Here's what one actor said about his class: "They teach you to be very self-indulgent . . . and a lot of psychotic behavior comes out."

- Is the class too disciplined? Too sloppy? A good laugh can be refreshing, but the class shouldn't be a barrelful of monkeys, either.

- Can the students question the teacher? Do they question him too much? If the teacher turns bright red with anger because a student disagrees, you're dealing with a bush-league Hitler. If there are constant challenges, either the teacher can't control the class or there is an underlying lack of respect for him.

- Does the teacher flatter or criticize too much? His critiques should be honest. Some pretty rotten actors have told us their instructor thought they were just marvy, dahling. We've also seen competent actors seriously damaged by whithering attacks and other "head games" played by their teachers. Listen to your gut. If a little voice tells you something's wrong, leave.

- Does the teacher care? Does he give you the feeling he's more interested in the tuition than the students? Do you get the feeling he's improvising what to do next, because he hasn't prepared for class? Does he constantly talk about himself, and how good he is? (Who cares? You're there to act.) Is he fully aware of the delicacy of his position, dealing with people's emotions, needs and hopes? How does he phrase things? "I don't think that worked because . . . "or "That stinks"? Is he out to show you how rough the business can be? (You know that already. You don't need his "help.") Is he straightforward? Non-manipulative? Bored or involved? Perceptive? Kind?

  Remember, keep your classes in perspective. No class is the end-all and be-all of your career. Nobody ever made a dime in an acting class. Your acting teacher is *not* your: agent, personal manager, buddy, guru, channeler, psychiatrist, group grope specialist, primal-scream therapist, lover or daddy.

MOVING ON

You may find a teacher with whom you'll want to study for the rest of your life, so arbitrary time limits aren't very helpful. Instead of asking "How long?", ask "Why am I still here?"

If the answer involves friendships with your fellow students, the fact that everyone thinks you're soooo good, or your fear of moving on — move on. You're nesting.

At the end of each "semester," ask yourself two questions: Have you grown? Can you learn more from him?

In general, though, move around. You'll learn different approaches, act with a more varied group of people, and, probably, keep your classes more in perspective. (If you find someone you don't want to leave, add other classes.)

And remember, study forever. Well trained? How about a seminar on film production or the emergence of the cable industry? A class on fencing? Dance? Horseback riding? Business? Directing?

Sound like a lot of time and money? You got it. Sounds like an actor never stops learning? You got it again.

VIII
MERRILY YOU ROLL ALONG

27 PUBLICIZING YOURSELF

There's nothing wrong with writing a critic . . .
especially to thank him for a good review.

John C. Mahoney, Drama Critic

You won't need or be able to afford a publicist until you really get rolling, so you're going to have to be your own. Your main concern will be to become known within the industry — in a positive way. Before you publicize anything, ask yourself, "What am I calling attention to? How will it affect others' perception of me and/or my career?"

ADS IN THE TRADES

Are trade ads worth it? Depends. Getting your name before the industry is valuable, but trade ads are expensive. A one-fourth-page ad (about as small as you should go) run *once* in either *Daily Variety* or *The Hollywood Reporter* will seriously crimp your vacation plans.

Anyway, if you're thinking about buying any ad, ask yourself:

What are you selling?

"Joe Idle, seeking representation" only tells the world you can't get an agent. "Super-Peachy Agency signs Ginger Keeny" (almost always paid for by the actor, by the way), has some value. You're reminding the industry you're alive, flattering your new agent, and telling any casting directors who are paying attention where you are. But it's only of passing interest.

"See Prudence Prindle in *My Best Friend's Bar Mitzvah* might be of value if you've got a decent part. But, as theatrical casting director Ron Stephenson says, "Don't take out an ad for a one-line part, please."

How are you selling it?

Tacky, amateurish-looking ads are worse than silence in an industry that thrives on style and status. Your ad should at least be one-fourth page (graphics savvy might permit you to go smaller); be uncluttered; contain your photo, name and agent; and sport copy that is not negative, silly, needful or excessively braggadocios.

NOTE: For addresses, phone numbers, websites, prices, fees of items mentioned throughout the book, see Appendix.

"Actors usually want to put review after review until nobody will read it," says an account executive for *Daily Variety* (who handles talent ads). "I always tell them 'short and to the point.'"

If you can't afford to have your ad done by a graphics house, the pros in the ad departments of both papers will lay out your ad at no extra charge, as long as it doesn't involve major artwork.

When/where should it go?

Readership is high on days when the production charts are published. That's the first and third Tuesdays of the month for *The Hollywood Reporter*, Thursdays (TV) and Fridays (films) for *Daily Variety*.

Unless you're paying for a specific location it's a rare publication that will *guarantee* where your ad will appear. But, what the heck, ask. Good spots: opposite production charts or any major column, on the right-hand side of any page.

GROUP ADS

Did the critics positively warble over your revival of *I Never Sang For My Father?* Get the cast to split the cost of taking out an ad for the production. Include pictures and a rave or two from the critics.

USING THE BREAKDOWN SERVICES

The same Breakdown Service that publishes casting breakdowns and the casting directors guide offers other services as well:

- *The "Go-Between"*: For a fee they'll hand-deliver your invitations and announcements to all casting directors; for another fee, to producers. It's a bit expensive, so you might opt for their cheaper alternative of label sets as mentioned in Chapter 8.

- *Delivery service for shows/theatres*: If you're in a show, and your group prints up an 8 1/2" by 11" flyer that includes the names of all cast members, the Breakdown Service will hand-deliver the flyer to agents and personal managers for yet another fee.

WRITING THE CRITICS

It's vital for the producer of an "Equity Waiver" play to get someone who knows what he's doing to work on publicity, especially in regard to the critics. Notices should go out two weeks before you open, followed by phone calls a day or so in advance.

"I try to tell people *we don't know they're opening*," says one critic. "Usually an actor is assigned to do publicity who doesn't know a thing about it . . . very often I'll get a call on Thursday night saying, 'Are your coming to our show tonight?' and I answer, '*What* show?'"

If a critic thought you were the cat's meow, there's nothing wrong with sending him a purring thank-you note. "That's no more than reasonable public relations," said Sylvie Drake, a drama critic for *The Los Angeles Times*. "My usual answer to thank-you notes is to tell the actors they have only to thank themselves . . . and the next time, if they get a bad review, they have only to thank themselves, too."

MAILING SERVICES

These services send photos and résumés as direct submissions for roles. They claim they're "selective," but casting directors tell tales of photographs arriving by the *pile*. Certainly these services vary in quality, but even without an agent you can do a lot of this work for yourself for only the cost of stamps and envelopes, and your photo will arrive by itself.

USING E-MAIL

As mentioned in Chapter 15, some casting directors have their own websites. Try notifying those who do about your play, movie, showcase etc., electronically. Just be sure you've got something to advertise.

IN GENERAL

Throughout this book we've talked about the importance of letting people know what you're doing through use of letters, postcards, news releases, ads, and even phone calls. Strangely, publicity is often neglected by actors. Take advantage of their foolishness by filling the void with positive, upbeat and continuous mention of your name. Show business is synonymous with publicity.

28 YOUR MANAGEMENT TEAM

Everyone should plan for success.

A. Morgan Maree, Business Manager

Ask an actor how he got a job and the word "friend" continually pops up. ("A friend told me about . . . ," "A friend of my sister knew . . . ") When we talk about the folks below, don't forget they're contacts too. Never underestimate the possibility of anyone helping your career. Entertainment attorney Michael C. Donaldson suggests, "When you hire a CPA invite him to every show you do, so he gets to know and care about you."

Your management team is divided into:

- People to obtain immediately;
- People to obtain later.

IMMEDIATELY

Certified Public Accountant (CPA):

For reasons best left to Merrill-Lynch to analyze, it's often tough to motivate actors to hire a good CPA. If you're at all skeptical as to their value, here's what actor Van Epperson has to say: "For years, we did our own taxes. Finally we decided to try an entertainment CPA. We still went ahead and figured our taxes, just for comparison. Well, he wound up saving us *literally ten times what we would have paid — and that was over and above what it cost us for his services."* That story is *typical.* Yes, his services will cost more than a guy seated at one of 33 desks in a storefront operation, but ultimately he'll save you money. Just be sure he's entertainment-oriented.

To find a CPA, ask bright Show Biz people you meet, including your agent, for recommendations.

Attorney

Eventually, someone's going to ask you to sign some gobbledy-gook with a lot of wherefores and whereases. And the worst time to go hunting for an attorney is when you need one. There's no need to pay a retainer, just establish a basic relationship with him for the future. Again, you'll want him to be entertainment-oriented.

NOTE: For addresses, phone numbers, websites, prices, fees of items mentioned throughout the book, see Appendix.

LATER

Personal managers

"The reason an actor needs a personal manager — and this is not meant detrimentally — is that agents are predominantly booking services. They get phone calls from casting directors saying, 'I want so-and-so; send me so-and-so.' In my opinion you need a personal manger and an agent in order to get full attention. A personal manager guides you on every facet of your career. We guide and direct and advise, from business management to publicity to selecting agents to opening bank accounts, you name it," says personal manager Melissa Tormé-March. "I'm sort of an architect, whereas the agent is sort of a realtor," says personal manager Roz Tillman.

Done a lot of theatre? A good personal manager makes sure you have an agent in New York. Sing? He gets you on the nightclub circuit. Offered a part at a theatre in Missouri? He makes sure you're happy with your dressing room. Offered a role on an episodic television show? He advises you whether or not to take it, based on how it may affect your career. Not sure your agent is submitting you? Your PM checks over his own copy of the Breakdown Service and calls you agent to nudge him a little. Need an agent with more clout? He helps you get one. "I do all the things the agent was supposed to have done in the first place," says personal manager Jerry Cohn.

And, on top of all that, he introduces you to important people. He opens doors that might be locked to you and even your agent. There have been cases where a personal manager has introduced a total newcomer to the right producer, and *zoooom!*

And, once you're earning more than $100,000 a year, a personal manager can very well catapult you into super-stardom. That's why we put them under the category of people to obtain "later," which, frankly, some would question. They'd say get a good personal manager first, have him get you an agent, and stand back and watch your career blossom. Otherwise, you might never get beyond being another drone. "I know an actor who has done 60 films and you still don't know his name," says personal manager Cathryn Jaymes.

However, others have mixed opinions or downright hate personal managers. "I don't think they're very valuable, unless they have access to packaging," says one producer. "They're only helpful if you're a star and they also can provide business advice," says another. "They're nothing more than ambulance chasers," says still another.

Ask an agent what he thinks, and watch smoke come out of his ears. Many agents think of personal managers with a fondness usually reserved for root canal work.

Why the mixed reviews?

Well, anyone can pick up a piece of wood, paint "Personal Manager" on it, and he's in business. He doesn't have to know a thing. He doesn't need a union franchise or a state license. He can charge any fool any percentage he wants. Then he can get on the phone and start making ridiculous demands of agents, casting directors, even producers and directors. The fact that he's destroying a career may never enter his mind.

Next, the going rate for personal managers is 15 percent (and upwards) of your gross income. Since he's not franchised or licensed, he can't negotiate a legal contract unless he (or someone in his office) is an attorney. "There are only three people in the state of California who may negotiate a contract," points out former theatrical agent David Westberg, "The artist himself, a certified agent, or a lawyer." In other words, with or without him, you're still going to need an agent.

Add the agent's commission to his and you're paying out (minimum) 25 percent — one quarter — of your income. And, if you think about it, you can do many of the things he does.

Next, even a top-notch personal manager isn't always going to be right. And his mistakes can be dillies. Maybe his demand for that fancy dressing room in Missouri is just enough to make the producer say, "Look, let's skip it." Maybe he nudges your agent once too often, and destroys a relationship you've been working on for years. Maybe he counsels you not to take a part, and you don't work for another year. Maybe he "manages" you right out of the business.

Yes, the general quality of personal managers has improved mostly because the good ones are policing themselves. But there are still a lot of sharks out there and, when it comes to helping you, toothless ones at that.

In any case, if you decide to look for a PM, it'll be easier if you're a teen heartthrob, glamor girl or handsome hunk, or are multi-talented (say, you sing with a band). Lesser beings will probably have to wait until they get hot — if they need one at all. Use the same methods we discussed in "Seeking an Agent." You might start with the Conference of Personal Managers, but bear in mind that not all (good or bad) personal managers are members. Other sources include *The Studio Blu-Book,* the *Academy Players Directory* (actors often list their managers) or the trades.

If a personal manager expresses interest in you, check him over with a microscope. He should have: been in business for at least a few years;

solid connections; at least one relatively well-known client; charge no more than 15 percent; and demand no money up front. Most agents and casting directors should know and respect him. He should have a maximum of ten to 15 clients. And, most important, his judgment should be solid and well-informed — that's really what you hire him for.

There's just no clear-cut answer to the value of a personal manager. In fact, only one thing is certain. As business manager A. Morgan Maree puts it, "Unfortunately today you get for 25 percent what you used to get for ten."

Business Manager

His title tells you what he does — he manages your business, helps you pre-plan tax deductions, suggests possible investments, arranges loans, puts together your portfolio and annual financial statement, etc. He should make his entrance when you're making upwards of $100,000 a year, and, if he's good, help you keep it and maybe make more.

Develop a good relationship with a CPA; he can offer business advice now and act as your business manager or refer you to one later. Some personal management firms also offer business management services.

With or without a business manager, learn some business. Stars have lost their shirts either through their own bad investments or those of a bad/shyster business manager. In college and thinking of becoming an actor? A major or minor in business will give you something to fall back on if it doesn't work out, and the background to make the most of your earnings if it does. Out of college? There are plenty of community college business courses and seminars available.

Publicist

Get rolling and a publicist can be invaluable. Through strategic planning, he can keep your name before the public, and, more important, the industry, for weeks, months and even years ahead. "Some publicists get you out to all the right parties," notes former theatrical agent David Westberg. He can keep everybody convinced you just never stop working and are in constant demand. As publicist Barbara Best puts it, "You'll know your publicist is doing a good job when people come up to you and tell you how well you're doing."

However, even if you can afford his monthly fee, no publicist can help if you're not doing anything worth publicizing. And a community theatre production of *Carousel* doesn't qualify. If you're thinking of hiring a "publicist" who claims he can get you on Jay Leno just because you're so cute, put your money on the longest shot at Hollywood Park instead. Besides, as editor Ruth Robinson put it, "Until you're famous, you can probably do the same things for yourself as any publicist."

29 GENERAL FINANCIAL

I know it's not very exciting or glamorous,
but if you want my best advice, keep records.

David Perren, Certified Public Accountant with
the firm of Barkin, Perren & Schwager

TAXES

- *Withholding*: Ugly shock time. When figuring your withholding, your employer follows a tax table that assumes you make what you're being paid for that acting job *every* week of the year. Chomp! There goes a substantial portion of your paycheck. And there's nothing you can do about it.

  In past years, to avoid this bite, some actors claimed 99 exemptions or wrote "exempt" on their tax forms. The employer then withheld nothing. No more. Oh, you can do it, but if you claim more than ten exemptions, or that you're exempt, your employer must immediately send that form to the IRS. The IRS can match it against your tax return, and if you don't qualify for what you've claimed, they'll send you a letter asking you to substantiate your claim. If you can't or don't respond to that letter, they'll tell your employer to withhold tax based on your being single, claiming zero exemptions. That will do for your paycheck what a T-Rex does for legs.

- *What's your line?*: It's a bit of a gray area as to when you can call yourself an actor on your tax return. Certainly you can if acting is your chief source of income. But if the amount of money made in any given year were to be the sole criteria to putting "actor" on your return, we don't have to tell you most actors wouldn't qualify. Therefore, the question seems to be: How much time did you spend trying to make money as an actor?

- *Keeping track*: Way back, we mentioned the importance of a daily diary in regard to filing your income tax. At least once a week, enter into your diary all the expenses you incurred as an actor. Did you "do" lunch with your agent on Thursday? Enter it. Did you buy *Your*

NOTE: *For a list of "typical" tax deductions and other financial information, see Appendix 6.*

Film Acting Career on Friday? Write it in. Not only will that diary serve you well if you're audited, but often it will remind you of forgotten expenses.

And keep receipts — even for items purchased by check or credit card. Without receipts, your deductions, no matter how legitimate, can be disallowed. Try attaching receipts directly onto the daily diary next to the expense.

- *Per diems*: When on location, you get a per diem for expenses. The IRS decides what your employer should pay you and, if he pays you more than that, it's taxable income unless you can prove that your expenses equaled what the employer gave you. If your expenses were greater, then you have a tax deduction (for the amount that was greater). In any case, keep records.

- *In case of an audit*: Don't jump off a bridge. Nobody's going to reserve a room for you at San Quentin unless you're defrauding the government, which has nothing to do with this book. Your return will be checked and you'll be asked to substantiate deductions. When notified about an audit, call your CPA. He'll advise you what to do, perhaps even take a power of attorney and go to the audit with your records, all by himself. The IRS will then: declare a "no change" (return accepted as filed); disallow certain deductions (for which you have the right to be billed at a later time); or maybe even give you a refund.

INVESTING

Ever hear of the concept of "paying yourself first?" Each month you pay your bills saying, "Well, I'll just use whatever's left over on myself." Reverse that. *Pay yourself first.* Before you pay any bill, put a ten spot in a savings account. Drop a fiver in a piggy bank.

And, if you get a small or large windfall, extend the concept. Before you buy shares in a diamond mine in New Guinea, invest in yourself. New pictures, an ad in *Variety*, that class you've been putting off, a good presentation tape, etc., will pay more dividends than stock on the Big Board.

A. Morgan Maree, business manager, suggests this order of investment:

1. You;
2. Insurance (especially if you have dependents);
3. A place in which you'd be comfortable living;
4. Other investments (and seek competent advice).

If the windfall is small, and you feel you might need the money sooner rather than later, you might look into a money market fund. Your funds won't be federally insured, but they pay higher interest rates and you can withdraw your money when needed. Some require a minimal initial deposit, others don't; the same is true for any succeeding deposits or withdrawals.

A WORD ABOUT INSURANCE

Achieve even a modicum of success and you may need more insurance on your car, house, etc. because actors are "target risks." See, it's a given that all actors are rich, so slam into someone with your car, have him recognize your face, and don't be surprised if he starts shouting, "Whiplash! Whiplash!" Ain't fame grand?

UNEMPLOYMENT COMPENSATION

We don't have the space to go into all the rules and regulations. Just don't view it as charity — you earned the money. As one actor put it, "I think of unemployment compensation as the National Endowment for the Arts."

To start, pick up the phone and call the number listed in your white pages under "California State of, Employment Development Department." Be ready to give them your Social Security number and the name and mailing address of your last employer. (If it was an acting job you'll need first to check with the producer's office as to who actually was your last employer — a production company, a studio, etc.) After they run a check you'll be notified of your "award" (no need to think up an "I'd like to thank the Academy . . . " speech): it's how much money you'll be getting each week.

It's computed like this: First, go back six months — you can't get unemployment on monies earned more recently. For the year prior to that time, your award will be based on the most money you earned in any quarter (January-March; April-June; July-September; October-December) of that 12-month period. Usually it takes a couple of weeks before the manna drops from heaven into your mailbox.

Bear in mind that, when you're receiving unemployment compensation, you must report any work and any income you get. That includes residuals, holding fees, etc. Don't fail to report a single dime. It can mean big trouble.

30 MISCELLANEOUS

Each actor is responsible for his own career
and I invite you to assume that responsibility.
It's your career. It's your business.

Roz Tillman, Personal Manager

SAG CONSERVATORY

A lulu of a bargain. Join (for how-to see Chapter 24) and you may participate in a host of free Conservatory programs held at the American Film Institute. These are put together by fellow union members and include voice-over workshops, improvisation workshops, cold reading technique classes, on-camera scene work with partner (called "job experience") workshops, even a once-a-month "open camera" where you can get up and do whatever you want in front of a camera (provided it's not X-rated). They even have summer seminars and workshops for children.

UNION SHOWCASES/SEMINARS

If you read Chapter 18, you know the importance of showcasing for casting directors, agents, etc. Well, both AFTRA and SAG offer showcases too, but with one slight difference: they're free to paid-up members. The rules and days for these vary between each union, but both hold prepared scene showcases for agents and casting directors. SAG's, for example, limits theirs to 24 actors per showcase, and both partners must be paid-up members of the Guild. SAG also offers casting seminars which sometimes include doing cold readings. Call each union's Info line for what's doing and when. (You can also find out about SAG activity on their website.) Used to be that it was fairly easy to get a showcase spot. No more. Be prepared to have to wait to get on the list and once you've done one you'll have to wait three months before you can apply again.

AFTRA/SAG FEDERAL CREDIT UNION

"The actor's savings and loan," it has two branches, one in Hollywood, the other in Studio City. You must be a member of SAG or AFTRA to open an account. Benefits include a slightly higher rate of interest on savings; lower interest on loans and their own credit card; interest check-

---

NOTE: For addresses, phone numbers, websites, prices, fees of items mentioned throughout the book, see Appendix.

ing, etc., all federally insured by NCUA. Best thing is that it's run by and for SAG/AFTRA members. That means they'll be a little more understanding if you get into trouble, and they'll even consider a part of your unemployment compensation as income when you apply for a loan. Try and get that from Louie the Loan Shark.

SAG FILM SOCIETY

It's open only to paid-up SAG members and sells out fast. (Don't wait when you see the application in the [usually early part of the year] SAG magazine.) For your membership, you and a guest get to see a first-run movie every other Friday or Saturday, at the Director's Guild of America. And you would be hard-pressed to find a better equipped, more beautiful movie theatre in the country.

Figure about 52 admissions to 30 new movies. Cost depends on whether you also buy pre-paid parking tickets for the year, or in blocks of 10 or 20 (see Appendix 2), but even including parking, that comes to about two bucks a ticket. Last time you saw a bargain like this was when Eisenhower fretted over his golf score. Two drawbacks, one minor, the other major. Minor: you don't get to select the movies. Major: no popcorn or Milk Duds.

GAME SHOWS

Brainless. Oh, not the shows — the financially-strapped actor who refuses to do them. In one month we met three actors whose winnings, added together, were over $100,000. Each was then able to pursue his career on a full-time basis for at least a year, without having to live on peanut butter. Actress Jan Hoag, who won $38,000 (her winnings are not included in the $100,000 mentioned above), says, "You still have to peel me off the ceiling. It certainly takes a weight off my shoulders for a while."

Aha, now you're interested. Okay, how do you get on a game show? Just pick up a phone. They really do need contestants and union members may play. AFTRA's news magazine *Diallog* includes a listing of game shows and their phone numbers. And, of course, a phone number is usually announced during the shows themselves.

But before you pick up that receiver, study the shows. Decide which show is best for you. Do they pay ten big ones to people who know the difference between a femur and a lemur? Do you? Do their contestants get apoplectic at the drop of a toaster? Can you? If you're slow hitting buzzers, pass on *Buzzing For Bucks!* You're limited to three game-show appearances so don't waste one.

Also, skip the shows that give more prizes than money. A new coffee table might be nice, but you're looking to support yourself — go for the gold.

What *they'll* be looking for, naturally, depends on the program. But they *all* want happy, warm, full-of-beans types with, above all, perk. It may be quiet perk, medium perk, or THE SCREAMING PERK FROM HELL — but *perk*.

Finally, once you know you're going to "COME ON DOWN!", practice. Rehearse like you're opening on Broadway. After all, if you're a "hit" it'll probably pay a helluva lot more.

AFTRA-SAG YOUNG PERFORMERS HANDBOOK

If Baby June is making goo-goos about getting into the Biz, she and her parents can benefit from this absolutely super booklet put together jointly by members of SAG and AFTRA. Includes parental do's and don'ts, child labor laws, info on unemployment insurance (yep, kids can qualify), etc.

Pick one up at either union, or simply write them for a copy. It's free. (It's also available on SAG's website on the 'Net.)

SAG'S ETHNIC PERFORMERS DIRECTORY

Here's a valuable freebie if you're SAG and are a member of a minority group. SAG publishes this directory at no charge to members in separate volumes for each group (African American, Asian/Pacific, Latino/Hispanic, etc.). You'll need an 8x10 glossy photo to submit. Call the SAG Affirmative Action Office for further information.

THE ACTORS' FUND/THE ACTORS' WORK PROGRAM

Old Wives' Tale #603J: A wealthy man dies. In his will, he leaves money in a special "shoe fund" for actors. Any actor needing new shoes need only ask. Reason? He felt actors tended to be paid less if they wore old and worn shoes. Isn't that just the most outlandish b.s. you ever heard?

Just one thing. It isn't b.s. or an old wives' tale. The person was Conrad Cantzen and "free shoes on request" is only one of the many services provided by the non-profit Actors' Fund of America to working pros who need a little help — and they don't charge for their services.

Other services? Well, want to keep acting but need to earn more money? (We know, what actor doesn't?) Thinking of hanging it up but don't know what to do next or who to turn to? Thinking of returning to school but need tuition advice, possibly assistance? If you're a union member The Actors' Work Program of the Actors' Fund might be able to help. Through their Services to Employable Persons (STEP) program, you can get emergency financial assistance, individual and group counseling about financial planning, career changes, etc.

Also, if you've got medical problems such as AIDS/HIV or substance abuse, they're a phone call away. They even have elder and disabled care services and run their own retirement and nursing homes in New Jersey.

So if the shoe fits . . .

"FREE" PHOTOS

If you're broke but need new pictures (modeling or standard headshots), try swapping posing services for cash at places such as the Art Center College of Design in Pasadena. You'll "donate" some hours of posing (no nudity) for student photographers, in return for which they'll give you a headshot session and possibly some free prints. (Also, they have an in-house casting book used by their students for student films they are doing.)

SEMINARS

College extension courses, open to the general public, can be a great way to fill gaps in your knowledge. So can classes offered by The Learning Tree, The Learning Annex, etc. You can learn anything from low-budget film production to belly dancing. Ask to be placed on their mailing lists. Also, *Back Stage West/Drama-Logue* holds a weekend expo for actors, usually in the Spring, they call ActorFest. Watch for their ads.

ACADEMY (OF MOTION PICTURES ARTS AND SCIENCES) FOUNDATION

Besides handing out the little gold statuettes you may have heard of, and publishing the *Academy Players Directory*, the Academy Foundation holds seminars, interviews, retrospectives, etc., many open to the public. You must write them and ask to be put on their mailing list. Also, look into their research library (at another location — see Appendix 5) on the film industry.

WOMEN IN FILM

An "old girl network" for career women in film and TV. Membership includes newsletters, guest speakers, workshops and the like. To get in, you'll need three years' pro experience in the industry and two WIF sponsors.

WOMEN IN THEATRE

Aiming to promote the performing arts, WIT holds showcases, workshops, seminars, mixers and the like. For a membership fee, anyone can join the fun.

HOTLINES

For hot tips on what's doing, off and on the unions offer hotlines. Give your union a buzz and see if they have one in operation.

A WORD ABOUT WEBSITES

Throughout the book we've been mentioning the Internet and the various websites on it specifically geared to the actor (for addresses see Appendix 4). If you've got access to a computer there is info galore available at the tweak of a mouse. Word to the wise.

HOOK, ON-LINE AND SINKER

You can subscribe to any number of on-line services. The hook? For a fee, you get your photos and resumes in front of casting directors via computer! The sinker? As it stands right now, only a small number of casting directors use computers at all. Anyway, remember that you are automatically put on-line via "the link™" when you place your photo in the *Academy Players Directory*, and at no additional charge. Only when and if — big IF — more industry people start using these services should you think about subscribing. For now, save your money.

STARTING YOUR OWN NETWORK

Throughout this book we've tried to point out the importance of taking your career in your own hands. Certainly one way is to get a group of actors together to form your own showcase, theatre, information-getting organization or what have you. It's been done in the past and can be done again. Also, you'd be amazed at the serendipity that occurs when you take on a project. You're working on project A and, boing!, someone comes along with project B. Work begets work, projects beget projects, ideas beget ideas. You're only limited by your imagination.

Some time ago, a group of guys got together to take their future into their own hands. The result was a little production called the U.S.A.

31 ASSESSING YOUR CAREER

In this industry you're either on the rise or falling — there's no standing still.

David Westberg, Theatrical Agent

We don't believe in arbitrary time limits, but at some point you'll need to examine where you are. Let's assume it's New Year's Day. Between toasts or kick-offs, you wander away for a mull. You have:

1. Gotten a good amount of work;

2. Gotten some work;

3. Gotten work in the past, but somehow your career has stopped;

4. Gotten nothing.

A GOOD AMOUNT OF WORK

Congratulations. If you earned $15,000 or more last year, you're in the upper 15 percent of the Screen Actors Guild. Think over what you've been doing right and plan to keep doing it. Then go back and toast yourself.

SOME WORK

Before you climb all over your own back, bear in mind that if you earned any money at all there are thousands of actors wondering just what you're complaining about. So make that a pat on the back instead.

Now: how to get more work? Look at the jobs you got. How'd you get them? What did you do right? Next, make a list of any career weak points and plan to solve them. Break that plan into weekly and daily goals. Need a new agent? Pictures? Are you showcasing yourself enough — especially in those cold reading showcases and "Equity Waiver" theatres? Are you keeping in touch with past employers? How about new contacts — did you nurture them? If you blow auditions, how about taking a cold reading workshop? A commercial workshop? A class in improvisation? Lost a role because you can't ride a horse? Or dance? Or do a French accent?

YOU WERE GETTING WORK, BUT YOUR CAREER HAS JUST "STOPPED"

We can't think of a more frustrating turn of events. If it helps, this is a phase all actors go through periodically. Everything is going swimmingly, then glub! Somebody pulls the plug out of the pool.

First, try figuring out what happened — unemotionally. Agent gone cold on you? Why? Been sitting back, waiting for him to do it all? Was your type "out" this season? Were there union strikes? Have you priced yourself out of the market? Maybe you need new pictures. Maybe you need to do an "Equity Waiver" play. And maybe, just maybe, you've become, through no fault of your own . . .

Yesterday's mashed potatoes: Hollywood is addicted to the new. Producers go anywhere from East Bochaboora to South Wales looking for "new faces"; all the while there are thousands of better-trained "faces" sitting idle in their own back yard.

It's as though you're given an indeterminate amount of time to become a "hot item." Exceed it, or "merely" become a pro who consistently does good work, and you may wake up to find you're passé. Old news. "Out." And typed to boot.

If that's you, you'll need to do one of two things:

- *Double your efforts*: Especially to meet new people. You're not passé to them. Find a play that shows you being different. Done nothing on TV but scroungy villains? Play a doctor reeking with distinction. Typed as a bookish accountant? Buckle a swash or two. Tired of playing Miss Goody Two-Shoes? Don't just say it, try doing: *Nuts*. Get "discovered" by those who don't know you, and "rediscovered" by those who do.

  You mean to say an established actor has to go back to work getting work? All the time. Otherwise you can really become past tense.

- *Turn bicoastal*: "The place to go is New York," said personal manager Larry Fonseca. "There, they'll take shots on people. The talent is what counts. Out here, they'll go for a name, or the (casting) precedent has been set." Selling like cold pancakes and sensing that casting directors yawn, "Oh, *him*?" Head east. You'll be new to an entire city. Even better, if you've got film/TV credits, you'll find it easier to interest agents. (A *lot* easier. Just as Hollywood goes ga-ga over New York credits, New York — whether it admits it or not — at least goes "ga" over Hollywood credits.)

Eventually, you'll get in a play, some Hollywood producer will see you, bring you out to L.A. for his next picture, and everyone will ask, "Where have you been hiding all this time?"

YOU'VE GOTTEN NOTHING

We don't have to tell you something's wrong. You're probably aching inside. Should you quit? Give it six more months? Keep going indefinitely? First, as voice-over casting director Andrea Romano puts it, "If you really want to do it, don't give up. There's always room for somebody new, if they're talented."

But, if you're beginning to feel, well, just not happy any more, note what theatrical agent Joel Rudnick has to say: "My biggest frustration is with actors who are unhappy. If it's always tense, and you always want to kill yourself if you don't get a job, and, when you do get a job you're unhappy with the dressing room . . . well, I mean, I just don't think it's worth it if it doesn't make you happy."

It boils down to one word: *love*. Still love it? You bet it's still worth it. As producer/director Buddy Bregman says, "After you've been at it a year or so, if you find it's totally negative and your ambition is *metza-metza*, it's time to think about whether you should carry on or not. Because sometimes persevering against a brick wall is a waste of time. But if you really think you've got the talent, and this is all you want, then don't stop; it would be wrong to stop."

If you decide to quit, happily quit. You're not a failure. If all you're doing is scratching, there's nothing wrong with racking your cue. This just wasn't your game. So what?

Besides, you took your shot. The rest of your life will be free from tortuous "What ifs?" That alone is an enormous gift to yourself — ask those who didn't try.

And remember, you're being relieved of all the problems, nonsense, and all those receivers being hung up in your ear. And, if you return home to another state, you'll be free from smog, traffic and 6.7 earthquakes. And you'll never again have to hear, "Leave your picture and resume and we'll get back to you."

And one other thing. Leaving acting doesn't have to mean exiting the film industry. You tried playing second base; how about catcher or short-stop? How about becoming an agent, casting director, gaffer, makeup artist, producer, director, stage-manager, writer, personal manager, continuity person, editor, lighting technician . . . there are hundreds of other industry jobs. Ultimately, you may find far greater satisfaction wearing a different hat. That's exactly what former actor, then theatrical agent, David Westberg did. Here's what he has to say: "I had been struggling with that decision for a long time. I mean, I loved acting, but it was between the jobs that drove me up the wall. I found myself becoming very negative and cynical about things. There seemed to be so many decisions that were out of my control.

"Finally, I reached an age when I didn't want to sit around for two, three months between jobs. And I decided that I could do more with my brain than wait for calls to come in. So I stopped acting.

"And, as soon as that happened, it opened up a whole range, a whole spectrum of colors came into play that I had never seen because I had always been so tunnel-visioned about acting. I could make decisions. And, all of a sudden I found myself receptive to people on entirely different levels. It was very exciting for me as a human being. And I love what I'm doing."

Don't forget, there are people ready to help you make the transition (see The Actors Fund, Chapter 30). And remember, the industry can always use more happy set decorators, fewer miserable actors.

32 CONCLUSION

> *Concentrate on your career, but have a*
> *personally enriched life along with it,*
> *which means dating . . . marriage . . .*
> *and having some fun.*

Viola Kates Stimpson, Actress

He lives in the South, working a typical nine-to-five job. He's a true fan of a famous actress. He even sent her a dozen roses once, when she won an Academy Award.

While he's talented and enjoys acting in community theatre, he has no plans to pursue a career as a professional actor. He's a rather shy person, reticent around strangers, so his interview technique needs some work. His cold reading technique, moreover, is nonexistent. He'll admit if he doesn't get the script long enough to memorize it, he doesn't have a chance.

He's non-union. He doesn't have any résumé shots or résumés — after all, what does he need them for? He *never* goes to L.A. or New York seeking work . . .

. . . And, on top of all that, he's partially handicapped.

One day, a local director asks him if he'd like to appear in a show being produced in that southern city . . .

Cut to: Manhattan. He's appeared on stage in a hit show for two years. His face has appeared on the front page of *The New York Times'* theatre section, and he's gotten excellent reviews.

He's been on a European tour, including performing for and meeting the Prince of Wales.

And, one night, his favorite actress happens to be in the audience. After the show, she goes backstage, tells him how much she enjoyed his performance . . .

. . . And then she gives him a kiss.

Sound like the script for a B movie?

It's all true. We know; it happened to a friend. Call it Fate, the Karmic Kosmos, or more things than are dreamt of by us Horatios. The point is, this business is just plain magically nutsy.

You can stand at a corner with a comic book in your hand, turn left, and bump into a guy with his shirt open to his navel who says, "You! You're perfect!" And zoooom.

Or you can be at the same corner with this book under your arm, turn right, and wind up struggling for 20 years.

Well, that's the job-getting business. At least you know the game a little better, which will cut the odds a bit.

In any case, whether you have that unlikely instant luck or the usual period of struggle, we hope you'll never forget the sheer joy of: a mustard-slavered hot dog at the ballpark; kissing your loved one for no good reason whatsoever; or just plain having a good laugh.

We also hope your acting coach never asks you why you secretly hate your little brother. We hope your agent calls you once a month desperate for more pictures. We hope the receptionists you run up against don't give you terminal frostbite. We hope casting directors sensitively understand why your hands are so clammy. We hope producers pay you all your meal penalties and directors only shoot you in close-up.

And, finally, we hope that blowhard who told you you'll "never make it" is backstage when your favorite actress walks up to you, tells you how wonderful you were . . .

. . . And gives you a kiss.

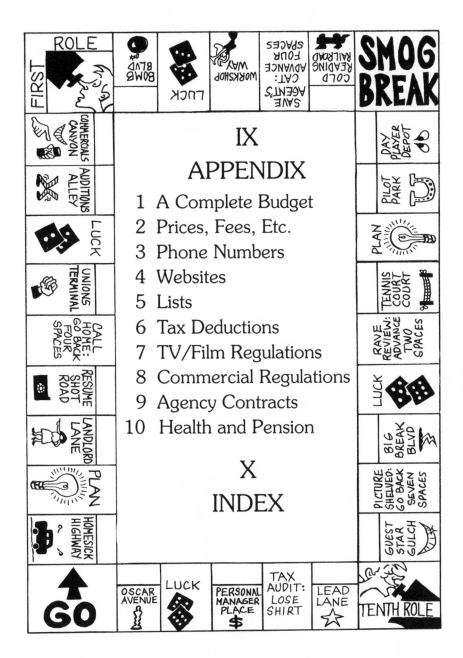

ROLE
FIRST

BOMB
BLVD

LUCK

WORKSHOP
WAY

SAVE
AGENT'S
CAT:
ADVANCE
FOUR
SPACES

COLD
READING
RAILROAD

SMOG
BREAK

COMMERCIALS
CANYON

DAY
PLAYER
DEPOT

AUDITIONS
ALLEY

PILOT
PARK

LUCK

PLAN

UNIONS
TERMINAL

TENNIS
COURT
COURT

CALL
HOME:
GO BACK
FOUR
SPACES

RAVE
REVIEW:
ADVANCE
TWO
SPACES

RESUME
SHOT
ROAD

LUCK

LANDLORD
LANE

BIG
BREAK
BLVD

PLAN

PICTURE
SHELVED:
GO BACK
SEVEN
SPACES

HOMESICK
HIGHWAY

GUEST
STAR
GULCH

IX
APPENDIX

1   A Complete Budget
2   Prices, Fees, Etc.
3   Phone Numbers
4   Websites
5   Lists
6   Tax Deductions
7   TV/Film Regulations
8   Commercial Regulations
9   Agency Contracts
10 Health and Pension

X
INDEX

GO

OSCAR
AVENUE

LUCK

PERSONAL
MANAGER
PLACE
$

TAX
AUDIT:
LOSE
SHIRT

LEAD
LANE

TENTH ROLE

APPENDIX

1 A COMPLETE BUDGET

In many cases these are average figures, all rounded off. You can raise or lower them to some extent.

- ### THE MUSTS

Telephone ($40 month, installation)	$500
Headshot session	$350
Headshot printing (500 theatrical, 500 commercial)	$300
Résumés (typing, printing 500)	$100
AFTRA initiation	$800
Equity initiation	$800
SAG initiation	$1,118
Union dues (assumes AFTRA & SAG)	$170
Postage (500 @ $.33 per 100)	$165
Envelopes (good-looking manila, some regular)	$50
Academy Players Directory listing (one year)	$75
Answering device/Voice Mail	$180
Good stationery	$75
Thank-you notes	$25
SAG agency list (free to members)	$1
Datebook	$20
Theatre, showcases, classes	$3,500
TOTAL	**$8,229**

- ### OTHER ITEMS

Card file & notebook	$20
Directories	$150
Working Actors Guide	$38
Trade subscriptions	$144

Postcards $300
Typewriter $200
Labels (blank or pre-addressed) $35
Beeper ($90 initial, $10 per month) $210
Videocassette (including air-check, stock, editing) $250
Passport (1st time; renewal $10 cheaper) $65

TOTAL $1,412

Total (The Musts) $8,224
Total (Other Items) $1,412

GRAND TOTAL $9,666

• CHICKEN SOUP

Desk $100
Computer/Printer $2,500
Fax Machine $250
VCR $300
Camcorder $600

TOTAL $3,750

Total (The Musts) $8,229
Total (Other Items) $1,412
Total (Chicken Soup) $3,750

DELUXE GRAND TOTAL $13,391

2 ALPHABETICAL LISTING OF PRICES, FEES, ETC.

(Prices do not include California sales tax)

Academy Foundation (mailing list for public programs): $5
(free to union members)
Academy Players Directory (per edition): $25
Academy Players Directory (per year): $75
Accent tapes (David Alan Stern's, per tape): $16.95
Actors Equity Association (AEA) initiation: $800
AEA (with parent) semi-annual minimum dues: $34
AEA (without parent) semi-annual minimum dues: $39
AEA Membership Candidate Program: $100
AFTRA initiation: $800
AFTRA semi-annual minimum dues: $42.50
AFTRA scale (principal, day rate, 1/2 hr. daily show): $482
AFTRA scale (principal, day rate, 1 hr. daily show): $643
AFTRA scale (principal, day rate, primetime drama): $559
AFTRA scale (3-day contract, primetime drama): $1,415
AFTRA scale (weekly contract, primetime drama): $1,942
AFTRA scale ("under 5" day rate, 1/2 hr. daily show): $228
AFTRA scale ("under 5" day rate, 1 hr. daily show): $280
AFTRA scale (extra, day rate, 1/2 hr. daily show): $99
AFTRA scale (extra, day rate, 1 hr. daily show): $128
AFTRA/SAG Federal Credit Union (minimum first deposit): $50
plus $5 Membership Fee
AGMA initiation: $500
AGMA semi-annual dues: $39
AGVA initiation: $600
AGVA (three-times-yearly dues): $24
Apartments ("single," one-bedroom): $550- $1,100
Apartment finders/real estate services (minimum): $40
Auto gas (average, unleaded, gallon): $1.30
Auto registration (add 2% of market value to): $35
Back Stage West/Drama-Logue, newsstands: $2

Back Stage West/Drama-Logue, (one-year subscription): $79

Back Stage, newsstands: $2.50

Beeper (average monthly): $10

Breakdown Services *Agency Guide*: $9.74

Breakdown Services "Go-Between" (agts., cast. dirs.): $80

Breakdown Services "Go-Between" (producers): $70

Breakdown Services (deliver flyers, agts., pers. mgrs.): $90

Breakdown Services *C/D Guide* (per quarterly issue): $6.75

Breakdown Services *C/D Guide* (per year): $41.30

Breakdown Services labels (L.A. agents): $17.32

Breakdown Services labels (L.A. casting directors): $17.32

Breakdown Services labels (L.A. comm. cast. dirs.): $9.69

Breakdown Services labels (N.Y. casting directors): $9.69

Buses (MTA): $1.35

Buses (transfers): .... $.25

Buses (monthly passes): $42

Camcorder: $600

Cold reading showcases (average, per session): $25

Commercial audition (every 30 mins. over 1 hour): $29.92

Commercial audition (3rd time for same commercial): $119.68

Commercial audition (4th time for same commercial): $239.35

Commercial creative fee, improv. audition: $175.70

Commercial scale for session, holding fees: $478.70

Computer/printer (possibly less): $2,500

Daily Variety, newsstand: $1.75

Daily Variety, one-year subscription: $197

Daily Variety, quarter-page talent ad: $756

DGA's Directory of Members: (drop in) $22

    (by mail) $25

Disneyland (adults): $36

Disneyland (kids): $26

Driver's license: $12

Equity-franchised agents (list): .... $.25

Equity-contract theatres (each list of LORT, etc.): .... $.25

Equity initiation: $800

Equity semi-annual minimum dues (with parent): $34

Equity semi-annual minimum dues (without parent): $39

Equity Membership Candidate Program: $100

Electricity bill (apartment, average month): $50- $60

Fax Machine: $250

Film Directors — A Complete Guide: $75
Gas (apartment, average month): $10
The Hollywood Reporter, newsstand:. $1.75 ($2.50 on Tuesdays)
The Hollywood Reporter, one-year subscription: $199
The Hollywood Reporter quarter-page talent ad:................... $650
Independent Feature Project/West (IFP) (per year): $85
Knott's Berry Farm (adults): $31.95
Knotts Berry Farm (kids): $23.95
La Brea Tar Pits (admission): (adults) $6
       (kids) $2
Los Angeles Times, newsstands: .... $.25
Magic Mountain (adults): $35
Magic Mountain (kids): $17
Mailbox rental (average, monthly): $15
Motel (average, per night): $70
Movie admissions: $8
Pacific Coast Studio Directory: $10
Publicists monthly fee (average, minimum): $2,000
Restaurant (inexpensive, dinner, one person): $10
Restaurant (moderate, dinner, one person): $10- $30
Restaurant (expensive, dinner, one person): .... $30+
Résumés typing (average): $20
Ross Reports Television (one edition): $5
Ross Reports Television (6 month subscription): $38
SAG Agency List (free to members): $1
SAG Conservatory: $10
       (children): $5
SAG extra work, daily: $86
SAG extra work, "special ability," daily: $96
SAG Film Society (basic membership): $65
SAG Film Society (with 10 parking passes @ $17.60): $82.60
SAG Film Society (with full-year parking @ $45.75): $110.75
SAG initiation (is double day scale, see below): $1,118
SAG semi-annual minimum dues: $42.50
SAG daily scale (until July 1, 1998): $559
SAG scale (3-day TV only; until July 1, 1998): $1,415
SAG weekly scale (until July 1,1998): $1,942
"Scale plus ten": Add ten percent to scale
SHOWFAX (per page faxing): $1.75
       (Max .... $12)

The Hollywood Reporter's Studio Blu-Book: .. (carry out) $70.31
.... (by mail) $76.31
Theatre tickets (average, "Equity Waiver"): $25
Theatre tickets (average, major theatre): $55
Thomas Bros. Maps: $16.95
Universal Studios Tour (adults): $36
Universal Studios Tour (kids): $26
VCR: $300
Videotape (average, blank, purchase): $3
Videotape (average, rental of movies per day): $3
Women in Film (first-year membership): $200
Women in Film (yearly membership): $125
Women in Theatre (artists' yearly membership): $60
Working Actors Guide: $37.50

3 Alphabetical Listing
Of Phone Numbers

Academy Foundation .... (310) 247-3000
Academy Players Directory .... (310) 247-3058
The Actors' Fund of America .... (323) 939-1801
ACTRA (Canada) .... (416) 489-1311
AFTRA .... (323) 634-8100
AFTRA Health & Retirement Fund .... (323) 937-3631
(800) 367-7966
AFTRA Hotline .... (323) 634-8263
AFTRA/SAG Federal Credit Union .... (800) 354-3728
(323) 461-3041
(818) 509-3690
AGVA .... (818) 508-9984
Airlink .... (310) 416-1116
Airport Transportation Information .... (310) 646-5252
AMTRAK .... (800) USA-RAIL
Art Center College of Design (ACCD) .... (626) 396-2200
ACCD,"free" résumé/modeling photos .... (626) 396-2250
Back Stage West/Drama-Logue .... (323) 525-2356
Breakdown Services, Inc. .... (310) 276-9166
Buses (MTA) (L.A.) .... (800) 266-6883
(213) 626-4455
Casting Society of America (CSA) .... (323) 463-1925
Columbia College .... (323) 851-0550
The Comedy Store .... (323) 656-6225
Conference of Personal Managers .... (310) 275-2456
Daily Variety .... (323) 857-6600
Dept. Motor Vehicles (DMV) .... (310) 271-4585
Dept. Water & Power (DWP) (electricity) .... (213) 481-5411
Director's Guild of America (DGA) .... (310) 289-2000
Disneyland .... (714) 781-4565
Larry Edmunds Bookshop .... (323) 463-3273
Equity (AEA) .... (323) 634-1750

Samuel French's Bookshop (Hollywood) .... (323) 876-0570
Samuel French's Bookshop (Studio City) .... (818) 762-0535
Info Line - Los Angeles .... (800) 339-6993
The Hollywood Reporter .... (323) 525-2000
The Improvisation .... (323) 651-2583
Independent Feature Project/West (IFP) .... (310) 475-4379
Knott's Berry Farm .... (714) 220-5200
La Brea Tar Pits .... (323) 934-7243
Los Angeles Times .... (213) 237-5000
Magic Mountain .... (661) 255-4111
The Oakwood .... (800) 888-0808
                                                                    (323) 878-2100
Producers Guild .... (310) 557-0807
Publicists Guild .... (818) 905-1541
SAG .... (323) 954-1600
SAG Affirmative Action .... (323) 549-6644
SAG Agency Information .... (323) 549-6737
SAG Conservatory (at AFI) .... (323) 856-7736
SAG Dental (Delta Dental) .... (800) 846-7418
SAG Events (24 hr. line) .... (323) 549-6650
SAG Film Society .... (323) 549-6658
SAG Film Society Hotline .... (323) 549-6657
SAG Hotline .... (323) 937-3441
SAG Pension & Welfare .... (818) 954-9400
SAG Residuals .... (323) 549-6505
SAG Seminars (gen. info, 24 hr. line) .... (323) 549-6540
SHOWFAX .... (310) 385-6920
Stuntmen Association of Motion Pictures .... (818) 766-4334
UCLA .... (310) 825-4321
Universal Studios Tour .... (818) 508-9600
USC .... (213) 740-2311
The Voicecaster (Bob Lloyd) .... (818) 841-5300
Writers Guild (WGA) .... (310) 550-1000
Women in Film .... (323) 463-6040
Women In Theatre .... (818) 763-5222

4 WEBSITES

Websites tend to come and go. We've tried to include only ones we thought might be around for a while. (Note: All are http://)

Academy Players Directory Online — www.acadpd.org/
The Actors Resource (general info) — www.onstage.org/
AFTRA — aftra.org/
Breakdown Services — www.breakdownservices.com
Castnet (on-line submissions) — www.castnet.com/
Daily Variety — www.variety.com/
Directors Guild of America — www.dga.org/dga/
E-Online (entertainment news) — www.eonline.com/
The Hollywood Net (various info) — hollywoodnetwork.com
Hollywood Reporter — www.hollywoodreporter.com/
Independent Feature Project/West — www.ifp.org/
"the link™" — www.submitlink.com/
Reel Props — www.reelclothes.com
Screen Actors Guild (national) — www.sag.com
SAG Calendar of Events — www.sag.com./calendar.html
SAG List of Franchised Agents — www.sag.com/agentlist.html
SAG Pension & Health — www.sagph.org
SAG (San Francisco) — www.aftrasf.org
SAG (Seattle) — www.aftra.com
SAG/AFTRA (Dallas/Fort Worth) —
    www.entertainment.com/org/dfwactor/asdfw.html
SHOWFAX — www.showfax.com
Women in Film — www.lag.net/~wifcf/
Women In Theatre — www.cybershowbiz.com./WIT
Writers website (scripts, software, books for tv & film) —
    writerscomputer.com/store/writing_production_software.html

5 LISTS

1. Acting classes
2. Bargains
3. Bookstores/newsstands
4. Equity theatres
5. Extra casting offices (union/no fee)
6. Photographers
7. Photographic print shops
8. Print shops (résumés, etc.)
9. Recommended reading
10. Showcases and cold reading workshops
11. Trade publications
12. Union branch offices
13. Videotaping services
14. Miscellaneous

1. ACTING CLASSES

There are scores more good ones than we have room to list.

COACHES/WORKSHOPS

A number of coaches and workshops have classes in more categories than are listed here.

• *On-camera acting*

Rae Allen
(310) 396-6734

Cherie Franklin
(323) 856-9604

Judy Kerr
(818) 505-9373

M.K. Lewis
(310) 826-8118/394-2511

- ## General acting

Corey Allen
c/o Margie Haber
(310) 854-0870

Paul Gleason
(323) 874-9967

Milton Katselas
(310) 855-1556

Tracy Roberts
(818) 623-9500

- ## Cold reading

Margie Haber
(310) 854-0870

M.K. Lewis
(310) 826-8118/394-2511

- ## Commercials

Pamela Campus
(310) 398-2715

Tepper-Gallegos
(323) 469-3577

- ## Dance

Conjunction Point Dance Center
(310) 836-3962

Debbie Reynolds Studios
(818) 985-4176/3193

The Dance Center
(818) 980-3336

- ## Dialects

Robert Easton
(818) 985-2222

Larry Moss
(310) 395-4284

- ## Extension courses

The Learning Annex
(310) 478-6677

Learning Tree University
(818) 882-5599

UCLA
(310) 825-9971

• *Improvisation/comedy*

The Groundlings
(323) 934-4747

L.A. Connection
(818) 784-1868

Harvey Lembeck Comedy
Workshop
(310) 271-2831

• *Savvy/seminars*

Sam Christensen
Savvy/Image
(818) 506-0783

Actorfest
(*Back Stage West/Drama-
Logue*'s expo for actors)
(watch for ads)

• *Vocal*

William and Irene Chapman
(818) 787-7192

Natalie Limonick
(323) 934-7472

Steven Memel
(818) 789-0474

Elizabeth Sabine
(818) 761-6747

• *Voice-overs*

Louise Chamis
(818) 985-0130

Robert Easton
(818) 985-2222

Bob Bergen
(818) 901-8714
(Animation v.o. technique only)

• *Foreign Students:*

Hollywood Acting Workshop
Andrea Balen & Petra Gallasch
2400 Silver Lake Dr.
Los Angeles, CA 90039
(323) 668-2685

OTHER ACTING WORKSHOPS

There are many other well-known acting coaches and workshops in L.A.,
including Film Industry Workshops, Eric Morris' Acting Workshops, Lee

Strasberg Theatre Institute, Van Mar Academy, Weist-Barron-Hill, etc. Also see *The Hollywood Acting Coaches and Teachers Directory* on sale at any drama bookstore.

COLLEGES/CONSERVATORIES

American Conservatory Theatre (ACT)
30 Grant Ave.
San Francisco 94108-5800
Degrees: MFA, Certificates

California Institute of the Arts
24700 McBean Pkwy.
Valencia 91355
BFA, MFA, Certificates

Los Angeles City College
855 N. Vermont Ave.
Los Angeles 90029-9990
AA, Certificates

Loyola Marymount
Loyola Bl. at W. 80th
Los Angeles, 90045-2699
BA (MA in film only)

Pacific Conservatory for the
Performing Arts/Solvang
P.O. Box 1700
Santa Maria 93456-1700
Certificates

Santa Monica College
1900 Pico Bl.
Santa Monica, CA 90405
AA

South Coast Repertory Theatre
655 Town Center Drive
PO Box 2197
Costa Mesa 92628-2197
Certificates

University of California, L.A.
(UCLA)
308 Westwood Bl.
Los Angeles, CA 90024-8311
BA, MA, MFA, Ph.D

University of So. California (USC)
University Park
Los Angeles 90089
BA, BFA, MFA

2. BARGAINS

• *Guides to bargains*

Buying Retail Is Stupid!
Tricia King-Crumley, Deborah Newmark, Bonnie Cunningham

Guide to the Los Angeles Garment District
Barbara Moe

L.A. Bargain Book
Jeff Hutner

L.A. *Weekly* (newspaper)
Los Angeles and
Valley editions;
lots of ads for bargains.

The Recycler
Weekly classified newspaper,
published every Thursday.

• *Clothing*

Garment District, downtown, roughly bordered by 7th St. on the north, the Santa Monica Fwy. (I-10) on the south, Broadway on the west, Maple Ave. on the east. S. Los Angeles is its "main street." Parking, however, is no bargain.

The Cooper Building
860 S. Los Angeles St.,
Garment Dist.
Seven floors of discount shops.

Loehmann's
333 S. LaCienega
(310) 659-0674
Women's wear

Men's & women's wear from
studio wardrobe departments:

It's A Wrap
3315 Magnolia Bl., Burbank
(818) 567-7366

Reel Clothes & Props
12132 Ventura Blvd.,
Studio City
(818) 508-7762

Reel Clothes & Props II,
the Sequel
13607 Ventura Blvd.,
Sherman Oaks (818) 990-2443

• *General merchandise*

(All below have locations thoughout the city.)

Appliances & electronics:

Best Buy
Circuit City
Costco
The Good Guys

Office Depot
Office Max
Pic 'N' Save
The Slauson Home Base

3. BOOKSTORES/NEWSSTANDS

• *Bookstores*

Samuel French's Theatre &
Film Bookshops
7623 Sunset Bl., Hwd.
(323) 876-0570
11963 Ventura Bl., Studio City
(818) 762-0535

The Collectors Bookstore
1708 N. Vine St., Hwd.
(323) 467-3296
(closed on Suns. & Mons.)

Larry Edmunds Cinema and
Theatre Bookshop
6644 Hollywood Bl., Hwd.
(323) 463-3273

Elliot M. Katt
Books on the Performing Arts
8568 Melrose Ave., West Hwd.
(310) 652-5178

Movie World
212 N. San Fernando Rd.,
Burbank
(818) 846-0459

• *Newsstands*

Al's Newsstand
370 N. Fairfax Ave., L.A.
(213) 935-8525
1257 Third St., Santa Monica
90401
(310) 393-2690

Centerfold Newsstand
716 N. Fairfax Ave., L.A.
(323) 651-4822

Sherman Oaks Newsstand
14500 Ventura Bl.,
Sherman Oaks
(818) 995-0632

Universal News
1655 N. Las Palmas Ave.,
Hwd.
(323) 467-3850

Westwood International
11737 San Vicente BL.
(310) 447-2080
(Other locations in West L.A.,
Westwood Village,
Sherman Oaks)

World Book & News Co.
1652 Cahuenga Bl., Hwd.
(323) 465-4352

4. EQUITY THEATRES

This list is a partial one and tilted towards Southern California, where you want to be most of the time, after all, if you're pursuing your film career.

League of Resident Theatres (LORT)
Letter of Agreement (LOA)
Small Professional Theatres (SPT)

American Conservatory Theatre
30 Grant St.
San Francisco, CA 94108-5800
(415) 439-2412
"A" house (highest pay scale, LORT contract)

Berkeley Repertory Theatre
2025 Addison St.
Berkeley, CA 94704
(510) 204-8901
"B" house, LORT

California Shakespeare Festival
701 Hinz Ave.
Berkeley, CA 94710
(510) 548-3422
"D" house, LORT

Dell'Arte Players Company
P.O. Box 816
Blue Lake, CA 95525
(707) 668-5664
LOA

El Teatro Campesino
P.O. Box 1240
San Juan Bautista, CA 95045
(408) 623-2444
SPT

Ensemble Theatre Co.
(Alhecama Theatre)
P.O. Box 2307
Santa Barbara, CA 93120
(805) 965-6252
SPT

Garden Grove Theatre Company
12852 Main St.
Garden Grove, CA 92640
(714) 636-7213/741-9554
SPT

La Jolla Playhouse
P.O. Box 12039
La Jolla, CA 92039
(619) 550-1070
Two houses, "B" & "C," LORT

La Mirada Theatre for the
Performing Arts
P.O. Box 1058
La Mirada, CA 90637
(714) 994-6150
Non-Resident Dramatic Stock (COST)
& Indoor Musical Stock (SMALL)

Lawrence Welk Resort Theatre
8860 Lawrence Welk Dr.
Escondido, CA 92026
(760) 749-3448
Member, American Dinner Theatre Institute

Mark Taper Forum
(Center Theatre Group)
Los Angeles Music Center
Los Angeles, CA 90012
135 N. Grand Ave.
(213) 972-7353
Two houses, "A" &
"Experimental," LORT

Old Globe Theatre
Balboa Park
P.O. Box 2171
San Diego, CA 92112
(619) 231-1941
Three houses, "B+," "B" & "C,"
LORT

Pasadena Playhouse
39 S. El Molino
Pasadena, CA 91101
(626) 792-8672
"B+" LORT

Sacramento Music Circus
P.O. Box 2347
Sacramento,CA 95812
(916) 446-5880
Resident Musical Stock

Sacramento Theatre Co.
1419 "H" St.
Sacramento, CA 95814
(916) 446-7501
LOA

San Diego Repertory Theatre
79 Horton Plaza
San Diego, CA 92101-6144
(619) 231-3586
LOA

San Francisco Shakespeare
Festival
c/o The Lone Mountain
Theatre
P.O. Box 640386
San Francisco, CA 94164
LOA

San Gabriel Civic Light Opera
P.O. Box 5004
San Gabriel, CA 91778
(626) 281-9444
LOA

San Jose Repertory Theatre
P.O. Box 2399
San Jose, CA 95109-2399
(408) 291-2266
"C" House, LORT

Santa Paula Theatre Center
125 So. 7th St.
Santa Paula, CA 93060
(805) 525-3073
SPT

Shakespeare Festival L.A.
411 W. Fifth St., Suite 815
Los Angeles, CA 90013
(213) 489-1121
LOA

South Coast Repertory Theatre
P.O. Box 2197
Costa Mesa, CA 92628
(714) 957-2602
Two houses, "B" & "D," LORT

Will Geer Theatricum Botanicum
1419 N. Topanga Canyon Bl.
Topanga, CA 90290
(310) 455-2322
LOA

5. EXTRA CASTING OFFICES (UNION/"NO FEE")

Central Casting
1700 W. Burbank Blvd., Burbank
(818) 562-2700
($20 for photograph)

Cenex
(non-union "branch" of Central Casting)
2600 W. Olive St., Burbank
(818) 562-2800

Producers Casting Agency
P.O. Box 1527, Pacific Palisades 90272
(310) 459-0229
(Commercials, union and non-union, $25 photo fee)

6. PHOTOGRAPHERS

David Beeler
(323) 464-4728

Ray Bengston
(818) 506-6868

Lesley Bohm
(213) 625-8401

Paul Gregory
(323) 852-0484

Michael Helms
(818) 899-8002

Michael Hiller
(323) 960-5111

David LaPorte
(310) 452-4053

Tom Lascher
(310) 581-1980

Michael Papo
(818) 760-8160

Tama Rothschild
(323) 658-7862

Mitchell Rose
(323) 462-8636

Buddy Rosenberg
(323) 874-2692

John Sanchez
(310) 275-5544

Alisha Tamburri
(818) 998-8838

Herb Weil
(323) 874-8492

Alan Weissman
(818) 766-9797

7. PHOTOGRAPHIC PRINT SHOPS

Anderson Graphics
6037 Woodman Ave., Van Nuys
(818) 909-9100

Custom Print Shop
1759 N. Las Palmas, Hwd.
(323) 461-3001

Duplicate Photo Labs
1522 N. Highland Ave., Hwd.
(323) 466-7544
12606 Ventura Blvd., Studio City
(818) 760-4193

Grand Prints
6143 Laurelgrove Ave., W Hwd.
(818) 763-5743
(By appointment)

Isgo Lepejian
2411 W. Magnolia Bl., Burbank
(818) 848-9001
(818) 843-9609
1145 N. La Brea Ave., Hwd.
(323) 876-8085

Prints Charm'n (3 locations)
9054 Santa Monica Bl.,
West Hwd.
(310) 288-1786

11020 Ventura Bl., Studio City
(818) 753-9055

1657 Sawtelle, West L.A.
(310) 312-0904

Quality Custom Photo Lab
142 N. La Brea Ave., Hwd.
(323) 938-0174

Quantity Photo
6660 Santa Monica Blvd., Hwd.
(323) 467-6178

8. PRINT SHOPS (RÉSUMÉS, ETC.)

Copymat
6301 Sunset Bl., Hwd.
(323) 461-1222
11988 Wilshire Bl., W. L.A.
(310) 207-5952
Many other locations;
some 24 hrs.

Copy Spot, Inc.
600 Wilshire Bl., Santa Monica
(310) 393-0693

Kinko's Copies
13321 Burbank Bl., Van Nuys
(818) 787-7271
601 Wilshire Bl., Santa Monica
(310) 576-7710
6157 W. Pico
(323) 655-9587
All open 24 hours.

Media Print and Copy
3915 Riverside Dr., Burbank
(818) 843-2679

9. RECOMMENDED READING

• *About L.A.*

LA/Access
Richard Saul Wurman

The Best of L.A.
L.A. Weekly Staff &
Mary Beth Crain, Ed.

Freeway Alternates
David Rizzo

• *Acting*

Acting Is Believing
Charles McGaw

Acting on Film
Michael Caine
(also has video with same name)

An Actor Prepares and
Building a Character
Constantin Stanislavski

Respect for Acting
Uta Hagen

Sanford Meisner on Acting
Sanford Meisner &
Dennis Longwell

• *Auditioning*

Audition
Michael Shurtleff

The Audition Book
Ed Hooks

How to Audition
Gordon Hunt

*Next! An Actors Guide to
Auditioning*
Ellie Kanner & Paul G. Bens, Jr.

• *The Biz of Acting*

Acting Professionally
Robert Cohen

Acting is Everything
Judy Kerr

An Actor Succeeds
Terrance Hines and
Suzanne Vaughan

*The Back Stage Handbook
for Performing Artists*
Sherry Eaker

From Agent to Actor
Edgar Small

*How to Sell Yourself
As An Actor*
K Callen

*How to Make It in
Hollywood*
Linda Buzzell

• **Commercials/voice-overs**

Acting in Television
Commercials
Squire Fridell

Word of Mouth
Susan Blu &
Molly Ann Mullin

• **Others**
The Power of Positive Thinking, Norman Vincent Peale; Think and
Grow Rich, Napoleon Hill; What Color Is Your Parachute?, Richard
Nelson Bolles, and any book on salesmanship.

10. SHOWCASES & COLD READING WORKSHOPS

The Casting Network
New Century Credit Bldg.
13201 Ventura Bl., Studio City
First class is your audition

In The Act
3361 Cahuenga West, Studio City
(323) 933-1178
By audition

Liason
2811 W Magnolia Bl., Burbank
(818) 705-0973
First class is your audition

One on One Productions
13261 Moorpark, Sherman Oaks
(818) 789-3399
By audition - call for
appointment

Reel Pros
13517 Ventura Bl., Suite 2,
Sherman Oaks (818) 788-4133

**Note: For Studios see
Studio Map, Chapter 3.
For Theatres see Theatre
Map, Chapter 25.**

11. TRADE PUBLICATIONS
KEY: (N) = Newsstand sales (S) = Subscription

Back Stage West/Drama-Logue
(N/S)
5055 Wilshire Bl., 6th Floor
Los Angeles 90036
(323) 525-2356

Back Stage (N/S)
Subscriptions: P.O. Box 5017
Brentwood, TN 37024
(800) 458-7541

Daily/Weekly Variety (N/S)
5700 Wilshire Bl., Suite 120
Los Angeles 90036
(323) 857-6600

Hollywood Reporter (N/S)
6715 Sunset Bl.
Los Angeles 90028
(323) 525-2000

OTHER TRADES OF INTEREST

American Film (N/S)

American Premiere (N/S)

Broadcasting (S)

Call Sheet (S) (SAG publication)

Casting Call (N/S)

Diallog (S) (AFTRA publication)

Entertainment Weekly (N/S)

Premiere (N/S)

State of the Arts (S):

California Arts Council

1901 Broadway, Suite A,

Sacramento 95818

12. UNION BRANCH OFFICES

ACTORS' EQUITY ASSOCIATION (AEA)
5757 Wilshire Bl., Suite One
Los Angeles, CA 90036
(323) 634-1750

165 W. 46th St.
New York, NY 10036
(212) 869-8530

MIDWESTERN:

203 N. Wabash Ave., Suite 1700
Chicago, IL 60601
(312) 641-0393

SAN FRANCISCO:

235 Pine St.
San Francisco, CA 94104
(415) 391-7510

THE AMERICAN FEDERATION OF
TELEVISION AND RADIO ARTISTS

6922 Hollywood Bl.
Hwd., CA 90028
(323) 461-8111

260 Madison Ave., 7th Floor
New York, NY 10016
(212) 532-0800

Excepting New York and L.A., SAG offices listed below also handle AFTRA. AFTRA also has hotines throughout the country.

AMERICAN GUILD OF MUSICAL ARTISTS
1727 Broadway
New York, NY 10019-5214
(212) 265-3687

Write New York office for list of AGMA branches nationwide.

AMERICAN GUILD OF VARIETY ARTISTS

4741 Laurel Canyon Bl., #208
North Hwd., CA 91607
(818) 508-9984

184 Fifth Ave., 6th Floor
New York, NY 10010
(212) 675-1003

For regional offices, write AGVA in New York.

THE SCREEN ACTORS GUILD

5757 Wilshire Bl.
Los Angeles, CA 90036-3600
(323) 954-1600

1515 Broadway, 44th Fl.
New York, NY 10036
(212) 944-1030

ARIZONA:

1616 E. Indian School Rd., #330
Phoenix, AZ 85016
(602) 265-2712

ATLANTA:

455 E. Paces Ferry Rd. NE,
Suite 334
Atlanta, GA 30305
(404) 239-0131

BOSTON:

11 Beacon St., #512
Boston, MA 02108
(617) 742-2688

CHICAGO:

1 E. Erie Dr., Suite 650
Chicago, IL 60611
(312) 573-8081

CLEVELAND*:

1030 Euclid Ave., Suite 429
Cleveland, OH 44115
(216) 579-9305

DALLAS:

6060 N. Central Expy.,
#302/LB 604
Dallas, TX 75206
(214) 363-8300

DENVER:**

950 S. Cherry St., Suite 502
Denver, CO 80222
(303) 757-6226

DETROIT:

27770 Franklin Rd.
Southfield, MI 48034-2352
(248) 355-3105

CENTRAL FLORIDA:

646 W. Colonial Dr.
Orlando, FL 32804-7342
(407) 649-3100

FLORIDA:

7300 N. Kendall Dr., Suite 620
Miami, FL 33156-7840
(305) 670-7677

HAWAII:

949 Kapiolani Bl. #105
Honolulu, HI 96814
(808) 596-0388

HOUSTON:

2650 Fountainview Dr., #326
Houston, TX 77057
(713) 972-1806

MINNEAPOLIS/ST.PAUL:

708 N. First St., #343
Minneapolis, MN 55401
(612) 371-9120

NASHVILLE:

1108 17th Ave. S
Nashville, TN 37212
(615) 327-2944

NEVADA:

3900 Paradise Rd., #206
Las Vegas, NV 89109
(702) 737-8818

N. CAROLINA:

321 N. Front St.
Wilmington, NC 28401
(910) 762-1889

PHILADELPHIA:

230 S. Broad St., Suite 500
Philadelphia, PA 19102
(215) 545-3150

PORTLAND:

3030 S.W. Moody, #104
Portland, OR 97201
(503) 279-9600

ST. LOUIS*:

1310 Papin St., #103
St. Louis, MO 63103
(314) 231-8410

SAN DIEGO:

7827 Convoy Ct., #400
San Diego, CA 92111
(619) 278-7695

SAN FRANCISCO:

235 Pine St., 11th Fl.
San Francisco, CA 94104
(415) 391-7510

SEATTLE:

601 Valley St., #100
Seattle, WA 98109
(206) 270-0493

WASH. D.C./BALTIMORE:

4340 E. West Hwy., Suite 204
Bethesda, MD 20814
(301) 657-2560

* AFTRA offices which also handle SAG business.
** Regional offices. DENVER also covers New Mexico and Utah. FLORIDA also covers Alabama, Arkansas, Louisiana, Mississippi, West Virginia, U.S. Virgin Islands, and the Caribbean. Puerto Rico is soon to have its own office.

13. VIDEOTAPING SERVICES — "AIR CHECKS"

Jan's Video
1800 N. Argyle, Suite 100, Hwd.
(323) 462-5511

Planet Video
11040 Santa Monica Bl., L.A.
(310) 473-2154

Propeller
2950 Nebraska Ave.
Santa Monica
(310) 586-1500

World of Video
8700 Wilshire BL., B.H.
(310) 659-5147
No air checks — copying and editing only

14. MISCELLANEOUS

Academy Players Directory
Academy of Motion Picture
Arts & Sciences
8949 Wilshire Bl.,
Beverly Hills 90211
(310) 247-3058

The Actors' Fund of America
4727 Wilshire Bl., Suite 310,
L.A. 90010
(323) 939-1801
Fax: (323) 939-1811
(Career guidance)

The American Film Institute
2021 N. Western Ave., L.A. 90027
(323) 856-7600

Breakdown Services, Ltd.
1120 S. Robertson, 3rd Floor,
L.A. 90035
(310) 276-9166

Sam Christensen's
Hollywood Headshot Gallery
Sam Christensen Studios
10440 Burbank Bl., N. Hwd.
(818) 506-0783

Greater L.A. Visitors &
Convention Bureau
633 W 5th St., #6000, L.A. 90071
(213) 624-7300

Independent Feature Project/
West
1964 Westwood BL, #205
Los Angeles, CA 90025
(310) 475-4379
Fax: (310) 441-5676

SAG's *Ethnic Performers
Directory*
c/o Affirmative Action
Department Office
5757 Wilshire Bl., 8th Floor
Los Angeles 90036
(213) 549-6644

SHOWFAX
2000 W Magnolia Bl., Suite 206
Burbank, 91506
(818) 556-5200

Women In Theatre
12417 Ventura Court, #2
Studio City, 91604
(818) 763-5222

"The Voicecaster"
(Bob Lloyd)
1832 W. Burbank, 91506
(818) 841-5300

6 "TYPICAL" TAX DEDUCTIONS
OF THE PROFESSIONAL ACTOR

We're not accountants or attorneys, and we don't expect you to use this material in place of a good CPA. Nor do we claim that these deductions are written in concrete. With the tax changes Congress is making in recent years, it's possible that, by the time you read this, none of these deductions will still be valid. Remember too that all deductions — in fact, your entire tax return — depend on your circumstances.

While some of these items may be totally deductible (your union dues and initiation, for example), others (such as your phone bill) are partially deductible depending on how much of the expense/use is business-related. Once again, what those portions may be depend on your facts and circumstances.

Also, certain items, such as television sets, typewriters, etc., may be wholly deductible in one year or they may have to be "capitalized" over a period of years — that is, a portion of the expense will be deductible each year, say, for seven years. ("Capitalizing" may ultimately prove more beneficial to you anyway.)

Also, for performers there are special rules involving "above the line" versus "below the line" deductions that are simply too complicated to go into here. Your CPA can explain this to you.

Finally, all deductions are applicable only to the extent that the cost *exceeds* any reimbursements, and certain expenses may only be 50 percent deductible.

- *Admissions to plays and movies:* Save your ticket stubs.

- *Attorneys/legal fees:* Only if the work pertains to your acting career.

- *Auto expenses:* First, you'll need to estimate how much you use your car for business purposes. An example: You're going out to make the rounds of studios. The drive to the first stop is *not* tax-deductible — that's part of your "normal commute." However, each stop after that is business use and therefore deductible, until the last stop. From the last stop to home is *not* deductible — again, it's part of your commute.

Here, too, keeping a daily diary can come in mighty handy. At the end of the year, look through it and figure out your deduction, based on one of the following two methods:

1. *The mileage method:* If you've got an older car, this is generally the best "tax break" way. Estimate the number of business miles you put on the car and multiply that figure times whatever the IRS is allowing for business miles that year. That's your deduction. (The IRS will not ask for receipts.)

2. *The usage method:* If you have a newer car, this may be more beneficial than using the mileage method. Along with your daily diary, keep receipts for everything — gas receipts, repair bills, insurance payments, etc. Add those receipts together and, using your daily diary, estimate the percentage of business use you put on the car. Take that percentage of your bills — that's your deduction.

- *Books:* As long as they pertain to the industry. *War and Peace*, no; *Your Film Acting Career*, yes.

- *Business gifts:* All gifts to agents, personal managers, etc., up to $25 per person per year.

- *Business meals:* This can be a picky area with the IRS. You'll need the receipt for the meal, a record of who was there, how that person or persons relate to your position in the industry, and, basically, what you talked about. Your daily diary can be worth its weight in gold here. If the meal was under $75, you don't have to have a receipt, but the IRS still will want to know why you deducted it. Be sure you can explain *each* and *every* deduction. (These expenses may only be 50 percent deductible.)

- *Classes:* Once established as an actor, classes that maintain or improve your skills as a professional actor are generally deductible.

- *Commissions:* Paid to agents, personal managers, etc.

- *Fax Machine*

- *Hairstyling/haircuts:* As long as it's directly related to a role.

- *Industry parties:* Probably the most difficult area to get the IRS to approve as a deduction. Not only do you need to be able to prove that the party had a direct bearing on your position in the industry, but you will have to keep a guest list and be able to explain how those guests have a direct bearing on your career. A *very* touchy area.

- *Magazine and trade publications: Daily Variety, Hollywood Reporter, Back Stage West/Drama-Logue,* etc., and any others as long as at least a portion of the publication pertains to the industry. If you buy these on the newsstands, get receipts and attach them to your daily diary. If you don't, an auditor could disallow these deductions.

- *Mailing expenses:* Stamps, envelopes, labels, etc.

- *Makeup.*

- *Office supplies:* Typewriter, staples, writing paper, etc.

- *Phonograph records.*

- *Plays.*

- *Publicity materials:* Anything that publicizes you as an actor. Presentation tapes, *Academy Players Directory* listing, postcards, ads in the trades, etc.

- *Résumés:* Typing, printing, and/or photocopying.

- *Résumé shots:* Session and printing costs.

- *Tapes.*

- *Telephone and related:* Your telephone bill, depending on how much it's used business. Also answering devices, voice mail, cellular phones and beepers.

- *Television and related:* The set itself, repairs, cable, satellite or pay TV, VCRs, videotapes (blank or rented), *TV Guide,* or other television magazines.

- *Union dues/initiations.*

- *Wardrobe: See* hairstyling.

- *Wardrobe maintenance: See* hairstyling.

. . . And anything else that is directly related to or associated with your profession. You'll need: receipts, a daily diary, and a good CPA*(also see* Chapter 29).

7 TV & FILM REGULATIONS

This material is based on the current contract which expires June 30, 1998. If you are reading this after that date, bear in mind that while almost all dollar figures will change, the actual regulations — hammered out over many years — will tend to have only minor changes if any at all.

WARDROBE FITTINGS

First, for all actors, if the fitting is on the same day you work, there's no additional pay, but the hour(s) you spend being fitted count as part of your workday.

- *Day player, $950 or less:* If you're called in for a fitting you get a one-hour minimum payment. Stay beyond one hour, and you're paid for each additional 15-minute period.

  Be sure to get and sign a voucher (indicating time in and time out) from the costumer.

- *Day player, more than $950 per day:* Sorry, no additional pay for being called in.

- *Three-day contract, television only:* The producer can call you in for two hours' "free" fitting time on one day.

- *Free-lance weekly:* Producer can call you in for four hours' "free" fitting time on two days if it's a film and three hours' time on two days if it's a TV show.

The agent only gets a commission on fees for wardrobe fittings if you're making more than scale.

WARDROBE ALLOWANCE

For supplying your own wardrobe: $11.50 per outfit, $17 formal wear. Your agent gets no commission.

MEAL PERIODS/PENALTIES

Meal periods (up to one hour) don't count as time worked. Your first meal break has to come six hours after you're called. (Six hours after returning to work from the first meal break, you must be given a second meal break.) If not, you're paid: $25 first half-hour, $35 second half-hour, $50 each half-hour thereafter.

Your agent gets no commission.

STUDIO/NEARBY LOCATION/OVERNIGHT LOCATION

- *Studio work:* That's working on a lot.

- *Nearby location:* Any place within a 30-mile radius of Beverly and La Cienega Boulevards (called the Hollywood Studio Zone) is a "nearby location." Either you'll report directly there or to the studio and be taken to the location by car or bus. In the former case, you're paid 30 cents per mile, based on the distance from the studio to the nearby location. If they're shooting next door you still must be paid as though you had driven from the studio to the location. Mileage can be paid in cash on the set or be included in your check.

  Your agent gets no commission.

- *Overnight location:* That's Georgia, Paris, Thailand, whatever. The producer must pay your transportation and your expenses (more later).

TRAVEL TIME/PAY

- *Studio:* Just like a regular job. You're paid nothing to get yourself there.

- *Nearby location:* If you're transported, the time spent traveling back and forth counts as a part of your day. If traveling takes you into overtime, it's paid at time-and-a-half.

- *Overnight location:* Depends on your contract:

  1. *Day player:* You get a full day's pay for traveling to the location and a full day's pay for returning.

  2. *Three-day contract $4,500 or less, TV only:* You go on salary the day you leave and remain on salary till the day you return.

  3. *Weekly player, Theatrical or TV: $4,500 or less:* Same as 2.

  4. *Weekly player, Theatrical or TV over $4,500:* Get to the location within 24 hours and you'll go on salary when put "on call." However, you can't go on salary any later than 24 hours after reaching the location.

COMPUTING OVERTIME

Your work day starts at the time you were first called and ends when you're excused. (Meal breaks don't count.) Whether or not you're due overtime depends on your contract and, in some cases, whether you're at a studio or on an overnight location.

- *Day player, $1,140 or less:* Overtime starts on the ninth hour, at time-and-a-half for the ninth and tenth hours. After that, it's double time. It's paid in "hourly units." That is, work 15 minutes overtime and you're paid for an entire hour.

- *Day player, more than $1,140:* Overtime starts on the ninth hour, but there's no double time. All overtime is time-and-a-half. Further, it's based on a maximum of $1,140 per day, regardless of how much more your salary might be. It's paid in hourly units.

- *Three-day player, $2,500 or less:* Overtime only starts after the tenth hour and goes immediately to double time, in hourly units. Also, if you work more than 24 hours (straight time) over the three days, you get overtime, at time-and-a-half, but it's computed in six-minute units.

- *Three-day player, more than $2,500:* Overtime starts after ten hours. It's paid in hourly units at double time, but will based on $2,500 no matter how much more you may be making.

- *Weekly/series players earning $4,500 or less, TV only:*

  1. *Studio week:* At a studio or a nearby location, your week is five days, 44 hours. If you work more than ten hours on any day, your overtime is paid in hourly units at double time. For two days, you may work up to ten hours without getting overtime. However, work more than eight hours on a third, fourth, and/or fifth day and you're paid overtime at time-and-a-half, in half-hour units, for the ninth and tenth hours. Past ten hours is double time, in hourly units.

  2. *Overnight location:* Your week is six days, 48 hours. Daily overtime is the same as a studio week. The longer week, however, requires the producer to pay a bonus four hours' overtime, whether you work those four hours or not. (That's the equivalent of a 44-hour week plus four hours' "automatic" overtime.) This "location premium" applies whether you work the full week or not.

- *Weekly player, $4,500 or less, theatrical or TV:* Work beyond ten hours a day is paid in hourly units at double time. Work beyond 44 hours in five days is paid in six-minute units at time-and-a-half. An overnight location workweek (six days) requires the producer to pay you four hours overtime, whether you work or not.

- *Weekly players, more than $4,500 theatrical or TV:* Daily overtime is paid after ten hours, in hourly units, at double time figured on the basis of $4,500.

- *"Pro rata":* When you're on a three-day or weekly contract, that's what the producer is actually paying you per day. He'll use that figure to pay you if you work a day or more beyond what you've actually been contracted for.

  Your agent gets a commission on overtime.

DROP AND PICK UP (DAY-PLAYER CONTRACT ONLY)

This option may be used only once, and can't be used at all if you start out on a weekly contract.

Let's say you'll be needed on March 21, but not again until May 24. To avoid keeping you on the payroll, "drop and pick up" is employed. You'll work March 21 and be dropped until May 24. You must be given an exact "pick up" date and must go back on payroll on that date, regardless of whether they use you or not. Also, at least ten days must intervene from drop day to pick up day. (If the production isn't domestic and isn't for theatrical or for TV 14 days must intervene.) They may pick you up on either a daily or a weekly contract.

REST PERIODS

- *Daily:* You must be given 12 hours of rest between workdays, with certain exceptions:

  1. If you're working on an overnight theatrical movie location, your rest period can be reduced to 11 hours for two days of an entire week provided those two days are not consecutive.

  2. If you're working outdoors ("exterior photography"), rest period may be reduced to ten hours once every fourth consecutive day. No reduction is allowed on the first day, however.

  3. If you arrive on an overnight location after nine P.M. (and don't work that night) your call to work can be after ten hours.

  4. If you fly for more than four hours, you must have at least ten hours rest from the time you arrive at your hotel.

- *Weekly:* Besides your daily rest periods, on a five-day week you must be given one weekly rest period of 56 hours. One exception: shooting at night, primarily exterior, that can be reduced to 54 hours as long as your call is not earlier than three P.M. and you're dismissed before midnight on the fifth day of the work week.

  On a six-day location week, your weekly rest period is 36 hours.

  Violation of rest periods is called a "forced call." Penalty is one day's pay or $950, whichever is less.

  To find out if you're on a "forced call," check "Time Dismissed Studio" against your next call.

  Your agent gets no commission on rest period penalties.

EXPENSES

On an overnight location, you must be provided:

- First-class transportation (you fly first class unless there are six or more actors on the same flight).

- $100,000 travel insurance (by plane).

- $250,000 travel insurance (by helicopter).

- A private single room.

- Meal allowances (per diems) of: $10.50 breakfast, $15 lunch, $27.50 dinner. Total: $53. The producer may deduct any meals he supplies. If the location is expensive (Tokyo, London etc.), the producer must adjust per diems upward.

Agent gets no commission on any of above.

SIGNING OUT

When wrapped, the second assistant director will hand you either a time card or a production time report, with times written in under the following headings:

- Date Worked
- First Time Call
- Time Arrived Location
- Lunch
- Dinner
- Time Dismissed Location
- Time Dismissed Studio

Be sure all times entered are in ink and correct. If on a nearby location, be sure he's given you enough traveling time from location to studio.

GETTING PAID

- *Day player:* Check must be postmarked within five days of date you worked. (Excluding Saturdays, Sundays and holidays.)

- *All others:* Your check must be postmarked no later than the studio payroll date (usually Thursday) of the following week.

Late-payment damages are $10 a day up to 20 days. If you don't receive your payment, contact SAG to file a claim.

Your agent gets no commission on late penalties.

GO GET YOUR MONEY — BUT USE COMMON SENSE

If your check is "light," go after what's coming to you. Explain it to your agent and have him call the accounting office or producer. If he's reluctant, call the union and think about changing agents.

However, sometimes it's wise to back off: An actor's check was missing a one-hour fitting fee and a 45-minute meal-period violation. He called SAG and was assured he was due the money. Then, the actor called his agent, who, after checking said, "Look, they say the wardrobe fee was an 'oversight,' but they're getting *very* uptight about the meal penalty. If you want, I'll go after the meal penalty, but it just may make them angry enough never to hire you again." The actor swallowed and said, "Skip it."

If a producer is one day late with your check, don't start screaming, "I want my ten dollars in damages!" Use your head.

A NOTE ABOUT AFTRA SHOWS

If the program is run on network prime time the work rules are almost exactly the same. However, daytime soap operas, syndicated shows — anything not shown on network prime time — have different rules and pay scales for each type of show. Call AFTRA for further information.

RESIDUALS

If your show was made for TV (other than pay TV) the producer is entitled to one run of the show. After that, you're into "subsequent runs" (re-runs). That's where residuals come in. What you're paid depends.

- *Television pictures, network prime time:* If your TV picture is re-run on network television between eight and eleven P.M. (that's "prime time"), you get 100 percent of your salary subject to "ceilings" (the *most* you can get):

Length of Show	Ceiling
1/2 hour	$2,053
1 hour	3,100
1 1/2 hours	3,225
2 hours	3,472
2 hours +	3,969

- *TV, network, non-prime time:* If the TV picture is re-run on a network but not in prime time, you get a percentage of *what union scale was when you worked*, regardless of what you actually were paid. If you worked one week in 1988 and were paid $5,000, you'll get a percentage of $1,385 as that was union scale for a week in 1988.

- *Syndication:* When a show goes into syndication, it's usually shown on independent stations. Again you'll get a percentage of union scale at the time you worked, and the percentages are slightly smaller.

- *Feature films to TV/cable TV/videocassettes:* You want complicated? Boy, do we got complicated! The important thing is pointed out by Mark Locher, former public relations director of SAG "A lot of actors believe every time their film is shown on television, they'll get a payment. Not necessarily."
  Now you could get SAG's latest figures on the producer's worldwide grosses, but then you'd have to know how to figure out how much of the percentage allotted to the entire cast is allotted to you. Just rely on SAG.

- *Foreign telecasts:* Occasionally you'll get small residual checks from a five-year-old show that's currently running in Zanzibar. The method of computing what you get is again too complicated to explain, but you won't get rich. (There's a bar in town that gives free drinks for silly residual checks. The record? One cent!)

- *Agents' commissions:* A theatrical agent gets a commission *only* on prime time network residuals of television shows Nothing else.

- *When/how you're paid:* With network re-runs, the producer's got 30 days from air date to mail the check. In syndication, he's got up to four months. Foreign telecasts mean up to six months. Since residuals are first sent to the unions, add at least another two weeks for handling. Hold off on the party.

We've barely scratched the surface of items that affect your pocketbook. We simply chose the most common rules. Obtain the digests of rules and regulations of SAG, AFTRA, and Equity and read them. Your banker will love you for it.

8 COMMERCIAL REGULATIONS

(This material is based on the current contract, which expires February 6, 2000.)

EXCLUSIVITY/HOLDING FEES (OTHER POINTS)

- Holding fees are due each 13-week anniversary of the day you shot the commercial. (These 13-week periods are called "fixed cycles." There are a maximum of seven during 21 months). The advertiser must send your "holding fee" within 12 working days of the beginning of each fixed cycle. If he fails to do this, his right of exclusivity is cancelled. (You don't need a release letter. However, have your agent call the advertiser just to be sure there haven't been any foul-ups.)

- You may permit the advertiser to later reinstate the commercial provided you haven't done a commercial for a competing company in the meantime. If you allow reinstatement, he must pay you a one-time double holding fee.

USE CYCLES

When a commercial first airs, that date starts what is called "use cycles." Therefore, if the advertiser airs the commercial, you'll have two different cycles running — a fixed cycle (for holding fees) and a use cycle (for "residuals" — use fees) and payments for each will be on different dates. However, the advertiser may credit only one holding fee against use fees in any fixed cycle.

USE FEES ("RESIDUALS")

- *Program usage commercial*: The commercial is shown on "interconnecting stations." You're paid each time it airs. Payments must be sent within 15 working days of the end of each week the commercial runs.

- *Wild Spots*: You're paid a flat fee every 13 weeks and the advertiser may run the commercial as many times as he likes during those 13 weeks. Fee depends on what stations (network, non-network) and what city/cities the commercial is shown in.

- *Cable Commercials*: You're paid *by the day* for use of the commercial. Advertiser may run the commercial as many times as he likes each day and only pay you a maximum of $11.11 per day.

- *Dealer commercials*: You're paid a flat fee that entitles the dealer to unlimited use of that commercial for *six months*. The fee depends on whether the commercial is a "Type A" (dealership is *not* owned by the manufacturer of the product) or "Type B" (dealership *is* owned by the manufacturer of the product) and where the commercial is shown.

    Your contract must stipulate that the commercial is to be used as a "dealer commercial" (as well as "test commercial" or a "seasonal commercial" — see below). In the upper-right-hand corner you'll see various boxes to be checked off telling you if that's the case. Farther down, there's another box to check if you don't consent.

- *Test commercials*: Your contract must stipulate you're doing a "test," and you must be told that *at your audition*.

    Since use fees are small, your agent probably will negotiate an "over-scale" session fee. Instead of the usual $478.70 payment, he'll try to get you say, $800 — and will try to negotiate the payment of that $800 every 13 weeks as your "holding fee."

    Usually you're released in the first 13 to 26 weeks or the commercial goes national, but in actuality one of three things can happen:

    1. The advertiser tests the commercial, decides he hates it and drops it. You're released.

    2. The advertiser continues to pay your holding fee every 13 weeks, keeping you exclusive for the maximum-use period of 21 months. (He may or may not use or decide to go national with it.) Sometimes your agent will negotiate a deal that gives you a guaranteed cut-off date prior to 21 months.

    3. The advertiser loves the commercial and goes national with it (called a "rollout"). It might then even go to program usage and wild spot.

- *Seasonal commercials*: This kind of commercial may only be used for 13 to 15 weeks. The advertiser may opt to pay you an additional holding fee and, the following year, reuse the commercial for one more cycle of 13 weeks. (That holding fee may not be applied against use.) After that, the advertiser may not use the commercial again without your permission.

AGENT'S COMMISSION

Your commercial agent gets ten percent commission on all session, holding, and use fees for the first 21 months. Then he must notify the advertiser (sometime between 120 to 60 days before the end of the maximum period of use) that the commercial is coming up for renegotiation. If he fails to do this, the commercial can automatically go into a second 21-month period with no change in terms. Should that occur, your agent no longer has a right to a commission.

If he wishes to continue to get his ten percent, the agent must renegotiate the terms of that commercial to above scale — at least "scale plus ten" (percent). You, of course, have the right to accept or reject any terms or simply say no to any deal.

9 AGENCY CONTRACTS

THEATRICAL

You'll sign two different contracts (three copies of each):

1. *SAG Motion Picture/Television Agency Contract:* Covers his representation of you in films and films made for TV. (We'll call this SAG.)

2. *Standard AFTRA Exclusive Agency Contract Under Rule 12B:* Covers his representation of you for taped TV shows and radio — not commercials. (We'll call this AFTRA.)

Both contracts are standard, with no "fine print." They protect you and the agent. Provisions in one contract are often similar to provisions in the other, although they may be found in different places.

Nonetheless, carefully read any contract. We're not attorneys, and we haven't the space to go into each contract point. Also, these contracts can change.

TOP OF THE CONTRACTS

At the beginning of both contracts, you'll find:

This Agreement, made and entered at (LOS ANGELES) by and between   (NAME OF THE AGENCY) , . . . hereinafter called the "AGENT" and (YOUR NAME), Social Security No. (YOUR SS#) . . .

TERM OF CONTRACT

Also on page one of both contracts — Paragraph (2) SAG; Paragraph (3), AFTRA:

The term of this contract shall be for a period of   (ONE YEAR) , commencing the   (DAY OF MONTH) day of   (MONTH) , 19 (YEAR) .

Your agent can't ask you to initially sign for longer than a year. Later, he may want you to sign for three years.

TEN PERCENT PROVISION

On the first page of both contracts — Paragraph (3), SAG; Paragraph (4), AFTRA — the number ten is typed in. That's his commission. No other number should be there.

Following this are paragraphs labeled alphabetically, (a) through (j) on SAG; (a) through (g) on AFTRA. These provisions include: when the agent gets no commission (wardrobe fees, meal penalties, etc.); that the agent only gets money if you do; fire an agent and you still owe him a commission on work obtained through his services; and so on.

PARAGRAPH 6 (BOTH CONTRACTS)

Perhaps the most important provision. It's the "out" we discussed in Chapter 12. It states that when you first sign with the agent, you must get ten days' work during a period of 151 days or you (or he) may fire the agent. After that first five months, you must get ten days' work in any 91-day period or you may fire the agent. In the SAG contract, Saturdays and Sundays are included.

Actually, the SAG contract permits you to fire an agent when you reach the 82nd day — on the 82nd day it would be impossible for you to get ten days' work in 91 days. However, this 82-day provision isn't in the AFTRA contract.

Also, the SAG contract states that during that first 151-day period, if you get no work at all, you don't have to wait 151 days — you may fire your agent after 120 days.

Following this are exceptions and additions to the provision. These include but aren't limited to:

- Leaves of absence don't count.

- You owe him commissions on work he helped you obtain.

- If production halts (say a strike) the period is extended.

- If you turn down a job while signed with your "old" agent, and later (within a time limit) accept it when signed with your "new" agent, you owe the "old" agent the commission. Time limit on the SAG contract is 60 days. However, on the AFTRA contract, it's 90 days, and is a separate provision, Paragraph (5).

- If you turn down a job at your "usual salary," and the job offer came "from an employer commensurate with the actor's prestige," as both contracts put it, the days you *would* have worked are counted as days you *actually* worked (Paragraph (c), both SAG and AFTRA).

PARAGRAPH (8) — BOTH CONTRACTS

There's a blank space to write in the name of the agent or agents representing you.

LAST PAGE — BOTH CONTRACTS

That's where you and the agent sign and date the contract. Below this, look for:

1. Your agent is licensed by the Labor Commissioner of California.
2. Your agency is franchised with SAG (or AFTRA).
3. The contract has been approved by the Labor Commissioner.
4. The contract has been approved by SAG (or AFTRA).

DIFFERENCES

There are differences between SAG and AFTRA contracts. We've touched on some, but there are others. One major difference is:

- *One year anniversary*: It's Paragraph (10) on the SAG contract. If you've signed a multi-year contract (usually three years), you may fire your agent on the anniversary of the day you signed by giving him 30 days' notice in writing — *regardless if you are working or not.* However, this provision isn't in the AFTRA contract.

PRODUCERS RELEASE FORM OR POWER OF ATTORNEY FORM

Call it "commission insurance." This form authorizes a producer to send your checks directly to your agent, and releases the producer from responsibility if the check is mishandled. The agent deposits your check into a "Client Account" and writes two checks against it — his check for ten percent and a check to you for the balance. He sends you this second check, along with your pay stub.

There's nothing wrong with asking you to sign this form. You can check his figures against your pay stub. Do you have to sign it? Well, no . . . and yes. As one agent put it, "If you refuse to sign it, as far as I'm concerned, you don't trust me. And if you don't trust me, I don't want you for a client."

COMMERCIAL

You'll sign the AFTRA contract mentioned above and the SAG Television Commercials Agency Contract, large sections of which have been "borrowed" from the SAG Theatrical contract.

Because of this similarity, we'll only touch on two points:

- *Paragraph (3)(b)*: Here's where it says that the agent gets no commission after the first 21-month "maximum use period." Immediately following are the exceptions, including if he notifies the advertiser no more than 120 days in advance that the commercial is coming up for renegotiation; renegotiates the deal above scale, etc.

- *Paragraph (6)*: The idea is the same as the theatrical contract, but the number of days has been replaced with a dollar amount. You must receive $3,500 in fees (use and holding) in 151 days when you first sign; the same dollar amount in 91 days after that, or you may fire the agent.

10 HEALTH AND PENSION

HEALTH

Back in the Jurassic period, dinosaurs roamed the earth and union health plans were relatively simple — you either qualified for coverage or you didn't, and the coverages were relatively simple to explain. Say bye-bye.

Today, not only do the major unions each have their own plans, but the eligibility requirements, coverages, etc., are about as simple as a DNA strand — and just as hard to explain.

We limit this section to SAG's because, as an actor working in film, it's more likely you'll qualify for their plans than, say, Equity's.

First understand that we can only generalize here so DON'T take this information as the final word. See the union for details, exceptions, etc. Second, since all plans are based on *earnings* (not merely being a member of the union), it's very possible there will be years when you don't qualify at all for health coverage. You must earn $15,000 a year to qualify for "Plan I," and according to SAG's figures, 85 percent of all actors earn *less* than that in a year.

Fundamentally, SAG offers three health plans. All three can cover you, your spouse, and any dependent children up to the ages of 19 (23 if they're still in school). However, how a particular plan works is not only based on your earnings, but also whether or not the treatment you get is from a doctor/hospital that is a Network Provider, and even whether or not you live in California.

- *Plan II:* (We've listed this first because it's the one you most likely will qualify for first.) For coverage, you must earn a minimum of $7,500 total in any group of four three-month periods (called your Base Earnings Period).

- *Plan I:* You must earn a minimum of $15,000 total in any Base Earnings period.

- *Self-Pay:* Once you have been covered by one of these plans, if you don't earn enough to re-qualify, you may opt to purchase your health insurance through SAG. If so, your benefits will change. Also bear in mind that, with certain exceptions, you will be limited to doing this for 18 months.

As we said, the particulars of each plan are different, and also are affected by whether you live in California or not. (For example, if you are under "Plan II," live in California, and go to a doctor who is not a Network Provider you get no coverage at all. If you live in California and are under "Plan I," the deductable is $100 per person, $200 for a family if you go to a Network Provider; $250 per person, $500 per family if you go to a Non-Network Provider.)

In any case, once you qualify for any of the plans, SAG will send you information as to the particulars. Take the time to read it.

PENSION

Compared to the health plans, qualifying for and understanding the SAG pension is simple: You must earn X amount of dollars in a cumulative number of years — currently ten. (The dollar amounts continue to change with inflation.)

Benefits start at age 65 (early retirement: age 55) and range from $220 to $4,000 per month.

INDEX

A

M.K. LEWIS OFFERS CLASSES IN:

• Acting for the camera   • Cold reading   • Film technique
For Information: M.K. Lewis Workshops
1513 Sixth St. #203
Santa Monica, CA 90401
(310) 826-8118/394-2511

Phone Orders for YOUR FILM ACTING CAREER: (310) 826-2299
Fax Orders for YOUR FILM ACTING CAREER: (310) 826-6966

ORDER FORM: YOUR FILM ACTING CAREER

Please rush me ☐ copies of YOUR FILM ACTING CAREER.

YOUR FILM ACTING CAREER: $ 17.95

Add $1.47 sales tax (California only):   _____

Shipping and handling: $3 for the
first book, $1 for each additional book: _____
(Allow 4 to 6 weeks for delivery.)

☐ (First Class Mail — Add $1)   TOTAL: $ _____

Name _____ Phone _____

Address _____

City _____ State _____ ZIP _____

Here is my: ☐ Check
                   ☐ Money Order in the amount of $ _____

Charge my: ☐ Visa
                   ☐ MasterCard

Card # _____ Expiration date _____

Signature _____

Checks payable to: Gorham House Publishing
1513 Sixth Street, Suite 203
Santa Monica, CA 90401

1 Hour Photo

Matte - Paper 8x11
White Border
Name ???
Width ???
1 inch - ½ inch
3 of each 3

ONE HOUR PHOTO WORLD
Headshots
Matte ————→ 8x10 9.95 (1 photo)
No Border
Name
14.95
10.00 lettering
10.00 to send
them

8x10